THE FERBEY FOUR

Marcel Rocque, Scott Pfeifer, Dave Nedohin and Randy Ferbey with Tankard after winning fourth title together at Edmonton 2005 Tim Hortons Brier.

Fab Four recreate Beatles' *Abbey Road* album cover they'd later present, framed and autographed, to Queen Elizabeth II.

THE FERBEY FOUR

Six-time Brier champion and four-time world champion Ferbey reflects on an amazing career. *Edmonton Sun*

Skip signs autographs at airport on return from 2003 world championship. *Edmonton Sun*

"Somebody get some hot water." Ferbs' tongue sticks to world championship trophy. *Andy Clark/Reuters*

THE FERBEY FOUR

Randy with son Cody returning with Ryan's Express team from winning 1989 Brier.

The Ferbey family. Wendy, dog Charlie, daughter Taylor, Randy and sons Cody and Spencer.

Who says it's no fun being a curling wife? Wendy at pool in Las Vegas.

Hamming it up at late-season charity golf event.

"Do they have skips in paintball?"

THE FERBEY FOUR

The intensity of Dave Nedohin, four-time Brier and three-time world champ.

Daughter Halle ready to throw out-turn?

"Hurry. Hurry, hard!"

Heather Nedohin with niece Miranda and nephew Tyler.

Dave with All-Star, MVP and Brier keeper trophy in 2002.

THE FERBEY FOUR

Señor and Señorita Nedohin in Mexico celebrating their fifth anniversary.

Starting them early—Dave gives Tyler and Miranda delivery lessons.

The Nedohin family. Dave, Heather and Halle. Baby Alyssa has since been added to the family.

"OK, I caught it, now what do I do with it?"

Barefoot waterskiing is Dave's passion.

Modelling for Asham Curling Supplies.

THE FERBEY FOUR

A study in success—four-time Brier and three-time world champ Scott Pfeifer also won a world title as a junior.

Immortalized on a Canadian stamp, which was issued to celebrate the 2002 Salt Lake City Winter Olympic Games.

Son Dominic toys with 2005 world championship gold medal and gets a peck from dad at airport reunion.

"Man, that beer looks good!"

THE FERBEY FOUR

Edmonton Sun

"Hey, a photographer!"

Michael Burns Jr.

The world junior curling champ.

Family photo

The Pfeifer family. Scott, son Marlow, Chantelle and son Dominic.

Family photo

Pfeifer with 1994 world junior champion teammates Kelly Mittelstadt, Colin Davison and Sean Morris.

Michael Burns Jr.

1994 Canadian junior all-stars Kevin Koe, Pat Simmons, Pfeifer and Todd Trevellyan.

THE FERBEY FOUR

Four Brier titles and three world championships is reason to smile for Marcel "Shot" Rocque.

Carry a big stick…and wear rubber boots?

"When are they going to show me on the Jumbotron?"

Overdressed for a future curler.

Coulda been a rodeo steer wrestler.

THE FERBEY FOUR

Nobody on Ferbey Four smiles more.

Coulda been a football hero.

Rocque family. Raylene, daughter Isabella, Marcel and daughter Gabriella.

Raylene with rock-heads Marcel and fan.

Gone fishin' with family on summer vacation.

THE FERBEY FOUR

The many faces of Randy Ferbey.

"That was awful."

"Perfect!"

"Now what?"

"Now we're having fun."

Edmonton Sun

THE FERBEY FOUR

"What a mess!"

"Hmmm. Maybe if we…"

"That one didn't work out."

"These guys are making me mad!"

"Yes! Sweep! Hurry!"

"Things aren't going well on Sheet A."

"Ouch! That one hurts!"

THE FERBEY FOUR

Queen Elizabeth and Marcel Rocque discuss the art of using a broom.

Denis Drever/Canadian Heritage

With fifth man Dan Holowaychuk (right), Ferbey Four honoured at Alberta Legislature by St. Paul MLA Denis Ducharme of Bonnyville-Cold Lake.

Government of Alberta photo

Ferbey rink at opening ceremonies of first Brier in Ottawa in 2001.

Team photo

THE FERBEY FOUR

Inducted to Edmonton Sports Hall of Fame by Alderman Ron Hayter (second from left) and Mayor Bill Smith (right).

2004 Brier all-stars Brad Gushue, Ferbey, Pfeifer, Rocque and Canadian Curling Reporters Association president Bob Garvin (right).

Motivational speakers at sponsor World Financial Group convention in Las Vegas.

Premier Ferbey! Randy Ferbey sits in Ralph Klein's throne in office of the Premier while Ralph himself takes a position with the rest of the rink.

"He's playing our song." Ferbey Four follows bagpipes in parade celebrating another Brier title.

Honoured by City of Edmonton with Alderman Ron Hayter (left) and Mayor Stephen Mandel (right).

THE FERBEY FOUR

2002, 2003 & 2005 World Curling Champions

WORLD FINANCIAL GROUP
A Member of the AEGON Group

CANADA

Official 2006 Team Photo

Noel Zinger

Official 2001 Team Photo

Team Photo

2002 & 2003 World Curling Champions

Official 2004 Team Photo.

Noel Zinger

THE FERBEY FOUR

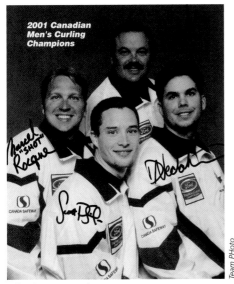

Official 2002 Team Photo.

Official 2005 Team Photo.

Official 2003 Team Photo.

THE FERBEY FOUR

Scott Pfeifer laying down on the job between ends at 2005 Brier.

"How are we going to get out of this mess?"

Randy Ferbey celebrates sixth Brier title with win over Nova Scotia's Shawn Adams (background) in 2005 Brier final.

Edmonton Sun

THE FERBEY FOUR

Huff & Puff, huffin' and puffin'.

Edmonton Sun

Arch rival Kevin Martin calls a shot while Nedohin and Ferbey look on.

Edmonton Sun

"The glare off Kevin's head is causing them problems."

Edmonton Sun

"I wonder if anyone's noticed that I shaved my moustache?"

Edmonton Sun

THE FERBEY FOUR

Edmonton's Jamie King looks on as Ferbey and Nedohin discuss a shot.

"Well, I thought you might have wanted to try to go for four here."

Ferbey with legend Ernie Richardson (centre) and son Jim at Continental Cup in Regina.

2002 Canada Cup champions in Kamloops.

2001 Edmonton Super League champions.

THE FERBEY FOUR

"The rocks go further if you sweep with your tongue out."

Classic Ferbey form.

Third provincial title in 2003.

THE FERBEY FOUR

"Call a time out."

Two heads are better than one.

Rock, paper, scissors.

"So you're big in this town, huh?"

"This sweeping is thirsty work."

Trophy from infamous "Rudy Spiel." Still waiting for $25,000 first place cheque (plus interest).

THE FERBEY FOUR

First provincial title in Stettler in 2001.

Old friend Don Walchuk hams it up with Ferbey.

Ferbey Four and Don Walchuk (in suit) honoured as Alberta's Curlers Of The Century at 2005 Edmonton Brier.

Second provincial championship in 2002.

Skip puts down the broom in the middle of a rock pile.

That's five provincial titles in a row.

Edmonton Sun

Fifth man Dan Holowaychuk about to get into a game.

Edmonton Sun

Rare shot of Ferbey and Kevin Martin smiling and shaking hands prior to leaving for 2006 Olympic Trials.

Edmonton Sun

THE FERBEY FOUR

Bird's-eye view of Ferbey in the house.

Ferbey celebrates another Brier title.

"I deserve a rest."

"Making you work today, eh?"

Nedohin and Ferbey on Tim Hortons Brier promotional tour.

Nedohin makes shot to clinch fourth Brier title.

Edmonton Sun

Finger-licking good game.

Edmonton Sun

Ferbey Four celebrates Brier win No. 3.

Team Photo

Newfoundland's Brad Gushue telling Ferbey he's thinking of adding Russ Howard to go for Olympic gold?

Edmonton Sun

Ferbey and Pfeifer in playful mood at photo op prior to Calgary 2002 Brier.

Edmonton Sun

THE FERBEY FOUR

Celebrity guest bartenders at Mo's Sports Bar in Edmonton.

Halle Nedohin, future water-ski champ?

Randy and Scott throw ceremonial pitches at Edmonton Trappers baseball game after winning 2003 world championships.

At the old course with Scotland curling legend Chuck Hay on January 5, 2005, Pfeifer's birthday.

In Grindelwald, Switzerland, in October 2000 with temporary teammate John Stewart.

THE FERBEY FOUR

Annual jam pail curling game with Edmonton Team 1260 radio host Jake Daniels (left).

Ferbey's Switzerland Shuffle?

Canadian Press/Calgary Herald (Colleen Kidd)

The Great Tricycle Race between Nedohin and Pfeifer before a game at Calgary 2002 Brier.

Heather Nedohin, Chantelle Pfeifer and Wendy Ferbey enjoy the pool while husbands attend a function.

What they'll do for a sponsor. Team wears Westjet hats at Calgary 2002 Brier.

THE FERBEY FOUR

Ferbey Four about to head out to various corners of the province for Alberta Centennial celebration webcast.

Edmonton Sun

Nedohin jam pail (OK, coffee can) curling.

Edmonton Sun

Edmonton Trappers honour team after 2001 Brier win.

Team photo

Everybody, except coach Brian Moore, on team cell phones during Brier semifinal.

Edmonton Sun

THE FERBEY FOUR

Fifth man Holowaychuk (second from right) at team table at 2002 Worlds banquet.

Team photo

Heather Nedohin with a little body language at 2004 charity 'spiel.

Family photo

Curling, beer and Mo's Sports Bar waitress at Brier send-off.

Edmonton Sun

Team about to go fishing with Edmonton Eskimo Hall of Famer Dave Cutler after winning Worlds in Victoria.

Team photo

Heather Nedohin, Chantelle Pfeifer, Wendy Ferbey and Raylene Rocque show off sexy gag photos in Las Vegas.

Team photo

THE FERBEY FOUR

Baby Halle Nedohin tastes gold for first time.

Ferbey welcomes Tim Hortons as Brier sponsor.

Dave tries prototype raccoon broom crutch at practice for M&M Skins game.

Brad Gushue rink members Keith Ryan, Mark Nichols and Jamie Korab (left to right in red and white) watch footage on scoreboard of Ferbey repeatedly trying to get out of bunker at St. Andrews between ends at 2005 Brier.

Autograph session at 2001 Worlds in Lausanne, Switzerland.

THE FERBEY FOUR

Team Photo

"Three Amigos," Pfeifer, Ferbey and Rocque in Las Vegas the last night Randy wore a moustache.

Edmonton Sun

Kirk Reiniger (second from right) gets to be member of Ferbey Four at charity golf tournament.

Team Photo

Kerry Burtnyk (left) gets to be member of Ferbey Four on European trip, which includes stop at Colosseum in Rome.

THE FERBEY FOUR

Victory walk down sheet after winning fourth Brier at home in 2005.

All Decked Out for 2007 Season: Well-sponsored Ferbey Four ready to go forward to the future.

THE
FERBEY
FOUR

The Kings of Canadian Curling

THE
FERBEY
FOUR

The Kings of Canadian Curling

TERRY JONES

The Distributor: Lone Pine Publishing
10145 – 81 Avenue
Edmonton, AB, Canada
T6E 1W9

Distributor's Website: www.lonepinepublishing.com

Library and Archives Canada Cataloguing in Publication

Jones, Terry, 1948-
　　The Ferbey four : the kings of Canadian curling / Terry Jones.

ISBN-13: 978-1-896124-12-4 (Dragon Hill Pub.)
ISBN-10: 1-896124-12-7 (Dragon Hill Pub.)
ISBN-13: 978-1-55105-570-1 (Lone Pine Pub.)
ISBN-10: 1-55105-570-8 (Lone Pine Pub.)

　　1. Ferbey, Randy. 2. Curling--Canada--Biography.
3. Curling--Alberta--Biography. I. Title.

GV845.6.J65 2006　　　　796.964092'271　　　　C2006-905668-4

A co-publication of Dragon Hill Publishing Ltd. and Lone Pine Publishing

Front cover photograph: Darryl Dyck *(Edmonton Sun)*
Back cover photographs: "fab four" *(Edmonton Sun),* "sweeping" *(Edmonton Sun),* "WFG team" (Noel Zinger).

We acknowledge the financial support of the Government of Canada through the Book Publishing Industry Development Program (BPIDP) for our publishing activities.

PC: P13

Table of Contents

Dedication

To Linda
Who deserves her own wife chapter.

Acknowledgements

This isn't an "as told to" book but the amount of time, effort and involvement provided by the members of the Ferbey Four was remarkable. Scott Pfeifer, Dave Nedohin, Marcel Rocque and Randy Ferbey made themselves endlessly available to take phone calls, answer e-mails and search for pictures. As their fans have found out, they're the real deal.

I am also indebted to *Edmonton Sun* curling writer Con Griwkowsky for his contribution of material and his editing. Longtime friend and running mate Larry Wood, editor of the *Tankard Times* and veteran of 45 Briers, also provided major contributions. Many thanks as well to curling scribes around the country for their questions in media scrums, especially those quoted throughout the book. Thanks as well to my sportswriting son Shane Jones for editing the first draft.

Without the exceptional support of *Edmonton Sun* publisher Gord Norrie and editor Graham Dalziel the extensive photo section of this publication would not have been possible. Many thanks to the *Sun* photographers themselves, particularly award-winning shooter Darryl Dyck who shot the majority of the *Sun*-credited pictures. Thanks as well to former *Sun* librarian Carolyn Woods who gave countless hours to the project.

I am also indebted to Terry Morris, Darwin Daviduk, the Northern Alberta Curling Association and the 2007 Ford World Championship organizing committee for their outstanding support.

Many thanks to Gary Whyte, Nancy Foulds, Carol Woo and Wendy Pirk for their editing of the book, to Gerry Dotto for his cover design and to Heather Markham and Willa Kung for their design and layout of the book.

CHAPTER 1

Up There With the Gods

Edmonton Sun

Randy Ferbey: Eight purple hearts.

Almost every great team in sport has that one, never-to-be-forgotten, defining moment when they make the leap from good to great.

Usually it involves a group of players—they're either holding a silver cup or have medals around their necks and the tears are running down their faces while their country's flag is being raised with their national anthem playing.

But the night it happened for Randy Ferbey, Dave Nedohin, Scott Pfeifer and Marcel Rocque, the night it kicked in that they'd gone from being a top team to an all-time team was, silly as it might seem, at a banquet.

It was the 75th Anniversary Brier in Saskatoon in 2004. The Ferbey Four were there, with 11 other rinks representing the provinces and territories, enjoying being part of the event that is as much a celebration of Canadiana as a sport. It's an event almost unique to today's sports world, an event where a butcher, baker or candlestick maker can go from playing in a cold curling club, with next to nobody watching, to playing live before an NHL-sized crowd, with hundreds of thousands watching on television.

The Brier banquet is, for the most part, like any other pre-event banquet in sport. But this one was different. It had gathered all the greats of the game.

One by one they called all the rock stars up to the stage, the men the Brier had made famous over the years, the men who had won the tankard three and four times.

Then they called the Ferbey rink up there, too, one by one—Ferbey, Nedohin, Pfeifer and Rocque.

It hadn't hit them until they were up there with the gods.

"I might as well have been standing up there naked," said Pfeifer of that moment of moments.

"You never picture yourself up there with those great curlers throughout Canada. It was indescribable. It was the best moment I've had at the Brier since I threw my first rock. I was 28 years old. It was one thing just to be up there with the legends, but for them to say what they were saying. That just beat the pants off anything."

Ernie and Sam Richardson, Matt Baldwin, Ron Northcott, Bernie Sparkes, Fred Storey, Pat Ryan, Don Walchuk, Bryan Wood and Rick Lang were all up there, waiting for the Ferbey Four to take their place, physically and symbolically, with them.

"It was overwhelming," said Ferbey. "To have Sam Richardson say over and over at the banquet that our team is the greatest team to ever play the game...I was so glad I didn't get called up there to speak. I'd have lost it."

Nedohin said it gave him goose bumps. "I'd never even been to a national championship until 2001. And to hear what they were saying. We were up there with all the greats of the game and they were coming up to me personally and telling me...well...what a great shot-maker I was. It blew my mind."

Rocque is the lead on the team. "It was a night to remember for the rest of your life. I couldn't help but compare it to another sport. I'm standing there thinking that this is the same as a hockey player standing up there with Wayne Gretzky, Gordie Howe, Bobby Orr...and these guys are telling us how good we are."

They made it to a fifth consecutive Brier, duplicated the Richardson record of four Brier titles in five years, won three World Curling Championships and became household names in a goofy game in which grown men sweep ice with brooms and throw rocks at houses.

"To be honest, I don't think I'll ever get used to the things they said that night and have been saying ever since," said Pfeifer.

The celebration of 75 years of curling turned into a celebration of four curlers from Edmonton who were honoured on the spot as the glory of their time—the greatest in the history of the roaring game.

"There's no doubt that they are the class of the curling world right now and I don't think they're finished winning yet," said the legendary Ernie Richardson, who at the time was the only skip ever to win four Briers. "A lot of guys take a holiday after a year or two. They want to win but they don't want to put the work in. Not these guys. They're consistent year in and year out."

Sam Richardson, the second on those great Regina rinks, seconded the motion. "Say what you will about them, that Ferbey team, there's never been a better one.

"At the Calgary Brier in 2001, I looked down at Bernie Sparkes and told him he was probably the best second who ever played—and that made me the second best. But today I think we both have to concede that Scott Pfeifer is as good or better than either one of us. He's fantastic. Fred Storey was probably the best lead ever, playing on those Ron Northcott rinks, and Marcel Rocque is probably just as good as he was. And my brother Ernie will tell you the same thing."

The Richardson team was the inspiration for the Ferbey Four's dream. They'd won the Brier in 1959, 1960, 1962 and 1963.

The Ferbey team was in Saskatoon to try to become the first team not just to win four—but four in a row. Unfortunately, they didn't. But a year later they won the most ballistic Brier in history, drawing a record-shattering 281,985 fans to the same arena where the Edmonton Oilers won five Stanley Cups, and only blocks from Commonwealth Stadium, home of the Edmonton Eskimos who won five consecutive Grey Cups, 13 in total. There they were, four curlers, being compared to those great teams.

Ferbey himself went where nobody had gone before. He'd won two Briers and a Worlds playing third for Pat Ryan. Six Brier titles. Four world championships. And who knows what he'll add to his resume before he calls it quits in 2010.

"I feel honoured to play with Randy," said Nedohin. "When he's done, he'll have the greatest accomplishments of all time."

Ernie Richardson agreed. "What Randy Ferbey is doing is fantastic. He's broken our record as a player and then set forth to break it as a team."

Easy to see and to say for Richardson.

"It's blowing our mind," said Rocque. "Ernie Richardson! Not one of us ever dreamed of the day we'd go to a Brier with a chance to do something like that, to equal a record like that. It's an incredible honour to even be in this position. It's unreal."

The Richardsons have been such a part of the Ferbey team's story line throughout their trip to the top—the thing they found most amazing about all of this was how the Richardsons seemed to be cheering for them.

"When I talk to Ernie, he seems to be as excited for us as we are," said Ferbey. "From what I know about the Richardson rink, I think we're a lot like that team in at least one way. When it comes to being a team, I think maybe we really do rank right up there with them and any team in history in terms of each guy being one quarter of the team."

Four Briers and three world championships as a team doesn't tell the whole story.

From 2001 to 2005, in qualifying out of Edmonton, the toughest town in all of curling, the Ferbey Four was 18–2.

Out of Northern Alberta, they were 24–4.

At the provincials, they were 38–1. The one loss was the claim to fame of Grande Prairie's Dennis Graber, which goes back to 2001. They'd win 40 straight at provincials.

Add the 57–8 record at the Brier and they were a mind-boggling 137–15 on the Brier path. And they've won three of four world championships with a record of 36–12 in doing so.

In Saskatoon 2004, when they won their fourth straight game to open their fourth straight season at the Brier, they beat a consecutive Brier-winning run by Manitoba in 1937–38–39 with one Spats Gowanlock going 9–0 in the middle year to make it possible. But that was put together by three different skips, not the same four guys.

The streak that started after Ferbey had lost to Newfoundland's Mark Noseworthy at the 2002 Calgary Brier finally snapped when, in Draw 13 in Saskatoon, they lost 8–7 to Mark Dacey. The old record belonged to Pat Ryan's Edmonton Express rink, which ran it to 14 in a row with Ferbey in tow. At the same time the Brier streak was stopped, it also snapped another streak—also 23 straight wins—dating back to a loss in the Edmonton zones prior to running the table at the Northern Alberta and provincial playdowns in 2005.

This is a rink that went 13–0 at the Halifax 2003 Brier with all four players named to the first all-star team at

Alberta's All-Time Greats: Ron Northcott, Matt Baldwin and Randy Ferbey honoured at 2005 Edmonton Brier.

their positions. They repeated the all-star sweep at their homecoming Brier in Edmonton in 2005.

"It all doesn't make sense," says Ferbey. "Considering the competition, that's a remarkable lack of losses."

"Not only doesn't it make any sense, it's wrong," said Rocque. "We should not have that record with the teams we've been trying to catch. In this day and age of so many top rinks out there, it's wrong."

It's staggering when you think about it.

"If somebody ever said that we'd put numbers like that together before we started, we'd have rolled on the ice laughing," said Rocque.

Not to mention the coins and stamps.

They hadn't really done anything yet when Pfeifer was put on a Canadian postage stamp.

Normally, you have to be either dead or sitting on a throne (or in the case of Elvis, both) to end up on a postage stamp.

But when Canada Post released a 2002 Olympic Winter Games set of stamps, the four-stamp set featured Pfeifer sweeping a stone to represent curling.

"At first I was actually contemplating not telling anybody and just surprising everybody when they saw it," said Pfeifer. "It's a real neat souvenir, a real novelty. It was more luck than anything that they selected my picture."

The problem with being on the stamp was that Pfeifer didn't get to the Salt Lake 2002 Winter Olympics.

"They needed to have the stamps done before the Olympic Trials. For the 2010 Olympics, somebody else can be on the stamp and I'll take the trip."

Then, two weeks before the Edmonton 2005 Tim Hortons Brier, Ferbey found out that his ugly mug was going to be on a coin.

As part of Alberta's 100th birthday celebrations at the 2005 Edmonton Brier, the three Alberta skips who had won three Briers—Baldwin, Northcott and Ferbey—were informed they'd each be honoured with a coin, the legal tender for the purchase of libations in the Brier Patch.

"I'd never had a pocketful of Randy Ferbey coins before," laughed Ferbey. "I had a lot of fun with that. When they told me I was going to have my own coin at the Brier Patch, I said, 'Great, because I do spend a lot of money in there.'"

But it was the idea of being one of the three coins with Baldwin and Northcott that caught Ferbey off guard when he was informed of the honour.

"It's kind of amazing. It came as a total shock to me. I don't put myself in the same shoes as Matt Baldwin or Ron Northcott. It's an incredible thing to be a part of something like this with two greats of the game."

It was Baldwin, at the Edmonton Gardens in 1954, who essentially did for the Brier what the 1948 Calgary Stampeders did for the Grey Cup, when the trainloads of fans and chuckwagons turned the football game into a major national sports event.

"In 1954 we had more fans than they'd ever had before," remembered Baldwin. "I was 27 and it was considered really something for a guy that young to win. Then Ernie Richardson kicked in. Then Ron Northcott… .

"Before I came along, nobody slid. They tossed them out of the hack and went about three feet and stood up.

"I think the Brier became something very important to Canada back then, but now it's the whole deal with the attendance, the TV cameras, the Brier Patch and people using coins with my face on them to buy their drinks."

Baldwin, for the record, loved his coin as much as Ferbey did. He said he was going to have fun with his for as long as he can still play golf. "I'm going to get a bunch of them and use them as ball markers. They're not a hell of a lot of good for anything but to prove you're a famous person," joked the oldest living, Brier-winningest skip.

"Lately, with all the guys I golf with down in Palm Springs in the winter, I'm in need of proving I was a semi-famous person a million years ago. The guys down there don't know what curling is and I can't wait for one of them to look at my ball marker and see my face on it," said the then 78-year-old Edmontonian, who won his Briers in 1954, 1957 and 1958.

"Curling is a pretty neat sport. I'm continually mesmerized that they never forget the older guys. I'm so honoured that they'd include me with these other guys. I could hold my own with Ron Northcott but I don't know about these Ferbey guys.

"Those guys are awesome. And that guy throwing last rocks…I'm amazed at Dave Nedohin's ability. He's calm and cool and makes just about everything. You drool when you think of having somebody like that throwing last rocks for you. He's the real thing, no question. I'm impressed.

"And Ferbey! I think he's a hell of a smart skip. He's obviously the catalyst, the guy who holds those guys together. He probably won't be the last guy to realize his place is better served on the team not to throw last rock. He's a winner.

"That kid Pfeifer sweeps like crazy and makes every shot. He's remarkable. In today's game you have to make all the shots from the start. Rocque makes all the shots. And sweep? My goodness, can he sweep!"

Northcott is from Calgary. With the sports rivalry between Edmonton and Calgary, the compliments don't easily flow between the two.

"My kids said, '*What?*'" said Northcott about the coin thing. "They said, 'It's the *Edmonton* Brier. You're from *Calgary*. They *have* to be kidding.'

"You never expect someone to call you up and tell you they're going to put your face on a coin. So, yeah, I was a little surprised. It was Edmonton doing it… that made it totally shocking."

Northcott, who won the 1966, 1968 and 1969 Briers, raves about the rink. "Dave Nedohin is as good as I've ever seen. He just does it. He's really cool. The guy has great finesse and weight control, which is what you have to have throwing last rock. He just doesn't miss. And he seems like an awfully nice kid.

"Randy Ferbey has eight purple hearts. What can you say about a guy with eight purple hearts?" he said of the crests the curlers wear over the hearts and on their sleeves representing eight appearances in the Brier. "I know a lot of guys who would have done anything to just have one. Major, major accomplishment."

If the Saskatoon banquet didn't tell the rink that they had become something special, another banquet, the one before the 2005 Tim Hortons Edmonton Brier, offered more for the Ferbey Four.

The Brier was part of Alberta's centennial celebrations, and the organizers chose a blue-ribbon panel from around the province and across Canada to select

Alberta's team of the century and Alberta's curler of the century. They chose Ferbey.

"I'm honoured. It's a phenomenal feeling. I'm at a loss for words for once," said Ferbey, who was supposed to deliver the thank-you from the curlers at the end of the banquet. He begged off instead and asked his old skip Pat Ryan to take his place.

"I found out I'm throwing out the first rock to open the Brier and I don't want this to be the Randy Ferbey show," Ferbey said as reporters surrounded him at the end of the proceedings.

He said it's the honour for the rink that he appreciated the most. And he admitted that while it all hadn't hit home a year before, everything was hitting home with the Brier in Edmonton.

"It's amazing. We do have something special with this rink. But to win this recognition and have Matt Baldwin and Ron Northcott standing there telling us we're special means even more."

Their record was beginning to make their reaction to compliments start to sound like false modesty.

"You put all the numbers together and it says something, I guess, that one day we'll probably appreciate," said Nedohin.

It's a team that has managed, throughout all of this, to live for the moment.

"We're just trying to accomplish as much as we can and for as long as we can," said Nedohin.

Whenever it comes time to write about the Ferbey Four and what they've accomplished together, Nedohin hopes people will look at the team component ahead of the talent component.

"I'd much rather people say we were a great team than we were a team of great players. Lots of teams are extremely talented. But only a few teams find the right chemistry. Egos often get in the way. All the egos of this team are checked at the door," says the guy who, throwing last rocks, traditionally would have his name on the team.

"In the end we all get more than our share of notoriety. Our front end probably has had more notoriety than any team in the history of the game. The reason why we've been so successful and why we've been able to get back again and again—it's our relationship with each other and how we deal with each other and adversity. Our biggest strength is that we're open to each other and communicate. We're all very different. And not many teams work at it as hard as we do."

Of all the honours and all the testimonials, it was maybe long-time Edmonton curling writer Don Fleming, the man who invented the shot-making percentage system and covered all those greats of the game, who put it best.

Fleming had just been inducted into the Canadian Curling Hall of Fame on the morning of what would be the Ferbey Four's fourth Brier title when he took his turn to tell the curling world that this modern day rink was, indeed, the best curling team ever.

"I think they're the best ever because they're the best at every position. Matt [Baldwin] never did have a strong rink in front of him. Even the Richardsons never had a strong lead. These guys are strong all the way down the line."

But the ultimate compliment came from Kurt Balderston, the two-time provincial runner-up to the Ferbey Four.

"I'm glad Randy and his team are all good guys because the way they put it to teams, you'd be awfully sick of them if they weren't nice."

CHAPTER 2

There and Back Again

Edmonton Sun

Those were the days: Pat Ryan and Randy Ferbey won two Briers and a World Championship together.

If Steve Ferbey had obeyed the sign at the Thistle Curling Club, his son might not have become the most successful curler in history.

"I remember the sign. 'Children Not Allowed.' But my dad took me anyway and I'd like to have that sign in my basement today. If we'd obeyed the sign, I might not be a curler today," said Randy Ferbey.

Then there was the ad in the newspaper.

"In some ways," said Ferbey, "I owe my curling career to the *Edmonton Journal*. Way back then, they had a Learn-To-Curl program that cost a dollar. It lasted about 15 to 16 weeks. I put up my dollar and learned to curl."

Boy, did he learn to curl.

Ferbey gets a lot of grief for being old. He'll be playing at the top of the world at age 50 if he makes it to the 2010 Olympic Winter Games in Vancouver or 47, 48 or 49 years old if he gets back to the Brier and Worlds to add to his titles.

When one of your claims to fame is that you used to play lead for the late, great Hector Gervais...well, you're old!

"I played lead one year for Hec," said Ferbey. "Now I'm playing with Dave Nedohin who has become the first guy ever to win the Hec Gervais Award as Brier MVP four times."

Ferbey says he was blown away when Gervais, winner of two Briers and a world championship, asked him to be his lead.

"I remember the day he asked me. I was two years out of juniors."

And Ferbey knows who was responsible.

"Darryl Sutton was the guy who got me on that team. He was one of the guys curling with Hector. Darryl played a big part in my career because he was always on me when I was a lead for Hector, encouraging me that I shouldn't stay a lead because I'd get labelled. He kept saying 'Randy, you are a third or a skip. That's where you should be playing.' Over and over, he'd be telling me that until I started to believe him."

Old Hector was having a tough time winning that year with young Ferbey at lead, so that might have had something to do with his becoming a third too. Ferbey is constantly ridiculed for his sweeping by his teammates. But what happened that year is not the least bit funny to Ferbey to this day.

"We struggled a bit. And I basically ran out of money. I left that team two weeks before the playdowns. I had to go up to Hector Gervais two weeks before the playdowns and tell him I couldn't get off work.

"I felt terrible to have to tell Hector that I had to quit like that. But he was great. He looked me in the eye and said 'Randy, curling doesn't put meat and potatoes on the table.' "

Ferbey treasures the times he had with the 1961 and 1974 Brier champion who became world champion in '61.

"It was fun playing with Hector and sweeping with those old corn brooms.

"With Hector you had to start sweeping when he was in the middle of that big backswing of his. You had to be sweeping long before he let the rock go.

"I remember we were in Haney, B.C., at a bonspiel and my hands were absolutely bleeding. I said 'Hector, look at these hands.' Hector looked at me and said 'Randy, you're here to curl. I don't care what they look like.'

"It was a different game back then. It was more of a defensive game. Hector had fantastic draw weight, as good as anybody back then. But looking back, the game wasn't as exciting. I didn't feel that way at the time, but it wasn't as good a game as it is now."

Ferbey said he learned a lot from the St. Albert potato farmer about how to carry yourself after you left the ice.

"He represented the best of everything in curling. If you were on Hector's team, wow! As far as I was concerned, I was a world champion, too, just sitting with him.

"When the games were over, all the other curlers were coming around to Hector's table. I learned a lot about how to treat people."

Big Hector's nickname in the media was "The Friendly Giant."

Ferbey always laughs when he hears that.

"Friendly Giant? That was horseshit. He was the most cantankerous guy out there on the ice. But off the ice, it was like he flipped a switch, win or lose.

"He was a miserable cuss out there during the game, but when the game was over, he would get along with absolutely everybody. Nobody disliked Hector, other than during the two hours they spent with him out on the ice."

To play for Hector Gervais, even though he had to quit, Ferbey considered it to be pretty good for a kid who started in the sport at the age of 10 with that trip to the Thistle in Edmonton with his dad.

"Late '60s," he said. "My dad played twice a week and I just liked being at the curling rink. I remember my mom and dad getting in an argument about me going to the 9 PM games because of school in the morning. I got caught up in curling at an early age. I worked at the Thistle. I spared any time anybody needed a guy. Sometimes two games a night every night for a week straight. It didn't matter who it was.

"My parents were very supportive. They never once said 'Don't play.' The first time I was successful and made it to the Brier with Pat Ryan in '87, I remember like it was yesterday. I know my dad enjoyed it as much as I did; he was there every day. He's travelled to every Brier in which I've curled except one. It puts a tear in your eye a little bit when you can see they're even happier than you are.

"My coach in junior was my dad."

And, at times, even Randy's teammate.

Forget six Briers and three world curling titles. For the longest time, Randy Ferbey treasured the tool kit he won with his dad.

"A tool kit was the first prize I won at a bonspiel. It was the 1970 Bruderheim spiel and I was playing on a rink with my dad. I think we finished second in the 'B' event."

While growing up, he had a choice of picking Hector Gervais, Matt Baldwin or Ron Northcott as his favourite curler. He chose Danny Fink.

"He was one of the younger guys. I thought he was the coolest guy I'd ever seen curling, and that's who I wanted to be like," said Ferbey of the Manitoba curler.

"Danny moved to Edmonton in 1978 and actually coached our team in 1979."

Ferbey competed in the Pepsi Junior playdowns, losing the provincial final in '78 to a Calgary kid by the name of Paul Gowsell.

"Things just progressed after that."

Ferbey has won four Briers as a skip, the guy with his name on the rink. But the count could have been six if he'd gone along with Pat Ryan's original idea.

"Pat had just lost the Moncton 1985 Brier final against Al Hackner. I'd beat him in the city zones on his way through to his winning the province. After Pat returned from the Brier, he asked me if I'd be interested in skipping his team. He said he wanted to play with me. I told him that I'd join his team as the third and he should stay as the skip."

Ryan had his name on the rink for the Brier titles in '88 and '89 although it was known in headline type as the Ryan's Express and the Edmonton Express.

"The best influence on my career was Pat Ryan," says Ferbey. "I think he was the best curler in the world. He certainly was the best teacher for a team there ever was. He definitely knows how to build a team."

Ryan put together a squad to win two Briers and a world championship with Ferbey playing third.

"We had a very, very strong team. Pat's idea was to get the best hitters in the game and we could win. He worked on putting that team together over and over again. He felt the team wasn't quite right and made a change. That's one thing Pat taught me. You can't always play with your friends in this game if you want to win. You have to continue to improve and become friends later."

You could make a case that Pat Ryan, Randy Ferbey, Don Walchuk and Don McKenzie did more to hurt curling than help, but Ferbey has most certainly made up for it since, playing a game that features more rocks in play than anybody.

Back then the goal was one rock in play. Theirs.

"It was mostly peel. In many ways it's a very similar team that we have now, just a different game. Scott and Don at second have a lot in common. And Marcel and Don at lead were almost identical personalities, always doing what's best for the team and giving it 100% all the time, every shot, every game.

"Dave and Pat are a little bit different. But back then the game was about hitting. I always said Pat was the best curler I'd ever play with. But now I'll say that Dave is the best curler ever to play this game. He's got them all beat. And he has such a great work ethic."

> **"The best influence on my career was Pat Ryan. I think he was the best curler in the world. He certainly was the best teacher for a team there ever was."**
> **—Randy Ferbey**

That said, Pat Ryan and Randy Ferbey have a special relationship that they'll have forever.

"I don't think Pat and I ever had a disagreement in all the time we've known each other," says Ferbey. "I'll always be a Pat Ryan fan. As long as we're curling in the same events, if my team can't win, Pat Ryan is the guy I'd love to see win."

Ferbey has a relationship with his rink that's difficult to describe. He's not really a father figure. As a rule, he's the most likely to make last call. There's respect. And yet the team loves to make fun of him.

"We always joke around and say Randy has the best of both worlds because when Ferbey wins, it's Ferbey and when Ferbey loses, it's Nedohin," laughs Rocque.

With Pat Ryan, it was always Pat Ryan. And for the longest time Ryan had the rep and the rap of being a choker.

After losing the Brier final to Al Hackner in 1986, Ryan decided to make changes and brought Ferbey on board to throw third rocks. Ferbey suddenly found himself on one of the best teams in the world and, before he knew it, in a hometown Edmonton Brier.

Winning that first purple heart was something special.

"It was the biggest and the best. That's the first thing you dream of as a curler. We'd lost to Ed Lukowich in the final the year before and we beat him in Fort St. John to get to the Edmonton Brier, which was a disaster. But winning your first purple heart, it's getting to a Stanley Cup or a Grey Cup for the first time. You dream of getting to the Brier before you dream of winning it. It'll always be a treasured memory."

It was 1987 and the Brier was being held in the 4,000-seat Agricom across the road from the arena where Wayne Gretzky and the gang played and where the next two Briers would set all-time attendance records.

Years later an Edmonton Brier would be the ultimate experience for Ferbey to that point of his career. But the '87 Brier didn't work out that way.

The rink didn't have a two-win day all the way and chased the Brier from start to end, finishing with a 6–5 record with a lot of catcalls from the home crowd.

"We stunk the place out," says Ferbey, simply.

The following year, the rink became the first in 11 years to emerge from the "C" event of the triple-elimination format, which was then in use, to win the province and make it to the Brier.

The rink went to Chicoutimi, Quebec, with an entirely different attitude from the year before in Edmonton.

"The year before, we wanted it about as much as you could want it," said Ferbey.

After what happened in Edmonton, Ryan and rink showed up in *La Belle Province*, unlike the year before at home, with no real expectations.

Two-time world champions Al Hackner and Ed Werenich (on a team with Paul Savage) plus 1981 champ Kerry Burtnyk of Manitoba were in the field.

"This is probably the best field there's ever been," said Ryan upon arrival. "There's enough world champions and Brier champions here. And I'd just as soon have them here. If we're ever going to win, this would be the crowd you'd want to beat out to win it."

But something was missing in Chicoutimi, 231 kilometres north of Quebec City.

"The excitement is definitely not here," is how Ferbey put it. "Maybe it's the language. Maybe the people here don't really relate to curling. It's just not the same."

Vive la différence?

They were 9–0 in the round-robin.

"So many people wanted a piece of us in Edmonton. Here we're one of 12 rinks. We're sort of glad we're away."

Ferbey would put both experiences in his pocket for use on another day. But for the moment, Ryan had a heck of a road team.

Having an 11–0 record at the '85 Brier in Moncton, Ryan with Ferbey on board would become the first rink to go 12–0 as a result of the extra playoff game added to win this one.

But in the end, it was: "Call it justice? Or call the cops?"

The victim of the "Miracle In Moncton" was the big benefactor of the "Catastrophe in Chicoutimi" in what may have been the choke of the century.

Eugene Hritzuk of Saskatchewan may have delivered the ugliest deciding shot ever.

Hritzuk was leading by two heading home. The fat lady had put away the microphone. And then the Saskatchewan skip came up so light with his final rock that it didn't even make the hog line. He was 20 feet short of the house. In total disgust he ended up kicking his rotten rock.

Ferbey and Walchuk jumped up and down and eventually ended up in each other's arms. The usually low-key Ryan kissed a rock.

"We lost the Brier the same way we won it. It doesn't matter how you win as long as you win and it all goes down in the record books as a win. We know that better than anybody."

Ferbey was over the moon that afternoon.

"I don't care if it was a miracle or wasn't a miracle, was good or bad shooting, our good luck or their bad luck. WE WON!" he said of Brier Win No. 1.

The rink then headed over to Lausanne, Switzerland to the World Curling Championships and ran the table again only to lose the final.

"Eigil Ramsfjell of Norway was in the same position in the 10th end with the world championship on the line. He didn't choke. He didn't come up short. He didn't present the game to Ryan on a platter. He drew in with his last rock to claim a 5–4 victory.

"Pat Ryan would walk away from the Worlds still hearing the same whispers he heard when he went undefeated at the Brier in Moncton in '85 and lost the final.

Ferbey had another experience to put in his pocket.

That December he had a flashback to the days when he played with Hec Gervais and had to tell him he was quitting the rink.

One day Ryan came up to his team and broke the news. He was leaving his job as an accountant in Sherwood Park to take a better position in Kelowna, B.C.

"Curling is a serious hobby," he said. "But it doesn't put bread and butter on the table."

Ferbey said it created the theme for the dream.

"We'll have to win everything this year because it's our last year together."

Ferbey himself came close to costing them a second Brier and another shot at winning the world title in the provincial playoffs against Doran Johnson of Calgary when he had a miserable game, guessing he curled 25% in the first game to create a sudden-death final. But then he was a perfect 100% in the final six-and-a-half ends to win it.

He curled 91% overall in the final against Johnson.

"It's the Polter-Brier…Weeeeeee're baaaaack!" said Ferbey after Ryan drew to the four-foot to beat Johnson 5–4.

The Brier in 1989 was in Saskatoon. And after losing their first two games, Ferbey went on record as saying maybe it was a good thing the rink was breaking up.

The magic, he said, was gone from the marriage. There's no spark left. No jazz. No pizzazz. No razzmatazz.

"We just don't have the fire anymore. And we don't know what to do to get it back. We're not hungry anymore. We don't want to win. We have no emotion out there. This is our last one together. It shouldn't be like this."

And then they got it going. They won eight of their next nine at the Brier, beating Rick Folk, the guy Ryan would hook up with to form a team in Kelowna, 3–2 in the final.

"It's funny," said Ferbey in the post-final media scrum. "But when Folk had to hit the house with his last shot, Pat turned to me and said 'He'll probably hog it and everyone will say we won by a fluke again.' I'm actually glad Pat had to throw his last one for the win. It's definitely a good feeling."

Ferbey had a great game in the final.

"I guess that's why I was on the second all-star team and he was on the first all-star team," said B.C. third Bert Gretzinger.

At the same time Kurt Browning was winning the World Figure Skating Championship in Paris, the rink made it a double celebration, triple, if you count LaDawn Funk winning the world junior women's championships, to keep the City of Champions sign up outside of Edmonton the first year after Wayne Gretzky left.

While it was a dramatic last-shot miss by Patrick Hurlimann of Switzerland for a 5–4 win, it was a win. It was the championship of the world.

"It was a fitting ending because we were able to go out on top," said Ferbey. "That team deserved to be world champions."

Ferbey had three purple hearts, two Brier titles and a world championship. The only Edmonton rink to have done it before belonged to Hector Gervais.

The team was breaking up, but what more could Randy Ferbey ask out of a curling career that, in many ways, started in his short stint playing lead for Gervais?

Ferbey curled 76%, 85% and 81% in his three Briers with Ryan, topping the charts at his position at the 1988 Brier in Chicoutimi. He shot 80% and 79% in his two finals.

With the Ferbey Four, he's gone 82%, 83%, 86%, 87% and 89% in the regular rounds of the Brier, topping the charts in Halifax 2003, Saskatoon 2004 and Edmonton 2005. In the finals, he's been 67%, 94%, 86%, 90% and 93%.

His mind isn't boggled by all that. It's boggled by the fact he ever had another chance to reach for the top after his days with Pat Ryan.

Between runs, there were what his rink has come to call "The Lost Years."

"In 1990 Don Walchuk and I played together. I skipped and Don played third."

Then Ferbey and Walchuk joined Kevin Martin and Don Bartlett for the "Dream Team." It was a nightmare and Ferbey split with Martin prior to the playdowns.

After the dream team blew up, Ferbey hooked up with one of the most unlikely rinks ever to enter the playdowns.

> **"Bruce Saville had the Edmonton franchise. I think he paid $50,000 for it. We did have one league game. It was at West Edmonton Mall. Kerry Burtnyk was New York. We were Anaheim."**
>
> **—Randy Ferbey**

The rink featured the late Wes Montgomery, a popular Edmonton DJ and sports commentator, former Edmonton Huskies and Edmonton Eskimo football player George Spanach, and Bruce Buchanan, a recently released television play-by-play voice of the Edmonton Oilers.

"How that team came together I have no idea. But it had to be Montgomery. It was a fun team. Buchanan spent all his time trying to sell cell phones to everybody we were playing. That was his new gig between broadcasting jobs. And...well, we didn't get to the Brier," said Ferbey.

Ferbey played on rinks with top local talents such as Brad Hannah, Gord Trenchie, Gary Greening, Rob Schlender and the like, and occasionally hooked up with Ed Lukowich and particularly Al Hackner for big-money spiels.

Ryan's Express: Pat Ryan, Randy Ferbey, Don Walchuk and Don McKenzie toast a title.

"I must have curled with Hackner in 10 of those. We'd round up a front end and off we'd go somewhere," he said of the 1985 Brier champion.

Then there was Merv Bodnarchuk. And the World Curling League.

"Bodnarchuk was trying to put together a super team and play lead. He was willing to pay three good curlers and have them carry him on to the Brier.

"He ended up in jail recently. But at the time he paid all the bills. I don't know that I got all the $30,000 I was supposed to get to curl with him but he paid for everything when we were curling. We lived great. We knew all along something was not right but it was an adventure. Pat Ryan was the skip. Ed Lukowich played third. I was the second. We did quite well. But Bodnarchuk was curling out of B.C. and we had to have a B.C. residence to be eligible for the Brier. Ed and I flew back and forth from Alberta. The whole thing actually went to court. It wasn't well perceived nor accepted by the curlers in B.C. One year we lost the semi-finals to get to the Brier.

"I took a six-month leave of absence from my job at NAIT and curled once a week at Bodnarchuk's curling club in B.C. We had an apartment at the airport. We flew in Monday, curled Tuesday and flew home Wednesday.

"It was an interesting situation."

There was also the World Curling League part of it.

"Would I do that again? With the same guy, no. But with 10 Merv Bodnarchuks who were all legit? Maybe.

"Bruce Saville had the Edmonton franchise. I think he paid $50,000 for it.

"We did have one league game. It was at West Edmonton Mall. Kerry Burtnyk was New York. We were Anaheim. They had all these nice jackets made up. And our commissioner was Bill Hunter. The opportunity to be part of something with Wild Bill Hunter made it all worthwhile," he said of the co-founder of the World Hockey Association, the founder of the Edmonton Oilers and the Canadian hockey legend who headed Canada in the '74 Canada-Russia Series.

"The bottom line was that the money didn't come through. Everything fell apart."

Everything, however, was about to come together for Ferbey again beyond his wildest dreams.

First he hooked up with David Nedohin, a curler, who told Ferbey at a bonspiel in Winnipeg that he was moving to Edmonton and asked if he might help find him a rink to join. Ferbey did—his own rink. The following year they added Scott Pfeifer. And a year later Marcel Rocque came on board.

The rest, as they say, is history.

You make it to eight Briers, win six and become a household name, you'd figure people would have a pretty good idea who you are and what you're all about. But Ferbey isn't so sure.

"I think a lot of people look at me as a very straight, very serious guy. The opposite is true. I have a good time. I'm always joking around. I love to go out and have a good time in the Brier Patch. On our rink, when the Brier schedule comes out, Marcel Rocque and I look to see what nights we don't play, so we'll be able to have a good night in the Brier Patch.

"A lot of people seem to be afraid to approach me. I'm very approachable. The whole team is very approachable. I think people seem to think I'm some kind of hard-nose tough guy."

Ferbey says there's lots that people don't know about him.

"Very few people know about my passion for baseball. I think baseball is the greatest game in the world."

His two sons, Cody and Spencer, were brought up to be baseball players and Ferbey, who has been involved in the baseball program in Sherwood Park where he lives, says his favourite thing to do is to watch his kids play baseball.

OK. That and watching his horses run at Northlands Park—when he had horses.

"When I was growing up, I had a part-time job as a pari-mutuel ticket seller at the track. I was intrigued by horse owners, and I thought it would be neat owning horses. Boy was I wrong.

"My first horse was Falcon Ripple. Don Walchuk and I bought it. I think the idea struck us at a bar in Viking. Why not buy a horse together? We put up $5,000 and we did OK, which is to say we didn't lose any money. We didn't win any either.

"Then we bought Yesterday's Wine for $40,000. We sold for $6,000.

"Then there was Trecento Hanover. That was $50,000. Horse went downhill as soon as we bought him. You could buy him today for $4,000. We got out of that at $30,000."

Ferbey then convinced Pfeifer to go in on a horse with him.

"Tierra Revo. We paid $10,000. In the first race the horse stunk. In the next race he won $5,000. Scott sold out after the win and made $3,000 in two weeks. He wanted nothing to do with owning a horse after that."

Ferbey is now completely out of horse racing and concentrates on watching his two sons play baseball and his daughter, Taylor, play soccer.

At least the kids occasionally win.

Randy Steven Ferbey may look like he's enjoying himself a lot more at the race track than he sometimes does on the pebble. But…

"I don't think he's going to win the Kentucky Derby," says Walchuk.

CHAPTER 3

Crockpot to Crackpot to Jackpot

Dave Nedohin: Best "draw-er" in the world.

His first curling experience was so traumatic, it's a wonder Dave Nedohin ever made it to his second game.

"I was six or seven. I can't remember for sure but I certainly wasn't very big.

"Don Duguid was running a program in Winnipeg. In the very first game, I burned a rock," Nedohin said of coming into contact with a rock in play.

"Somebody asked if I'd burned the rock and I lied. I said 'no.' The other skip said 'yes.' All of a sudden I started to cry. I ended up sitting on Don Duguid's lap crying. I'm bawling on the lap of Don Duguid and

he's patting me on my back saying 'It's OK. It's OK to say you burned a rock.' "

That would be the same Don Duguid who won back-to-back Briers in 1970 and 1971.

Hard to believe now, that Dave Nedohin was that kid sitting on Duguid's lap crying.

Actually, Nedohin started even younger. If jam pails count.

"I remember it vividly. I was five years old. It was Charleswood Legion jam pail curling," says Nedohin.

Curling entered his consciousness even before that.

"In Winnipeg, a curling rink is like day care. My mom would take me to the rink when she curled and I'd play with all the other mothers' kids.

"My dad has been a big influence on my curling career. Both my parents, Neill and Kris, have been a big influence on everything I do."

The first prize Nedohin won in curling was a crockpot and some drinking glasses.

"It was a spring mixed event our family entered," he remembers.

"It was the Assiniboine Memorial, an event our family entered every year. Our team included my parents and my brother. This was one of those great memories of the whole family, even if Sean and I thought we were the heart of the team. It didn't matter if we won candy bars; we looked forward to it every year."

At ages 12 and 13, Nedohin won the big Christmas tournament for his age group two years in a row and received a lot of ink.

"I was supposed to be great," he said of predictions people were making for his future in the game in Winnipeg, which at the time was considered the capital of curling in Canada.

"Funny how it worked out. I never made it to a national championship until we made it to our first Brier."

David Neill Nedohin says he's all-Alberta now. But he does honour his Winnipeg roots.

"I curled third for my brother over an eight-year period in juniors. We were pretty successful overall but we never did get to the national level.

"As mere 13 and 14 year olds we were pretty proud of winning that Christmas tournament which typically had over 100 teams entered. As staggering as it was to win at that age, we went back the next year to defend our title and won it again a couple of years later. Only one other player in history, Mark Olson, had ever won it three times. But with all that early success, and eporters in Winnipeg writing that we were destined to win the province and maybe nationals, it never happened. We were always close, losing to James Kirkness, Lyle Hudson, Brent Braemer and many other great teams from Manitoba.

"Eventually Sean played men's and I hooked up with Chris Galbraith, again playing the third position. When that happened we were supposed to be the provincial champions without even playing. In my first year at provincials with this new powerhouse, we went out in two straight. For my last year we again had a tremendous season, not losing more than a handful of games throughout the year. Again at the provincials we were a major disappointment. And my junior career was over."

Failing to live up to all the hype as a junior, Nedohin never wore the stylized buffalo on his back. The bigname Winnipeg touring teams were not competing to sign up this kid Nedohin to lead them to the promised land and to be the next Kerry Burtnyk in Manitoba.

Burtnyk was Nedohin's guy as a kid.

"He won the Brier when I was only eight years old," remembers Nedohin. "Ever since then he was the guy I looked up to."

When Nedohin grew up he was delighted to find out Burtnyk was just like the guy he had envisioned him to be.

"He's a gentleman, a leader and one of the greatest shotmakers of all time. His team, especially in the mid-90s, epitomized teamwork to me. I don't know if the team, player for player, was the best in the world. I think there were plenty of players with the skills of his group. But as a team they were a machine. They weighed pretty heavily on the amazing shot-making of Kerry, but that can't win alone. Burtnyk had a team I always wanted to emulate. And I think we have for the most part. Our team tries to do what Kerry's team always did and that's bring out the best in each other."

Nedohin says if you look at the success stories in sports, most of them are greatly affected by the people who touch their careers along the way. Of all the people who touched his, Arnold Asham gets one of the biggest assists.

"In '94 I hooked up with my brother Sean again and his new skip Arnold Asham. I went from being a big shot on the junior scene to a nobody on the men's scene.

"As a rule of thumb, only the provincial champions from juniors were considered for a top-level team, which Arnold's team was not. As it was, playing for Arnold's team was the best option I had and it meant I could play again with my brother.

"The first thing I noticed was the confidence my new teammates had in me. Arnold moved Sean to second and had me playing third. He felt this was my position and that I should stay there.

"The season went just as everyone predicted—a complete bomb. Until the provincial playdowns. We managed to sneak into the provincials and actually do pretty well. It was an important part in my decision to play for Arnold again the following season."

To outsiders, young David Nedohin was nuts.

"It seemed crazy to most. I mean, we went 0–10 in qualifying in bonspiels. We lost a lot of money. And I was jeopardizing my schooling for this? But I just had a feeling things were about to change. I believed very much in Sean and learned a lot from Arnold over the year. He was not so much a teammate as he was a coach. It didn't take long for me to understand the wealth of experience he possessed and to figure out I could learn from him.

"Arnold committed us to practice schedules, mental training and physical training. This was where I began to realize the importance of practice, where I began throwing 100 to 125 rocks per day, six days a week, during university. Our practising went as far as going into bonspiel days, finding ice to practise on at local clubs between games.

"The following season we went from the donators at the cash events to the top-winning team in the province over the season. That took everyone on the curling scene by surprise except for our team and for Arnold who always believed in us.

"We continued our run the following year. Once again we made it on top of the leaderboard in Manitoba for money earnings and really continued to surprise people.

"At the beginning of that '95–'96 season, we headed to Switzerland for a trip we'd earned by winning the Manitoba tour title the year before. We ended up winning it," he said of the Bund Trophy in Bern.

They came home and found themselves leading the World Curling Tour money list. They headed straight to the West Edmonton Mall event they had been invited to attend at the last moment.

"I still remember sitting in the change room and nobody knowing who I was. Wayne Middaugh was sitting there and joking with his team about how crazy it was that Asham of all people was leading the WCT standings at the time.

"We didn't win the West Edmonton Mall event but our team qualified for the tour championship three years in a row, lost the provincial semi-finals and won a pretty reasonable amount of money on the tour.

"We really were the most unlikely team to be successful considering we had two brothers who never made it out of the province in juniors and a curling supplies magnate who began throwing with no broom, something that we got a lot of ridicule over, too."

Asham sells curling brooms. But he stopped using them.

"The broom thing, or the lack of it when he throws, I can take credit for. Or blame, in the minds of most, probably. But what do they know? We were practising one day and Arnold left his broom at the other end of the ice. But he had another rock to throw. So he threw it without the broom," says Nedohin.

"I noticed right away how square his shoulders were, something he continually struggled with because the weight of the broom would often turn them on him. I made the comment he should throw like that more often. I was half joking. But he thought about it and it made sense to him.

"We got into our next game and we went to throw. I didn't know about his decision not to use the broom anymore. And I'd forgot about the whole incident at practice. I mentioned to him when he headed down the ice that he forgot his broom. He reminded me that I told him not to use it anymore.

"We were laughed at and teased. But we were the ones laughing when we sat on top of the World Curling Tour standings a month later.

"Everything was like that.

"It was the same when we wore the 'dirt bike moto-X' style gloves for the first time instead of the traditional curling gloves or mitts. Boy we got laughed at. Now everyone wears them.

"Right again, Arnold. A lot of people viewed him as a crackpot, but he's been absolutely the most creative mind in the sport.

"He's an amazing individual," says Nedohin. "He breaks the mold, remakes it and breaks it again. Arnold is one of a kind. He's been maybe the most

influential person in my career other than my parents. It would be difficult to go through all the things I learned from Arnold, but I can certainly say that because of him I stopped worrying about what other people thought of what I was doing or how I was doing it. I stopped thinking I had to do something a certain way because that's what the 'experts' say. I can't even imagine the number of times we were chuckled at by other players because of things we would try. Sometimes they worked. Sometimes they didn't. However, everything we did we always learned from and certainly we promoted our team well beyond what anyone ever gave us credit for. We were the Oakland 'A's of curling.

"To that end, he is also responsible for the start of the World Curling Tour. A lot of people don't know that."

Nedohin says making some moves from one team to another are easy and some are tough. Leaving Asham was tough.

"I left Arnold with a heavy heart. We had become the best of friends. I respected what Arnold had to offer. He is one of the most innovative and creative people I have ever met. Based simply on Asham's success with his curling supplies business, I had an immediate respect for him. He grew up in a poor family and is a self-made success. He has native roots that he cherishes and creates avenues to support his heritage, not hide it.

"I think Arnold appreciated the fact that I respected him, and we had a mutual admiration for each other. Mine, because of who Arnold was and Arnold's because of who he thought I could be."

And it was becoming who he thought he could be that made Nedohin switch squads.

"I wanted more. And I thought Dale Duguid was my ticket there."

The kid who had started in the sport crying on Don Duguid's lap was now playing for his son.

Too cheap to buy waterskis? Dave Nedohin comes off a jump barefoot waterskiing

Edmonton Sun

"I felt that was my best chance at an Olympic Trials spot and decided to play with him despite everything I had heard regarding how tough he was to play for. The rumours around Winnipeg were that he would blame everyone but himself for the losses and take all the credit for the wins.

"According to some of his ex-teammates, if he could have curled alone, they were sure he would have.

"That next year was, overall, pretty successful. Dale turned out to be a great shot-maker, although we probably lost six games through the year that if we'd won one of, would have put us in the 1997 trials.

"Our team was ready to give it our last shot at the tour championship when the rumours came true. I was cut from the team, citing the fact I could not draw, according to Dale."

Anytime one of the top curlers in the game suggests Nedohin is the top draw maker in the game, perhaps the entire history of the game, he loves to think of Dale Duguid.

"It was tough but I guess I knew it was the risk I was taking playing with Dale. As it turned out, I had enough points by myself to get into the tour championship. I hooked back up with Arnold and my brother Sean for one final event and, although we didn't qualify, we had a good run.

"Knowing then that I was not in the following November trials, I had now graduated with my engineering degree and decided to head west in search of employment.

"However, before heading to Alberta, I ran into Randy Ferbey at that tour championship in Winnipeg and talked to him about the possibility that I might head out that way.

"I didn't know Randy except to say hello and I was a little intimidated by his growly appearance. But Randy was nothing short of extremely helpful, indicating he'd be more than happy to find me a team if I ended up in Edmonton.

"Right there I decided I would definitely call Randy if I ended up in Edmonton and see what he could do to find me some decent players."

It was 1996. Nedohin had just graduated from the University of Manitoba in civil engineering and found out that having a degree and a job were two different things.

"There were no openings for a junior engineer in Manitoba. After committing the 1996–97 season to curling, I decided my future was in Alberta, so I packed up and moved to Edmonton in the spring of 1997 and knocked on doors.

"In Alberta I ended up with three job offers. Two were in the oil field and one was in the consulting industry. The oil field jobs were going to pay twice what the consulting job was going to pay. But if I took one of the oil field jobs, I was not going to be able to curl. For someone who had never been to a national championship in curling, it might seem like an obvious decision. But I knew I had to play at an elite level in curling and I wanted to continue it."

It might have looked like the wrong move to most, but Nedohin took the consulting job and then phoned Ferbey to find out if he'd live up to his promise of finding him some people to play with.

"He helped find me a team, all right. And he was on it."

In short order, he'd be a world champion.

"When we won the world championships in Bismarck, N.D., I called Arnold Asham immediately after the win. This was part of the promise I made to Arnold after I left Winnipeg. I had told him to expect a call from me immediately after I win the world championship. I'd never even been to a Brier at the time but he believed that day would come for me, and I certainly honoured that with the call."

A second career move for Nedohin came when the rink decided to dedicate themselves to winning a fourth Brier and third World Curling Championship along with preparing for the 2005 Olympic Trials.

The idea was to quit work and concentrate on curling. Not working gave birth to a new business for Nedohin.

"As it happened, an associate of mine, Chris Sealy, was in a position where he was looking for a change. I'd managed to get to know Chris really well over the previous three years as he worked for Denmar Energy Services, one of our sponsors. He was responsible for the design of the Ferbey image, the logo and the marketing.

"Chris was also responsible for the development of our web site. Now Statusfirm, our new company, builds and updates the site, www.ferbey4.com.

"As far as team sites, or most curling sites in general, Team Ferbey set the standard in this area. Our team

and Statusfirm take a lot of pride in the image of the Ferbey Four, partially because we all think it's important to look like champions, but also because Statusfirm is in the business of branding and image development. We have designed promotional CDs and presentations to make sure the team is always at its best.

"Chris was a previous entrepreneur in the skateboard industry and he had an itch to go back to doing something on his own again.

"Chris called me that spring and we thought about an idea for the National Hockey League Players Association where we would be responsible for a massive interactive marketing initiative. We started the business on very positive conversations with the NHLPA. Just when we were ready to go, the NHL lockout came along. No more hockey. Chris and I were already committed to a business of some sort and we knew we had to come up with other ideas. Through our design of the NHL project, we connected very well with a couple of businessmen in Edmonton, Bruce Saville and Don Metz."

Saville, one of the owners of the Edmonton Oilers, a member of the board of directors of the Edmonton Eskimos and a long-time sponsor of Kevin Martin's rink, made millions with software development for the telephone industry. Metz built Aquila Productions into one of the most successful sports video concerns in the world with projects involving most major networks around the world, sports teams and leagues, and major corporations. Aquila handles in-stadium video boards for the Edmonton Oilers, Edmonton Eskimos and the Grey Cup, and has done major documentary work, some of the most notable involving Wayne Gretzky.

"Bruce was integral in connecting us with the people we work with today and is still an important advisor of Statusfirm," says Nedohin. "Metz saw the initiative that we had in the interactive side of production and saw the potential that would benefit both companies, if we made a synergy between the two. Since that time, we have worked on some significant projects including CurlTV and Alberta's centennial celebrations. Statusfirm and Aquila are both in production. Statusfirm is based on the Internet while Aquila is television-based."

In a year in which Nedohin was taking off from work, he went from a partnership to a firm of 10 with plans to add four more.

Eventually Nedohin may be bigger in his new business than he is in the curling game. But the question is if he's ever going to be bigger in barefoot waterskiing.

Nedohin has one goal he wants to accomplish in his athletic career beyond curling. And the clock is ticking on that one.

"I've always had a passion for barefoot waterskiing," he says.

Edmonton waterskiing enthusiasts may remember the 13-year-old who won the junior national championships at Shalom Park near Devon, Alberta.

"I've been doing it since I was just a kid. Because of curling, I had to quit completely. My last nationals was in 1999.

"Before that, I used to train in Florida and act as an instructor. One of my goals is to ski at another world barefoot waterskiing championships before I'm done," said Nedohin, who competed at the worlds from 1992 to 1996.

The guy has not only won four Briers, he's won four Hec Gervais MVP honours at the Brier. And if there were MVP honours for World Curling Championships, he'd

probably have three of those to go with his three world titles.

His percentages for a last rock thrower in finals of the Brier—90%, 89%, 96%, 84% and 88%—are going to be almost impossible to match by anybody, including himself, in the future.

While his numbers at the world championships have not been a study in consistency, he's consistently in the top three at the position where you have to make all the toughest shots and do it under the most pressure.

This is almost certainly Phase I of his career, like Randy Ferbey had Phase I of his career winning two Briers and a World Curling Championship with Pat Ryan's Edmonton rink, but hopefully without the 12 years in limbo.

Ferbey is convinced his record six Brier championships and four world championships are only being held in trust for Nedohin to come along and break at a later date.

"The other curlers know he's the reason we win," says Ferbey.

"He's a phenomenal shooter. I've never seen a better player at throwing the draw in my life. He's the best thrower in the game today and he's only getting better.

"He's only 31, which is young for a curler, and there's not a shot that scares him.

"Twenty years from now, when all is said and done, you'll say Dave Nedohin was the best curler ever to play the game."

Puff—The Magic Curler

Scott Pfeifer: All-star's all-star.

Scott Pfeifer's two kids have been his inspiration. Their names are MVP and Torino.

"Our oldest is Marlow Vincent. He's our MVP," he said of the kid's initials.

"My youngest son is Dominic. His middle name is Torino. I was hoping to tell him how special his middle name is because that's where his daddy won a gold medal in the Olympics."

Sadly, Torino 2006 didn't happen, so Pfeifer will have to name his next kid Vancouver.

But their daddy has already won four Briers, earned four consecutive Brier first team All-Star spots and a second team selection from his first trip to the big show. Before that their dad was a world champion in junior, and he has now won three big-time World Curling Championships to go with it. How many guys are four-time world champions at anything? And he is already being viewed as the all-time all-star at his position. And that's not to mention their pop is on that postage stamp.

"Scott is not just a talent at the game; success follows him everywhere he goes. He has the mentality for the game that most people try to achieve in a lifetime," says Dave Nedohin.

"He was the most spoiled talent in curling history. He'd been successful since he was 16 and won a World Junior championship. He didn't really know what it was like to lose," says Randy Ferbey.

Not bad for a kid from St. Albert who started curling because no matter how hard he dreamed, he couldn't conjure up an image of himself as Wayne Gretzky.

Now he has young curlers trying to conjure up an image of themselves as Scott Pfeifer, the second who has curled 87%, 83%, 87%, 89% and 89% in the round-robins of his five Briers and 89%, 86%, 86%, 88% and 88% in his five Brier finals.

Scott Michael Pfeifer never dreamed of having sports statistics that would end up in newspapers and eventually in a book.

"I started when I was 11. I was too small and scrawny to play hockey. I'd been out to watch my dad, Brian, a few times at a few bonspiels," he said.

The first prize Pfeifer won in curling was a Sony Walkman.

"It was in a junior bonspiel at the old Edmonton SportEx. That was for winning the entire event. Can't remember what the second place rink received."

Pfeifer didn't take long to figure out he'd found his sport.

"I turned out to be pretty competitive right from the beginning. After my first year I was either at Northerns or provincials pretty much every year.

"My first skip ever was Jamie King," he said of the skip of the Edmonton rink that met the Ferbey Four twice in the provincial final, once taking them to an extra end that almost interrupted their record run.

"I started playing in the Tuesday afternoon junior league at the St. Albert Curling Club, and we played three-handed all year and managed to win the 'A' section. Woo hoo! I was also voted most sportsmanlike player. Double woo hoo!

"In 1991 I played with Jamie, Tony Paine and James Symyrozum and we lost the 'C' final of Northerns to Neil Heck.

"I watched the '91 Pepsi Juniors in Leduc that year and decided I definitely wanted to play in a Canadian championship sometime, somewhere one of these years.

"The next year it was myself, the two Jamies and Chris Keown and we lost a heartbreaker as Chris Hassall literally squeaked around a guard on last rock in the 11th end to deny us the right to represent Alberta at the Pepsi Juniors in Vernon, B.C. I was 15 at the time and was very disappointed.

"The year after, I met my wife Chantelle and started dating. The breakthrough year after when Colin Davison, Chantelle's brother, asked me to join their team. The other rinkmates were Kelly Mittelstadt and Sean Morris. Sean now lives in Aberdeen, Scotland, and we still keep in touch.

"We went 8–3 in the round-robin at nationals that year, beat Quebec in the semi-final and the Yukon/ Northwest Territories in the final. The final involved a highly controversial finish with a burned rock that decided the game.

"It was an extra end. They half missed their final shot. After the rock stopped, their second, Mark Whitehead, kicked the rock. We couldn't measure it.

"Warren Hansen of the Canadian Curling Association had to determine who won the game. It's not the way you want to win a championship. And there's been a lot of debate all these years since then about whether or not that rock was shot. But Hansen declared us the winner."

Scott Pfeifer was off to the Worlds.

"The way it worked out, the rules changed on going to the world championships that year because of Shawn Adams' team's drinking fiasco the year before. A bunch of juniors at the Canadian championships went out drinking at a bar. That was strictly forbidden even though some of the individuals in the tournament may have been of age," said Pfeifer.

Adams' rink had won it but was suspended. Normally, back then, the rink that won the Canadian championships one year couldn't compete for Canada in the World Junior until the following year. Because of the Shawn Adams fiasco, the winner would go directly to the World Junior three or four days later.

"Every single person at the Canadian juniors that year had to bring a passport."

Pfeifer had brought his. But when it came time to produce it…

> **"He was the most spoiled talent in curling history. He didn't really know what it was like to lose."**
> **—Randy Ferbey**

"I'd lost my passport the night before we were to leave for Bulgaria. And we'd won. With a few frantic phone calls, someone took a second set of my passport photos to the airport. My dad was waiting at the passport office in Edmonton. My mom was waiting at Vital Statistics when they opened. Stuff was faxed to the Brantford, Ontario, office. It was all processed in an hour and a half after I landed in Toronto. They had a lawyer sign the declaration of lost passport and everything. I caught my flight to Frankfurt with a brand new passport."

He was off to Sofia, Bulgaria.

Not the curling capital of the world.

"Sofia was a culture shock. It was dirt cheap and fairly dangerous all combined into one. We had to take cabs to the 3,000-seat arena where we were playing, a place normally used for figure skating, and we used to challenge each other to take certain cab drivers because some were just insane. Colin's cab got into an accident before the semi-final. And one time we took a bus, we drove right by a dead person lying on the road. No word of a lie.

"We found one good place to eat that served lasagna and calzone pizzas and ate there as often as we could. Other than that, I ate from the big suitcase of candy that the Shamrock Curling Club sent over for us.

"I remember the junior girls team, skipped by Kim Gellard, getting all their stockings and panty hose stolen from their room. Stockings and panty hose were very difficult to get over there at the time.

"A few other items also went missing from our hotel room.

"But the ice was real good, made by Dave Merklinger of Canada. Well, there was one game when the roof started to leak and we had to put a pail on the ice. I'll never forget Kelly hopping the pail while sweeping one of my rocks.

"The closing banquet featured a well-known 'plate dance' featuring Peter Lindholm, the Swedish coach and two guys from Norway, one of whom turned out to be Lars Vagberg who would go on to be third for Pal Trulsen. The plate dance featured three less-than-sober guys dancing on stage with nothing on except a plate in front of them in each of their hands trying to cover each other up. Unsuccessfully, I might add."

The rink went 6–3 in the round-robin, beat the U.S.A. in the semi-final and Germany in the final.

Huff and Puff: Scott Pfeifer is Puff and Marcel Rocque is Huff.

"We lost to both of those teams in the round-robin. We were down 4–1 after five, playing the U.S., and came back. We won the final 6–2 over Germany but it was like a relief getting it over. One thing I remember about that one was that the girls started their game earlier and they stole two on the 10th and stole the 11th end. We were still on the sixth end when we watched them celebrate. That provided us all the extra motivation we needed."

Scott Pfeifer was a world champion.

"Physically and emotionally it was very tough. We were in Truro, Nova Scotia, from March 17, had to deal with the kicked rock controversy and didn't get home from Bulgaria until April 11. That was almost a month away from home and I'd never left the country before. The toughest part was flying into Toronto and seeing the girls' team from Ontario get off the plane to go home and know that we still had another four-hour flight to go.

"It made it all worthwhile, however, when there was a huge pipe band and hundreds of people waiting for us at the Edmonton airport. That's when it sunk in what we'd accomplished.

"I still remember the closing banquet. Celebrating our world championship, we had to be very careful. We knew what happened to Shawn Adams at the Canadians the year before. We weren't allowed to consume any alcohol regardless of our age. I remember all the other tables at the closing banquet having bottles of wine. We drank Fanta pop. Woo hoo!"

Pfeifer would learn a few years later that curling is a small world.

"I played with Blake MacDonald in '96 in juniors," he added of the last-rock thrower on the Jamie King rink.

"Actually, I played on two teams that year. Colin and I started off with Justin Coderre and Blayne Iskiw and our team split up in November. We had a lot of personality differences. We were oil and water. We decided to go our separate directions.

"Colin and I finished the year with Blake MacDonald skipping and Jason Lesmeister at lead. We lost the provincial semi-final to the young Kennedy brothers, Marc and Glen."

In 1997 Pfeifer teamed up with Ryan Keane, Blayne Iskiw and Peter Heck.

"Ryan skipped and threw third rocks while I threw skip rocks and swept. Now you know where Randy Ferbey and Dave Nedohin got the idea. I was doing Dave Nedohin's job and he was doing Randy Ferbey's job before they started doing it that way.

"We beat Carter Rycroft in the provincial junior final and went 10–2 at the Canadians in Selkirk, Manitoba. We beat John Morris in an extra-end final. No burned rocks this time."

The names Kelly Mittelstadt and Blayne Iskiw in there may ring a bell.

"Kelly Mittelstadt was one of the players on that junior rink. We played against each other at the 2005 Edmonton Brier. He was with Nova Scotia. It was déjà vu all over again," says Scott. "I'd previously played against Blayne Iskiw, a former junior teammate of mine when we went to the world championships in 1997. He played for Paul Flemming of Nova Scotia against us in the 2001 Brier but he's moved back to Edmonton now."

Pfeifer says he loved wearing the blue and yellow Alberta uniform from the git-go. It's second only to the one you get if you win.

"It was just a thrill to represent Alberta the first time. Wearing the Maple Leaf on my back was an amazing feeling the first time even if it was kind of culture shock in Bulgaria. It never gets old."

After beating Morris at Canadians, Pfeifer's second trip to the Junior Worlds in 1997 was to Karuizawa, Japan, the pre-Olympic event, with Keane.

"That was a fun trip. It was a test event for the 1998 Nagano Olympics. You had to go through everything the Olympic curlers and all the officials, volunteers and everybody would at the same site a year later.

"People there had never seen the sport before. It was a big deal.

"It was really a contrast from when we curled in Sofia at my first World Junior. It was one of the most fun trips I've ever taken.

"Even in my junior career, I faced some pretty good curlers. Ralph Stockli played for Switzerland."

After losing in the semi-final at the Junior Worlds, Pfeifer decided to take the next year off.

"I wasn't curling, and Dave and Randy had hooked up that year and asked me to spare in the 1997 Poor Boys at the Shamrock.

"Obviously that went well. At the end of the year they came and asked me if I wanted to play with them.

"How can you foresee what we've accomplished happening back then? You couldn't. But it didn't really take long after we started playing together that you could tell *something* was going to happen."

In their first year together, Carter Rycroft was also a member of the rink. Then Rycroft split to join Kevin Martin and a large lad by the name of Marcel Rocque showed up at lead.

"Huff & Puff" were born.

"It all started in 2002 at the Calgary Brier. It's stuck ever since," said Pfeifer of the nickname, which started as "Huffer & Puffer" in print and refers to them losing their breath sweeping so hard. It then was shortened to "Huff & Puff" on the telecasts.

"Marcel and I probably get asked 1,000 times a year which one is Huff and which one is Puff?

"I tell them just think of Puff Pfeifer. That pretty much straightens it out for everyone."

The two are amazing enough with the out-of-this-world shooting percentage numbers that they've put up in their careers so far, but most curling fans view them as a twosome, a pair.

"I don't think we try to outdo each other, but when Marcel gives it his all out there, it's hard not to follow," says Pfeifer.

Normally leads and seconds have about the same kind of profile as offensive linemen in football. But when you're on an all-time team and people suggest you're the key to a rink that could become the most successful of all time, it's a different deal.

The thing about Ferbey, Nedohin, Pfeifer and Rocque, which has been said again and again, is that they're better at every single position than every other rink at every event they play. And if you look up and suddenly see Rocque and Pfeifer on fire, forget about it.

"I'll never get used to hearing that," says Pfeifer.

"If Marcel and Scott are on, it makes it very difficult for other teams to combat that," says Ferbey. "They're the best in the game. And when they're on…"

The front end don't disagree with the shot-making side of their jobs.

"If Marcel and I make our shots, I really like our chances," said Pfeifer.

When Rocque and Pfeifer show up at the rink for a big game, unlike a lot of rinks where the front end players are looking for the last-rock thrower to win the day, they believe they can win it.

"It's a snowball effect," said Rocque. "Especially the way Randy calls the game. It can really set up the big end. With the four-rock rule, if I win my match-up and Scott wins his, we believe we're going to win the game."

But Rocque says the whole rink swings off Pfeifer more than anybody.

"If he has his magic, it snowballs to Randy and Dave. Scott is the key."

Puff, like Huff, didn't get much ink in the first few years with the Ferbey Four. With Ferbey the skip and Nedohin throwing last rocks, they'd both be brought to the media scrums after the games and Pfeifer and Rocque would walk by without notice. Then their numbers and the "Huff & Puff" thing got attention, and finally their own separate characters started to surface. Now it is rare if Pfeifer doesn't get stopped for a quote on the way to the dressing room.

With each year and each success, Pfeifer has gone from the no-profile position of a second to a recognizable sports star, especially in Edmonton.

"I still can't get used to it. It's been great meeting so many people and everything, but as much of that as I get, it still stops me in my tracks when I get it. Like one day I was at a store and a guy comes up to me and remembers some shot and asks me why we played that shot. It's not that I don't want to talk to the guy about it. But I'll be damned if I could remember the shot."

CHAPTER 5

"One More Word and You're Mine!"

Edmonton Sun

Marcel Rocque: A household name?

When Marcel Rocque's cell phone rings and he's not there to answer, the leave-a-message recording kicks in.

"Hi. This is Shot Rocque…"

Shot Rocque? The guy is a *lead*. Lead rocks seldom stay shot.

When asked to sign his autograph in the Brier Patch, the "Huff" in "Huff & Puff" signs it "Marcel 'Shot' Rocque."

Again. The guy is a lead.

"I didn't give the name to myself," says the junior high school teacher who has curled 88%, 88%, 91%, 93% and 88% in the regular rounds of the last five Briers and been 90%, 94%, 88%, 95% and 88% in the finals, but hasn't had a whole lot of his shots actually end up on the scoreboard.

"It was a game playing with Don Walchuk and Gord Trenchie against the Park brothers of Edmonton in Smithers, B.C., when I first joined the team in 1992. I had a rock in the eight-foot that miraculously turned out to be shot rock—the winning rock. That's where it started. All of a sudden they started calling me 'Shot Rocque.' It kinda stuck.

"When I started signing autographs in the Brier Patch, and eventually almost everywhere, I started signing it that way. So if you've got my autograph and it doesn't say 'Marcel Shot Rocque,' it probably isn't authentic," he laughs.

Leads signing autographs? What has the world come to?

"It's worse than that," says Heather Nedohin, wife of the Ferbey Four last-rock thrower. "When the boys printed up player cards to give out to fans, the first ones to go were the 'Huff & Puff' ones."

The ultimate, said Rocque, was when the team was in Heathrow Airport in London, England.

"They are the best team on the planet from lead to skip and I give a lot of credit to Marcel. There damn sure isn't a better lead than him."

—Del Shaughnessy

"We were on our way to Scotland. A stranger walked right up to me. Obviously, he was a Canadian. He pointed his finger in my face and he said 'One more word and you're mine!' And then he walked away. He didn't introduce himself or anything."

You see, Rocque was caught on television late in the 2004 Saskatoon Brier telling a fan who was heckling Dave Nedohin in the hack, "One more word and you're mine!"

"I remember leaving West Edmonton Mall with my wife Raylene. We were in the parking lot when a 17-year-old kid was running up to me, gasping for air. He'd seen me from a distance. He asked me for my autograph. That's the kind of thing you don't expect. It's not that I wasn't used to signing a few autographs, but usually they are for people who are a lot older. And they don't run after me to get one. I don't know.

For some reason I found it really neat that somebody who was 17 wanted my autograph.

"One of my favourite stories was when we were asked to drop the puck for the ceremonial face-off at an Edmonton Oilers game. I was driving in the right lane on Wayne Gretzky Drive and four guys in a truck drove up beside me. Raylene was driving and I was the passenger. I love to tell this story on her because the guys were hooting and hollering and staring and she's getting a bit bothered thinking that they're doing it at her. All of a sudden they roll down the windows and they all start hanging out of the windows making sweeping motions. That was great. I loved those guys."

Recognition and autographs are one thing, but when the mayor of your old hometown calls…

"The Mayor of St. Paul wanted newspaper articles on me to put in their time capsule for the Alberta 100th centennial. Somebody is going to look at that 100 years from now!"

Rocque says it's getting less and less of a shock when stuff like that happens. But the part he likes best is the way things have changed in the curling community itself.

Rocque is a four-time Brier champion and three-time world champion but for any top lead, he says, there's now a new respect out there.

"It was a position on a curling team which was seen as not being as valuable or integral in the past. But since the rule changes with the free guard zone, it's made my position more important."

That said, there's absolutely no getting used to being talked about as a great in the game when you play the position he plays.

"They are the best team on the planet from lead to skip and I give a lot of the credit to Marcel. There damn sure isn't a better lead than him," said Del Shaughnessy, the lead on Kurt Balderston's provincial rival rink.

His teammates agree.

"He's the ultimate No. 1 team person in curling today. And he's a fun guy. He's my roommate. He's never negative. And he plays with so much passion," says Randy Ferbey.

"Marcel has fire in him. He has more desire to win than anybody. Nobody works harder. He's consumed by trying to be the best lead he can be," says Dave Nedohin.

"Marcel puts forth more effort than anybody I've ever seen in my life," says Scott Pfeifer.

Rocque takes all those compliments and throws them back.

"Dave is the best ever, by far. Randy just knows so much about the game. And Scott is just an amazing talent. I keep pinching myself that I'm along for such an incredible ride with them."

Marcel Louis Rocque has not only won four Briers, he's been named the All-Star lead at the last three of them.

In the beginning, all Rocque really wanted was a few trophies like his brother-in-law.

"I was babysitting my sister's kids in St. Paul and was looking at all the trophies he'd won. I was probably 10 years old. I decided I wanted to be a curler," said Rocque who lists his first curling prize as an antique rifle.

"At first, I couldn't get the rock to the other end. And my brother-in-law wouldn't let me push it because he said that developed bad habits. When the ice was keen, I managed to get a few down there. Then I grew a little bit and figured a few things out and I was getting them down there regularly."

Rocque says curling started out as a family thing.

"My whole family learned how to curl in St. Paul. My dad, Roland, started with my twin sisters Lea and Rhea and my brother Victor when they were very young. They went out in rubber boots. At least by the time I came along I was able to score some really good curling equipment from my older siblings.

"Victor is the most competitive older brother that I have. He continues to take a good run at Zones and Northerns. He's been real close to a provincial berth on a couple of occasions. I think he'd love nothing better than to beat us in a big game.

"My brother Roland Jr. and I started at the same time with my dad and my brother-in-law, Gerry Looy. That was the rink where I had to kick dad off the rink for missing too many games and meetings.

"My brother-in-law Gerry was the most instrumental. I was 10 years old and he was insistent on the fact that I not develop any bad habits so he suggested that it wasn't important that I make many shots. He always had me focussed on technique."

Coming out of St. Paul as a competitive curler isn't easy.

"There weren't any junior leagues. And to play, I needed people to drive me to the rinks. I kept my brother on the team so he could drive me."

But he fired his father.

"He was on the town council and he missed too many games. I was instrumental in removing him from our rink. I, uh, actually moved up and took his position."

Despite being fired, his dad was supportive. Mom, too.

"I was able to go with them a couple of times to the 'Four Foot' curling camp run by Glenn and Elaine Jackson out in Osoyoos, B.C.

"I moved to Sherwood Park to live with my Aunt Denise in order to curl. They also allowed me to move from St. Paul, during a teacher's strike, to Sherwood Park. I was in Grade 11. I felt I had to be near the city in order to be more competitive and maybe get on a good team one day."

It's ironic that a young man who grew up to be a teacher would consider the turning point of his career to be a teacher's strike.

"It was there I met Tara Brandt (Weaver) who was on this junior team out of Sherwood Park. She introduced me to Trevor MacGregor. Trevor and I hit it off.

"Both Tara's girls team and Trevor's boys team were coached by Pat Batty and her husband Joe. I'm still grateful to the two of them for all the time and dedication they had for us in juniors. I was able to skip a junior mixed team in 1989–90 back when Randy Ferbey was playing in the Brier with Pat Ryan. That was the last Alberta Junior Mixed ever held. And we won it."

The same year he teamed up with MacGregor and went all the way to the Provincial Men's Junior, losing to Rob Schlender.

"That was the first of 10 years curling with Trevor. To this day that's longer than I curled with anybody else."

Rocque's junior career was over, and it looked like his competitive curling career was toast, too.

"I took a year off and didn't know what I wanted to do. I didn't have any offers. I played with Trevor in the men's league at the Granite. We made the semi-finals against Gord Trenchie. I had no idea that he'd curled in a Brier final with Pat Ryan or that Randy Ferbey would end up taking his place on Pat's rink.

"All I knew was that he was an old guy who wanted to play eight ends so they could go upstairs for beer.

"It was the second game of the night and Trevor told me the opposition's plan was to quit after eight and Trevor didn't like the idea. This was the club championship, after all. We would have agreed during regular league play but not for the club championship.

"The other players sent Gord to me. He asked me about playing eight ends at the start of the game. I told him, still not knowing who he was, 'You guys are old. We're going to keep up with you for eight ends and then win the game in the ninth and tenth ends.' I figured they were more experienced than we were and we'd need the ninth and tenth ends to beat them. Gord stormed away and never spoke to me the rest of the game. They were ticked off. But that's what happened.

"We won on the tenth end and went on to represent the Granite at Edmonton Club Champions Bonspiel."

It blew Rocque away when Trenchie called that summer inquiring about their services.

"He called Trevor and told him that he appreciated our competitive fire, loved our spirit and that we were just the type of players he was looking for to play on a front end with him and Don Walchuk. Don wanted to try skipping and had asked Trenchie to play third. They had agreed to develop a front end and we were it. What a dream come true.

"I had idolized Fast Eddy Lukowich during all those years of the Battle of Alberta against Randy and that Ryan's Express rink and here it was right in front of me. Wow!"

For Rocque it wasn't an easy adjustment.

"It was a big learning curve. I hadn't played competitive curling at front end and the next thing you know we're playing guys like Vic Peters, Russ Howard with Wayne Middaugh and Peter Corner on the rink, Ed Werenich and Lukowich himself.

"We lost in the provincials in 1992 after beating Randy's team in the 'C' event final of Northerns.

"Gord retired and we picked up Brent MacDonald to play third. We must have qualified in every bonspiel we entered out of the 'A' event. We lost the provincial finals to Lukowich to go to the Red Deer Brier in 1994. I was starting to think I wasn't meant to win.

"I had some unbelievable experiences curling with that group of guys. Not only did I learn a lot about curling, I learned a lot about life. Gord Trenchie and Don Walchuk will always be great contributing factors to any of my personal successes and I am forever indebted to them for the willingness to take a chance on us and being patient with us. I think Trenchie knows how to pick 'em as he seems to be a step in front of everyone when it comes to spotting players with potential."

Rocque managed to get to a provincial final with Walchuk. And he knows what it feels like to be on the other side of the ice when a top team with a first-rate rock thrower is intent on getting to another Brier.

"I was tied for the highest percentage of the week. Guess who I was tied with? Ed Lukowich. He was absolutely on fire. It's one thing for a lead to curl 94%. But Ed was curling 94% as the skip.

"In the first end we were all over them. In the second end we were all over them again. We were laying two

Morning draw? Marcel Rocque yawns between shots at provincials.

Edmonton Sun

and he has no shot. And he missed his shot. It was a miss, but it went through the port. Wick. Wick. Redirect. We had hammer. We had to go way out in the weeds. We were looking at a real good chance for three and instead were down 2–0. That put the wind in their sails and knocked the wind out of ours. He didn't miss anything after that."

When Walchuk decided to give it up as a skip and return to play second for Kevin Martin on a rink featuring Randy Ferbey at third and Don Bartlett at lead, Rocque was in limbo again.

"When Walchuk went to form the Alberta dream team as it looked at the time, I didn't know what that might mean for me. I'd been together with Trevor for so long that I figured we should continue to stay together and work at it. We played a season with Rob Schlender and Shane Park. Then we went back to being skip and third. That's when Trevor injured his back and had work restrictions. He moved away for work and I was left with uncertainty.

Walchuk would end up winning three Briers, two with Ryan and one with Kevin Martin, not to mention an Olympic silver medal with Martin.

"That spring I was asked to play in 'The Rudy' qualifying bonspiel to get a berth in the big $250,000, or should I say the $0 cash spiel Rudy Ramcharan, from Kevin Martin's rink, promoted.

"Gary Greening, Les Rogers, Garth von Hagen and myself felt we had a good chance of qualifying as a group so I went along for the bonspiel in Leduc. We happened to play Randy, Dave and Scott in the final of 'The Rudy' qualifying spiel and we beat them. Not long after that I got a call from Randy. We met and I was on the team. So I always brag to the guys telling them that I was the glue that was missing.

"They'd just lost the provincial final to Ken Hunka, who went on to represent Alberta at the 1999 Edmonton Brier, and they'd lost Carter Rycroft to Kevin Martin for the next season. They were looking for a guy and trying out different players. I played the last bonspiel of the season with them and…"

Shot Rocque was born.

Shot Rocque became Huff and met Puff and the two have become welded together as an entry in curling history.

"It's been kind of neat. Scott Pfeifer and I have become, we keep being told, the most well-known front end ever.

"We're both proud of that because it means we've raised the profile of those positions in the sport."

Rocque says he learned something from watching Martin's lead, Don Bartlett.

"He took pride in being a lead. I decided I'd take pride in being a front-ender, that I could be happy playing that position on a quality team. I believed if I found the right three guys in front of me, I could play lead for a long time. I decided I'd try to be the best I could possibly be at that position.

"Now I'll probably retire as a lead."

Bartlett curled 91%, 88%, 79%, 81%, 80% and 89% in his six Briers for Martin. Rocque has never been below 88% and averaged 92%.

Rocque says he has to credit his sweepers.

Being a lead, that gets a laugh. But he's serious.

First, he has Puff. And then he has Nedohin, who he says sweeps harder than your average last-rock thrower. A lot harder.

"I don't know if sweeping with Scott and me has inspired Dave but he sweeps very hard and that's a credit to the fact every shot counts," he told John Chaput in a *Tankard Times* interview one year.

As the Canadian Curling Association TV commercial goes, "a lot of sports are games of inches, but in curling sometimes you wish you had inches."

"If we've barely rubbed a guard after I've swept it, I always ask myself if I could have managed a couple more strokes in there or gone a little bit harder to maybe get it by. Rarely at provincials or a Brier can I answer that question with a 'yes' because I'm giving it my all and Dave and Scott are doing the same.

"My expectations are that if I don't shoot in the high 80s, then I haven't done my job. Consistency has to be there for a lead because your shot repertoire is very limited. Once you figure out how to play those shots, you really have no excuses."

Rocque can talk. It took a couple of years for the curling writers to discover that fact. As a rule leads are to be seen and not heard. But Rocque became a media go-to-guy as the wins began to mount and the titles accumulated. One day, at a Ford World Curling Championships, Hall of Fame curling writer Larry Wood, who had scribbled the odd quote from a curler before on the subject of beer, ended up interviewing Rocque at length on wine.

"My wife, Raylene, is an X-ray technician at a hospital and there are a couple of doctors who are wine experts. They got me into wine tastings. Then somebody gave me a book on how to start my own wine cellar. Mine isn't a perfect one, but I hope it will be someday.

"My wine mentors gave me a 1990 Dom Perignon champagne to take to the Brier in Halifax to celebrate with the team if we won it. You could price out this baby. It was expensive stuff. So we're in Halifax and we've won three straight, then five, and it keeps going.

"So I'm thinking about that bottle and then I say to myself 'Hold it. Why waste this stuff?' We wind up winning 13 straight and the Brier—and I still haven't opened it. The bottom line is, I decided, I'll drink it myself. I'll get the guys together with a bottle of Baby Duck. They won't know the difference."

A lead being quoted at length about wine?

Signing autographs? Being famous?

Putting It All Together

See-through champions: Ferbey Four with provincial trophies.

Edmonton Sun

In most sports, you draft, you trade and you sign free agents.

It doesn't work that way in curling. Teams come together in a lot of weird ways —few more unusual than the birth of the Ferbey Four.

Randy Ferbey, two-time Brier champ and one-time world curling champion, had been floating around in limbo for years after Pat Ryan moved to the B.C. interior.

"I floated around until, one day at a curling rink in Winnipeg, I met a kid by the name of Dave Nedohin," he said.

"He came up to me in the dressing room and told me 'I'm moving to Edmonton. Do you know anybody I could curl with?' I was kind of committed to curling with Ken Hunka that year," continued Ferbey. "But something told me to call Hunka to tell him that I'd changed my mind, and that I'd decided to play with a kid from Winnipeg by the name of Dave Nedohin. To this day, I don't know why. Kenny was a bit disappointed. But the way it worked out, he beat us in the provincial final and went on to play in the 1999 Brier in Edmonton."

Ferbey said it didn't take long for him to know he'd made the right move.

"I saw right off that he sort of had that stubborn mentality, like Pat Ryan. He hates to lose. He stews about it a bit and then comes back strong after that. There's nothing wrong with that."

For his part Nedohin said it didn't take him long to figure out this was the right move for him, too.

"I couldn't imagine getting this much experience—of being with such a good player—from anyone else. Getting together was the best decision I ever made. Nobody practised more than I do and sometimes I feel like I carry the load of it a little too much. But all of a sudden I had good guys around me who could joke and lighten the load."

Today they all look back at the way it came together and almost giggle.

"I still can't believe calling Randy, when I accepted that consulting job, to take him up on his offer to find me some people to play with. To my complete surprise he decided to play with me as long as I would skip," said Nedohin.

"I had never skipped before, but I thought 'Why not?' I decided to give it a try."

Nedohin knows that Ferbey did his homework a bit on him.

"I think having Arnold Asham as a friend helped in me hooking up with Randy. Ferbs was considering the rebuilding process with me when I first moved to Edmonton but needed some references on whether I was the guy or not. Arnold was certainly instrumental in talking with Randy about our coming together."

That year, the 1997–98 season, they hooked up with Aaron Skillen and Pat McCallum.

"The year went pretty well," remembers Nedohin. "We managed to get close in a few spiels. About the third spiel our front end suggested that Ferb call the game and that I sweep but still throw last rock. This simply used the best of all our skills, allowing me to sweep and burn off extra energy. I was fairly wound-up

back then. It used Randy's experience in the house. It was a GREAT call by our front end."

Ferbey said it worked for a while.

"It wasn't too bad. He started calling the game. One day we went to a spiel and we were struggling a bit and Pat McCallum suggested I hold the broom. Stay at third but call the game and hold the broom. We did quite well and Dave and I knew we had something."

The problem, however, was that the guy who suggested the idea and his mate on the front end weren't the right idea.

"We didn't make it to the provincials. That was a major disappointment," said Nedohin.

This is where it gets interesting with curling teams. You spend a winter together, travelling the frozen tundra, sharing hotel rooms and bar tables in curling clubs and small arenas. You have to be more friends than teammates to really make it work. And then at the end of the year…

"You make a change," said Ferbey of Skillen leaving on his own and cutting McCallum.

"They were two very good curlers. But they didn't fit in with what we were trying to accomplish," said Ferbey of their first-year front end. "One wasn't as committed and one wasn't the right fit to get where we thought we could get."

Besides, he had his eye on two hot shots: Scott Pfeifer and Carter Rycroft.

"We picked up Carter for a bonspiel and he agreed to come on. Scott came along after him," remembers Ferbey.

"Scott wasn't as committed in the beginning. He was busy with university and wasn't sure he wanted to go into curling as a senior. We sort of had to beg him a little bit. In his first spiel with us he made $10,000. Then he thought, 'This is pretty good.' "

There was success. The rink won the Edmonton Super League title and made some money.

"Again it was a pretty good season," remembers Nedohin, whose name was still on the rink in some coverage despite the change in skip, at least in terms of calling the game if not batting order of rock throwers.

"We won our first World Curling Tour event. And we made it to the provincial finals only to lose on an impossible shot to Ken Hunka."

Actually, it was the Ferbey rink that sent the Hunka gang to the provincials in the first place. Hunka jumped on miscues by both Ferbey and Nedohin for a three-ender to win the "A" event at the Northerns to qualify for the provincials in Grande Prairie. That snapped a seven-game losing streak. But the rink bounced back to win the "B" event and watched Mark Johnson win the other spot, leaving Kevin Martin and the rest of the best from the area out in the cold.

Martin won $30,000 in a skins game the next week but Walchuk was quoted as saying "I'd give it all back if I could still be in the Brier chase."

It was Hunka, 48 at the time, not Ferbey and his boys, who was the sentimental favourite. And when Hunka won, the Edmonton Brier committee was celebrating.

"Kenny has been such a popular curler. It's going to be very special," said Brier organizing committee member Darwin Daviduk.

Thirty-three years earlier Daviduk had coached Hunka to his first title as a high school curler.

"I had tears in my eyes," said Daviduk.

It was a last-rock shot of a lifetime for Hunka to beat Ferbey, Nedohin, Pfeifer and Rycroft.

"I was praying," said Hunka.

Blake MacDonald was begging.

"Curl," he demanded. "Curl, rock, curl."

Finally it did. Hunka never saw it. But suddenly he saw brooms go up in the air.

Twenty minutes later, Hunka had recovered for the presentation and looked at Randy Ferbey's young rink and named them all by name.

"You guys are all younger than me," he said. "You've got lots of time, man. That's all I've got to say."

It was one of the most interesting provincials of all time involving a plethora of tie-breakers and the Ferbey rink playing five games in a span of 29 hours only to lose the final on the last rock.

Ferbey said he felt for Nedohin more than anybody.

"Dave played well. Kenny made a hell of a shot with his last rock. You can't do anything about that. It was a great shot. The whole game came down to one shot and he made it. But Dave kept us in for 10 ends. I can't take anything away from him."

Ferbey said it was one of those rare occasions when losing was made easier because of who had won.

"You don't mind losing to a team like that. We've gone a lot of miles with these guys. We've played them six times and haven't managed to beat them once. And it's hard not to be happy for Kenny."

Ferbey, Nedohin and Pfeifer were spectators at the 1999 "Last Shootout of the Century" Edmonton Brier which busted all previous attendance records.

"We ended up as spectators but, you know, I didn't mind it. I knew I had my opportunity. I was still a curling fan in addition to being a curler. I had a great team. I was a Ken Hunka fan. He'd never been to a Brier and I already had my purple hearts. I didn't sit there resenting the fact he was there and I wasn't," said Ferbey.

Rycroft, after one year with the rink, left to play with Kevin Martin.

"He defected to our arch enemy in the curling world. That's how we looked at it," said Nedohin.

Ferbey was steamed. It wasn't the beginning of the Kevin Martin feud with this rink, but it fueled it.

But what do you do? Martin had used Ferbey for his farm team. And Ferbey had to recruit somebody else.

"We played four games with four different leads, four very good curlers. But in each case it was like 'Something isn't right here.' That's when Marcel walked in. The guys said it right then. That guy! That guy right there! A light went on with everybody. That guy! He wasn't one of our four guys. Marcel was in the bonspiel playing for somebody else. We totally didn't think about him at all. He walked right by us and said 'Hi, Randy.' We looked at each other and you could see us all thinking the same thing. We all liked him. Bingo! There he is," remembers Ferbey.

"We called him later that week. I'm not sure he jumped at it."

Individually, everybody but Pfeifer had spent a significant amount of time out of the limelight.

"Counting my time in Manitoba going back to when I started curling as a kid, I think I'd been in 15 or 16 provincial championships," said Nedohin.

"When we lost to Ken Hunka in the 1999 provincial championships, that really fueled our fire to get to the Brier."

Here's looking at you: Randy Ferbey and Dave Nedohin pose with another championship trophy.

Despite leading the World Curling Tour in earnings in 2000, the team lost to Kevin Martin and Mark Johnson in their first two games of the Northern Alberta playdowns to end up in the 'C' event and didn't even manage to make it to provincials.

But already, the rink was well on their way to creating one of their many legacies.

Rinks started noting the way they were calling their shots.

"Six!" Rocque and Pfeifer would shout as the rock headed down the ice, indicating they figured it had the weight to end up to the top of the four-foot.

"It was actually something I brought to the team when I moved to Edmonton," said Nedohin.

"Arnold Asham had suggested our team use it in Winnipeg when I played with him, another thing we did in Winnipeg that people thought was crazy."

Nedohin says playing all the games on TV with commentators being forced to explain the system made most of the curling world adopt the same system.

"As soon as we made it popular on TV and as soon as any curler tried it, they saw the benefits of the system. Of all the competitive teams, about 90% of them are now using it or a very similar numbering system. The only ones who aren't using it or an adaptation of it, I believe, aren't because we're the ones who made it popular."

Numbers one through three are guards, one being the top third of the free guard zone, two being the middle third and three the closest third to the house. From there each number represents a ring color. Four is the top 12-foot. Five is the top 8-foot. Six is the top 4-foot. Seven is the T-line and so on. Ten is the back 12-foot. Actually it's not a 10-number system, it's 11. Eleven is just enough weight to throw it through the house.

As they started winning regular money on the tour and started to put it all together, all of a sudden the Ferbey Four became five, six, seven and eventually eight, with the addition of Henry Hwang, the team doctor who joined them in 2004.

Curling, en route to becoming an Olympic sport, added coaches and alternates. And that explains those other guys in a lot of their pose-with-the-trophy pictures.

One of them is Brian Moore. He's the head coach.

The definition of head coach in curling depends on the rink. But it hardly relates to other team sports. Especially in the case of Moore. With Ferbey around, there's not much need for coaching.

But that isn't to say he hasn't been a valuable member of the team.

"Brian was very instrumental the first couple of years, especially with Dave assuming the position of last-rock thrower," said Pfeifer.

"He was Carter Rycroft's coach in juniors. It was more of a Carter thing than anything," said Ferbey.

"Brian ended up helping Dave more than anybody. Dave's emotions in early years were kind of questionable. Brian was the perfect guy and he helped him a ton. He was a dual coach for Carter and Dave in the beginning, but then mostly for Dave in the first few years.

"From a technical aspect he doesn't help us that much. It's more of a mental aspect. Each coach is different. Jules Owchar, for example, knows Kevin Martin's slides from juniors. He knows him better than anybody. He probably has a lot of input in that area. Brian keeps us loose on the ice and we have fun with him. We don't talk to him a whole bunch during the year. He's mostly just around at provincials, Briers and Worlds.

"A lot of coaches are there to keep you thinking curling. This might sound strange but one of Brian's strengths with this team is almost exactly the opposite. He's a real prankster. He keeps us NOT thinking curling. A lot of those teams are thinking curling 24 hours a day. We're the other way. We try not to think about it until it takes our complete focus about an hour before the game.

"Forget about it. Have fun. That's the kind of team we are and Brian knows when and how to keep us loose."

"Exactly," says Rocque.

"Brian quickly realized his role early on. He really did a lot of work with Dave who was very hard on himself. Brian really worked channelling the negative emotions out. He played a big role in Dave's development and growth.

"In recent years he's seen what we needed as a team to reduce the demand on our time at a Brier, for example. It gets to be so much at times, you need someone to deflect it. Radio people are calling Randy's room at 5 AM to do a morning show in Toronto. Sometimes Brian will set it up so all those calls go to his room. A managerial position during big events has become quite important. When you get off the ice at 11 PM, you want to go to the Patch for one or two beers. But you also want to get out of there by 12:30. He'll have our driver at the front door and the team meeting at a certain place. Sometimes it's hard to leave people talking to you. He'll come up to groups maybe talking to Randy or Dave and say 'the guys are waiting for you in the van' and make it easy for them to get away. He has a real intuition about when he's needed."

Dan Holowaychuk is the fifth. He's been with the team from the first Brier, has actually appeared in three of them, and has outstanding percentage numbers for his appearances. And while other rinks heading to the 2005 Olympic Trials were picking up big-name curlers to add as their fifth man, the Ferbey Four said, nope, Holowaychuk was their man.

"It was strange how we came to selecting Holowaychuk as our fifth man," remembers Pfeifer. "We were looking at all these different players. In the beginning, we were looking more at their accomplishments, and then one day at the curling rink when we were talking about it, he just happened to walk past our table and…"

Holowaychuk had no accomplishments.

"We weren't really looking to choose someone who was going to replace Nedohin or Ferbey if they were injured so much as someone who fit in with the group personality-wise," remembers Rocque.

"We sat around and threw a few names around, talked about it, mentioned a lot of great guys we felt deserved to go to a Brier who hadn't been there.

"We kind of decided you are who you hang around with. We didn't want to be associated with guys who thrashed around on the ice and broke brooms, who were poor sports. We wanted to pick someone who was a reflection of who we thought we were."

And when Holowaychuk walked past the table, someone said "a guy like him."

"He understands the game. He has a lot of heart. He'd been to the provincials several times. He could play most positions and not hurt you," Rocque said. They all agreed.

But his real position has been as organizer.

"We hit a home run with Dan," said Pfeifer. "When we're at the big event, he's the constant organizer on the team. There is no one anywhere in the entire sport better at preparing a team before you get to the event, for one thing. He takes care of all the logistical things. After a few years it's become a routine."

Ferbey said Holowaychuk has been a fantastic fit.

"He's become more of a manager who can play. He's one of the best organizers I've ever seen in my life. Give him a job and he takes care of it. He and Brian are a good fit together.

"And he's an above-average curler. He's very good but he's just never managed to get on the right team to win. We don't throw him in often, but he's performed well every time we've used him."

Jim Waite would become the other member of the team when they'd reach the World Curling Championships. For a dozen years he's been the official head coach of every Canadian team to play internationally.

But he can only be as much a part of the team as the team will allow.

"He's the national coach. He's appointed to you. He's very knowledgeable. He comes in for the Worlds. He knows everybody on the other side of the ocean. He's invaluable. Some teams maybe don't use him for what he can offer. But our team certainly accepted him and he's really helped us," said Ferbey.

"He's there to try to help Canada win gold. He's a phenomenal resource but only if you can get the personalities out of the way for him to do his job," says Rocque.

"We hope that he feels more a part of our team than any team he's gone to the Worlds with over the years," says Pfeifer.

But they'd have to wait for Waite. And the others.

Nobody needs an official head coach, an official fifth man and, especially, an international head coach, when they're just another team out there trying to get to the Brier.

In early 2001, they looked like they were headed to a similar fate as the year before. In trying to get out of the city zones they lost 7–5 to Kevin Martin in the 'B' event.

But this time, thanks to a wild 9–5 win over Shane Park in the 'C' event, the Ferbey Four was headed to the provincials in Stettler.

> ## "It's been 12 years since I've been back there. I can't explain how emotional I am right now. I can't say anything. I'm speechless."
> ### —Randy Ferbey

That's actually the time and place they became the Ferbey Four, although no one was calling them that yet.

Kevin Martin was the man to beat as he went to the Central Alberta community gunning for an unprecedented seventh title. But it was Ferbey and Dennis Graber who were the only two teams to emerge from the first day at 2–0. Ferbey ran the record to 4–0 while Martin struggled at 2–2 through day two.

Not much was made of it at the time because it was an early draw and Ferbey beat Martin 9–4 in the evening to create the story line for the day.

But Ferbey lost 7–6 to Graber when Nedohin's draw to the button to win it hit a flat spot to give Graber the steal and, as time wore on, his claim to fame. The Ferbey rink went five years without losing a game at the provincials since losing that one.

The next day Ferbey made his own headlines. He announced his impending retirement.

Ferbey said curling's grind no longer held the same allure for him as it did in the past and that he was much more into being a minor league baseball coach in Sherwood Park where he could spend time with his kids.

"This is probably my last year," he said.

"I've been thinking about it the last couple of years. I don't get up for these things or look forward to them like I used to 15 years ago. I was like 'Let's go!' about bonspiels. I've got a family that wants a little bit of my time and I want a little bit of their time."

Nedohin said there was one way of keeping the old guy with the young team. "He's not done yet. If we win this, he's stuck with us for another year."

Nedohin's prediction came true in a matter of hours. They beat Martin in the final.

Tears flowed from Ferbey when it was over.

"It's 12 years since I've been back there," said the skip. "I can't explain how emotional I am right now. I can't say anything. I'm speechless, to be honest with you. It's a big win.

"You know, beating Kevin Martin, one of the best teams in the world… I'm ecstatic about this win. It's huge. In curling, you have to be patient, take your time and hope good things happen to those who take care of it. Tonight we did. We played well."

Nedohin made the last shot on 10 to run Martin out of rocks.

"I just went down and Scott said, 'Take your time,' and I told him, 'I'm not going to take any more time than I normally do,' " said Nedohin.

"This is, absolutely, the sweetest. Losing to Ken Hunka two years ago just fuelled the fire to get back here. I couldn't wait to get here again. We got into the final and we knew we were playing well. It was such a calming game. It never crossed my mind we could lose that game. We were in a zone."

Pfeifer, who had represented Canada twice as a junior, said he was happiest for Nedohin and Rocque.

"Dave and Marcel haven't been to a Canadian championship and Randy hasn't been back to the Brier in a while. I'm just happy for all of them. They played awesome."

Rocque, who had been a member of Don Walchuk's rink that lost the provincial final to Ed Lukowich in 1994, said it felt fantastic.

"I have three of the best curlers in front of me. Scotty is just unbelievable. When he's firing, he's amazing. Randy doesn't make many mistakes. I told Dave if he gives us a solid game, we'll be there. He definitely did. He earned it. I'm just glad to be on their coat tails."

It was the beginning of a wonderful ride.

CHAPTER 7

What a Time to Go Potty

Looking for pigeons? Ferbey had to keep his head up.

It had been so long since Randy Ferbey had been back to the Brier...

How long was it?

"I haven't been there in such a long time we were still wearing sweaters back then," Ferbey laughed when he received his new Alberta duds, baseball-style jackets and golf shirts that had become the style for curlers everywhere.

Ferbey had been wandering in the curling wilderness for a dozen years.

"Twelve years! It doesn't seem like it was that long ago. Time has gone by quickly," he said before taking the trip to Ottawa and the big show.

"I remember a lot of things about it just as well as I remember things that happened last year. It's nice to get back after 12 years because it just goes to show you how tough it is to get back and play in that thing."

Ferbey remembered getting $800 for playing in the Brier in 1989. In Ottawa each rink would receive $20,000.

"It's so true, in the purest form, when people say they'd pay to play there. After not being back there for such a long time, I understand where they're coming from. I can understand the top teams' viewpoint, too, but in a sense they're spoiled," he said of a growing discontentment with the lack of cash at the Brier.

"There are players and teams that have never had the opportunity to play in the Brier that would absolutely love to go there whether they get $10 or have to pay."

Ontario's Wayne Middaugh, Quebec's Guy Hemmings, Manitoba's Kerry Burtnyk and Northern Ontario's Al Hackner headlined the 2001 Nokia Brier and nobody was sure what to make of the Albertans.

Larry Wood's *Tankard Times* morning line had Ontario at 6 to 5, Manitoba at 2 to 1, Quebec at 3 to 1 and even New Brunswick's Jim Sullivan ahead of them at 5 to 1. Behind Ferbey at 6 to 1 was Northern Ontario, Saskatchewan's Doug Harcourt and Nova Scotia's Mark Dacey all at less than 10 to 1.

And some of these guys were chasing history, like Ian Tetley, Middaugh's second going for his fourth Brier title. Hackner and Burtnyk were looking for their third Brier titles as skips.

"I don't see why a playoff spot isn't realistic," said Ferbey. "Curling is a funny game. Would it surprise me if we go 9–2? No. Would it surprise me if we go 4–7? No."

For the others, they weren't thinking of it so much in terms of the big picture as the experience of walking out there behind the bagpipes for the first time.

"I get butterflies just thinking about it," said Nedohin. "I'm sure with all the lights and all the people it's going to be exciting.

"I don't know if I'd consider us a rookie team because we have so much experience. The only thing we're a rookie to is the Brier instead of another bonspiel. But we knew that until we got to our first Brier, we weren't going to be considered one of the top teams in the country. You can win all the money in the world but until you're at the Brier, you're not in the public eye as one of the top teams."

When you get to the Brier the first time, before you think about winning it, you worry about making a mess of it.

"You come to these things and think you're going to go 0–11," said Ferbey after his first day at the Brier in 4383 days.

The Albertans, despite finding themselves down 2–0, scored two in the seventh and another two in the 10th to beat Dean Joanisse of B.C. for openers in a game Nedohin, Pfeifer and Rocque would remember forever, it being their first.

"This is something," said Nedohin before going back on the ice and defeating Sullivan's New Brunswick Herring Chokers 5–2. "This is my first time at a Brier and I looked around out here and there isn't a single team that can't beat you. But to tell you the truth, I was more nervous in the provincials, actually. That surprised me because we were losing most of the time in our first game and we were able to tell ourselves to stay patient. We always played it that way and if I have a shot to win it on the 10th end every game, I'll be happy."

Ferbey was back in his element and having fun with the day. "Now, the worst we can be is 2–9," he said when his re-entry was over.

"Everybody was nervous and everybody played phenomenally for the first day at the Brier—especially Dave Nedohin. I was concerned about him.

"Personally, I stunk early on. I turned it up and the team stayed in there. Generally, when somebody's playing bad you have to work through it and hopefully come through it. That's what a team is all about."

After the day was over and they'd won the second one, Nedohin breathed a sigh of relief.

"It feels great now," he told reporters. "I was trying hard not to think that it was our first Brier game, our first Brier day. I was just trying to think of it as another game and another day of curling. I told Randy when I threw that last rock I didn't feel as stressful as when I was throwing it in the morning."

Ferbey knew the pressure was on his rookie last-rock thrower and worked on trying to reduce it.

"In the ninth end of our first game, I turned to Dave and said 'You know what? This Brier is over right now.' He laughed and it seemed to settle him down. The atmosphere is something out there."

There wasn't a big buzz about the Ferbey Four on the first day at the Brier. Most of the attention was aimed at Quebec's Guy Hemmings. The Albertans were cool with that.

"This is the Brier," said Ferbey. "The crowd's cheering for Hemmings. You have to work through that."

In their third game, they were going against a big name and a legend in the game—Al Hackner of Northern Ontario.

Ferbey was relaxed playing Hackner—"The Iceman"—having been part of Hackner's rink on the cashspiel circuit. But this was a test for Nedohin, Pfeifer and Rocque.

Hackner had Ferbey down 4–1 after three ends, but Alberta bounced back with a 9–5 win in their only game in the second day of the event.

With a 3–0 start to the first Nokia Brier, the team had won 10 of their last 11 starts on the Brier trail, had their opening day jitters behind them and had just knocked off somebody who was a *somebody*.

"Those other three guys have never been to a Brier, so now they should be proud of themselves," said Ferbey of his young guns.

"We've talked about what it's like to play in a Brier and they've played well. After the first three games Dave is throwing as well as I've ever seen him throw and that's the key. If the last rock is on, you're going to do well here. He's had to make all types of shots—hack weight, draw weight, draw the button—and Dave has made them all."

For his part, Nedohin nodded.

"I didn't really know how I was going to react or feel when I got out here. I was hoping I would play like it was another bonspiel or another game. But it's hard to do when you're playing in front of 10,000 people. I think I've been pretty calm from the get-go, so I don't think I'll have to change anything in my approach to the game."

Nedohin, the next day, was put to the test on all of that.

It was the ninth end against another big name in the game—Ontario's Middaugh—and Nedohin had just settled into the hack for his final shot on the eighth end when a beeping (some might say "bleeping") fire alarm started to sound.

This was nothing new to the Ottawa Civic Centre, which had a whole host of such happenings at hockey and figure skating events held in the building. It was, however, all new to Nedohin.

He played it like an old pro.

Nedohin sat out the wait for five minutes before the alarm stopped and then made a huge shot—a double takeout for three. It was the shot that made the difference in a 9–6 win over Middaugh and raised their Brier profile even higher.

"Actually, I didn't mind the fire alarm because it gave me another chance to see if that double was even there," said Nedohin. "When the alarm went off, it gave me some time to go down and have a talk with Randy and the other guys to see if it was going to work or not. It actually didn't hurt us. It helped us."

Ferbey admitted he was concerned that Nedohin's leg might have stiffened up during the unscheduled rest, but it really didn't matter.

"He made the shot," said Ferbey of the inch-precise double kill by his last rock dispenser.

But Alberta lost 7–3 to Doug Harcourt of Saskatchewan on a day when all three undefeated teams from the opening weekend found their way into the "L" column.

"The Express record is still intact," laughed Ferbey of his Ryan's Express rink's 12–0 run in his previous Brier life.

The Albertans would bounce back with two more wins, knocking off future foe Mark Dacey's Nova Scotia Bluenosers and getting a game from Steve Moss and the Territories' Polar Bears, who would go through the Brier without a win but kept it close in a 6–4 loss to Ferbey.

"They're right into it now," said Ferbey of his boys.

"My experience as far as teaching them or telling them what to do doesn't matter any more. I was expecting them to be a bit more jittery with the crowds, the cameras and the media. Any time it's a first, they have to be nervous. All three have held up quite well."

Ferbey hadn't just taken his team to school on how to handle the Brier you watch on television but with the Brier you don't see unless you're on the scene.

"I told them to go with the flow, to make sure they had some fun. If you win, you win. If you lose, you lose. Just go to the Brier and have some fun because you never know when you're going to get back."

This meant visiting the Brier Patch, the gigantic entertainment layout that is part and parcel of any Brier, where the competitors have a post-game brew with the customers, a concept that hasn't caught on yet in the NHL.

> **"If you win, you win. If you lose, you lose. Just go to the Brier and have some fun because you never know when you're going to get back."**
> **—Randy Ferbey**

Curling involves celebrating Canadiana with the odd shout of "Sociable!"

To many, because the Brier brings together fans from every province in the country, it has, in a way, replaced the Grey Cup as the so-called Grand National Drunk.

Not that the Ferbey Four was going there for "aiming fluid," but they were definitely making sure they made themselves part of the scene and they enjoyed it.

"What Randy told us is that if you come to the Brier and concentrate 100% on curling and don't get out and enjoy the atmosphere a bit, you're going to go home and not remember how much fun the Brier was because you never saw much of it," said Nedohin.

"We're kind of picking our spots. We're going to the Patch for an hour here and an hour there. We're really getting into the atmosphere and having a blast."

They also didn't have to pay for too many drinks. As is the case with the Grey Cup, there's a decidedly high percentage of Albertans who go to every Brier, and the last few years prior to the Ottawa Brier they'd been crying in their beer.

Other than two titles from Edmonton's Kevin Martin, an Alberta rink hadn't won the Brier since Ferbey and Ryan won back-to-back in 1988 and 1989.

Harold Breckenridge of Calgary went 4–7 in 1990. Greg Ferster of Leduc went 4–7 in 1993. Ed Lukowich of Calgary was 5–6 in 1994. Tom Reed of Edmonton was 5–6 in 1998. Ken Hunka of Edmonton was 5–6 in 1999. Kevin Martin was 6–5 in 2000.

Alberta fans had been getting used to being a Brier power again. Heading into the last two days of the round-robin with Ferbey sporting a 6–1 record, the team was being chased by a trio of luminaries—Burtnyk, Middaugh and Hemmings.

Not that anything was a lock here. They were reminded of that when, after making short workout of Keith Ryan of Newfoundland in the early draw, they met crowd favourite Hemmings in the nightcap and lost.

"If we see them again, if we play as well as we did tonight, we'll beat them. We were all over those guys. There's no question about that. They know it. We know it. Guy played tremendously and once those breaks were given to him, he got the job done," said Nedohin.

Hemmings could have had Montreal Canadiens hockey legend Guy Lafleur's No. 10 on his back for the way they chanted "Guy! Guy! Guy!" when he executed an angle-raise double takeout with the out-turn in the fifth end of what was then a 2–2 tilt.

Nedohin wrecked on a guard with the last rock and it was a steal of four for Quebec and a shake-hands-after-nine 9–5 win.

After Alberta's 8–7 extra end win over Peter MacDonald's Spud Islanders they met the challenge in another name game—this one for first place—against Burtnyk's Buffalo Boys from Manitoba. The way it worked, by the time they got to the game in the final draw, both teams knew they'd made the final four with Middaugh and Hemmings, a final four with as much mustard as you could have possibly manufactured. The question was who would end up where and who would have last rock advantage through the playoffs.

Alberta won it 7–3 to end the round-robin at 9–2.

"Not bad for an old man and a bunch of kids," said Ferbey. "Make that a really old guy. I feel tired right now. That game drained me. Any time you play Kerry Burtnyk for first place in the Brier it takes a lot out of you. But I'm sure I'll be ready to go again."

The condition was shared by Nedohin: "It feels great to be the No. 1 team. I'm really excited. But I'm tired right now, too. There's a lot of stress in these games and you're drained when you're done."

By finishing first, the Ferbey Four moved into position "A" in the Page playoff system, which features a 1–2 game and a 3–4 game. First plays second. The winner advances direct to the final. The loser drops to play the winner of the 3–4 game to determine the other finalist. It's about as intelligent a playoff system as there is in all of sport.

Ferbey & Co. were just happy to be playing when they played Ontario's Middaugh (who also finished at 9–2 but lost his round-robin game to Ferbey) in the playoffs in the 1–2 game while Quebec's Hemmings would meet Manitoba's Burtnyk in the 3–4 elimination game.

The "You're Nobody Until You've Won A Brier" theme was in there somewhere, too.

"If we're still underdogs coming in, that's fine," said Ferbey. "Guy hasn't won either. But Guy is Guy. There are hundreds of teams out there who are willing to shine and we're just fortunate to be here."

Ferbey knew it was like forging steel. And he knew this was a much more secure squad than he took to the pebble on the first day of their first Briers. They all knew it.

The team had put together some impressive statistics in their first Brier round-robin together, not the least of which was a Brier record of 23 steals.

While their shooting percentages weren't what they'd be in subsequent Briers, Nedohin's 81% was only four percentage points short of top-percentage man Burtnyk. Together with Ferbey's 82%, Pfeifer's 87% and Rocque's 88%, it put them at 84% as a rink. None of them led at their positions. None of them were far behind the leaders. In a Brier field loaded with experience, they were happy with that.

The security heading into the playoffs didn't come from the stats but rather from beating the big-name rinks along the way.

"We played every team now. We know what to expect. We've been on TV a few times. I'm sure people are getting sick of looking at us," said Nedohin. "I've just gone through this relying on Randy's experience. I may never be back. The Brier has been exactly what I expected it was going to be. Mostly it felt like it was a long time coming.

"It feels great to be the No. 1 team. That means the hammer throughout and we'll take it. Our aim was to make the playoffs and this is a bonus. I know a lot of people here don't know who we are and haven't seen us play. I guess they're surprised. I'm happy to surprise people."

The next day in the *Tankard Times*, Larry Wood referred to them as "the unheralded Alberta juggernaut."

In a spectacularly curled game, the Albertans found themselves down 3–2 to Ontario after four but

regained control with a three-ender on the fifth, shaking off Ferbey's fourth hog-line violation in the seventh to help preserve the win.

"I came back with a good one after that anyway," laughed The Ferbs.

Nedohin gave the Brier a video clip for the ages in the 10th end when he lost his gripper, slipped and somehow managed not to end up falling on a rock pile.

"I just did anything I could to get my body and broom out of the way. It would have been a horrible time to burn a rock. We're in the game you've dreamed about your whole life. I can't imagine what it would have been like if I'd burned a rock and cost us everything."

There was a bonus to go with the win, one that the rink hadn't given much comment or thought to, as they worked their way to the Brier final.

They became the third Edmonton Ottewell Super League team to qualify for the 10-team Olympic Trials in Regina, joining Kevin Martin and Kevin Park, to win a chance to represent Canada at the 2002 Salt Lake Olympic Winter Games.

"We celebrated for about 10 minutes," said Nedohin, who watched the 3–4 game on TV with Ferbey while Pfeifer and Rocque toured the Parliament Buildings.

"We opened a bottle of Perrier and had a cheers toast to that. I think our wives were more excited than we were. We were getting ready for a game."

Nedohin wanted to play it immediately. "I feel wonderful. The way we're playing, we're to the point where we're expecting to win. I sure hope we can put out the same performance we did in the 1–2 game and hope that's good enough."

Middaugh, the way the Page playoff system works, still had a life and ended up against Burtnyk, who beat Hemmings 9–7 in the 3–4 game.

Hit and run: Dave Nedohin was in the bathroom when first Brier was won.

Now, in all of sport, how many times have you heard an athlete ask which team or individual he hoped to play in the final? And has anyone ever said anything other than "It doesn't really matter to us?"

But Ferbey made no bones about it. He didn't want to play Middaugh again.

Despite knowing that whoever he'd play he'd have the hammer—last rock advantage to start the game—Ferbey wanted Burtnyk.

"It scares me if they beat Kerry," he said. "I'd rather play Kerry in the final right now. Beating a guy like Wayne Middaugh three times in a row is extremely difficult. I don't know if anybody has ever done it."

It's not like Burtnyk was one of those guys who somehow managed to get to the final because of a bunch of breaks or something. The guy had become Manitoba's all-time winningest skip—and Manitoba was the cradle of curling in Canada for most of the 20th century.

Burtnyk, then and there, was chasing the same history the Ferbey Four would end up chasing in a couple of years. He was attempting to become only the fifth rink in Brier history to win three titles. The Richardson rink with their four and Manitoba's Ken Watson and the two Alberta skips, Matt Baldwin and Ron Northcott, had won three each.

Not only that, it was the 20th anniversary of Burtnyk's first Brier when he was a 22-year-old.

Burtnyk and teammates Jeff Ryan, Rob Meakin and Keith Fenton had also created the monster match in terms of a bigger picture. Burtnyk hadn't been back to the Brier since winning it all in 1995 and following through with his second world championship.

"I've come here a few times," Burtnyk told the curling writers after his 6–5 win over Middaugh in the semi-final. "This is my fourth trip. If we manage to win the third one, I couldn't ask for more than that. If we don't, I'll have two wins and a second. Either way, it's going to be pretty good. But it would be a lot sweeter with a win."

Burtnyk was hoping his team's experience and the "Manitoba mystique" would offer an edge. "There's no doubt. Our team has been to the Brier final before. Randy Ferbey has the experience of playing and winning but the other three haven't. They're going to have a little different nerves than we're going to have going in. When it comes down to crunch time, you never know."

Manitoba versus Alberta is the longest-running rivalry in the game. Combined, the two provinces had won 44 of the previous 71 Briers. Manitoba led 26–18. In sudden-death Brier showdowns for the title, this was the 13th. Manitoba had won nine. In 1996 Kevin Martin lost the final to Jeff Stoughton and in 1997 Martin bounced back to beat Vic Peters in the final.

Even though Burtnyk suggested all the pressure was on Alberta, Ferbey scoffed at that. "I say he's full of it," he said. "The pressure is on him. He's the former world champion. The team has been together for seven years. They're one of the best teams in Canada ever. We're still up-and-coming. I view it as a Randy Ferbey–Kerry Burtnyk final and not the whole weight of the province on our shoulders."

For Nedohin, the final presented an entirely different perspective. Burtnyk was his boyhood hero growing up in Winnipeg.

"I've always idolized Kerry," he said. "Playing him in a Brier final is just a phenomenal feeling. I couldn't have picked anybody that I'd rather play against. It's really exciting for me.

"He's one of the best shot-makers in the world and they are a really nice team. I enjoy spending time with all the members of that team. Their team, in my mind, represents more what a curling team should be like. They're not four individual players. Shooter for shooter they might not be the best in the world, but they are as a team."

When he still resided in Winnipeg, Nedohin had approached Burtnyk about joining the foursome when Jeff Ryan was contemplating retirement.

"They didn't break up because they had a bad year," said Nedohin. "They've stuck through it, and they know the friendships you develop off the ice translate on the ice."

It was a mutual admiration society throughout the line-up.

"It's great to be able to play Kerry," said Ferbey. "With Kerry, we're good friends. Losing to him won't bother me at all. It'll be quite a friendly game. They're just four nice gentlemen to play against. I'm a Kerry Burtnyk fan more than a Wayne Middaugh fan."

That said...

"It would be special to win. It would give me a third Brier victory. It would be a nice touch to end my career," said Ferbey.

Ferbey said it wouldn't be easy to tell his rink to relax. First he had to sell himself.

His team seemed loose enough. They passed on a chance to practise and instead decided to attend the Ottawa Senators–New York Rangers hockey game.

"I know I'm going to be nervous because I am right now," Ferbey said. "The other guys may have to settle me down. Sure, I've been there. But they've held up pretty well this week. I've always been like that in all the years I've played the big games. It'll be nothing new to me. But there will be butterflies the size of eagles."

OK. Maybe pigeons.

Brier history is littered with a lot of unusual happenings, and as previously pointed out, Ottawa's Civic Centre has it's own quirky past. When a pigeon somehow managed to get into the old rink overnight, it became a sidebar to the final.

"One Flew Over The Brier Nest" was how *Edmonton Sun* curling scribe Con Griwkowsky phrased it in his story:

> Flapping around overhead, the pigeon dislodged a piece of ceiling asbestos that fell on the ice early in the second end. Hans Wuthrich and his icemaking crew were called upon to perform the unusual task of sweeping off what was assumed to be the result of pigeon poop.

"Can you imagine if they cancelled the final of the Brier because of a pigeon?" said Ferbey. "Where's a cat when you need one?"

The pigeon, again as Griwkowsky put it, "continued his work of trying to single-wingedly bring down the house, repeatedly targeting the sheet the game was being played on."

Burtnyk turned to Ferbey in the third-end cleanup. "How come he has to pick on our sheet?"

Earlier in the week, it was raining in various parts of the building as melting snow somehow found its way through cracks in the aging barn. There were "waterfalls" that cleared out one section of spectators and a stream that chased a reporter off the media bench. In addition to the building's troubles, there was also the incident when Middaugh took out his frustrations on a leather-lunged fan by flipping him the middle finger.

It was as entertaining a final as they come and not just because of the pigeons and the curling.

There was Nedohin returning from the fifth-end break wearing a Guy Hemmings jacket.

With the crowd, which had been cheering Hemmings all week, now solidly on their side, Nedohin scored what would prove to be the winning deuce in the sixth end.

Ferbey, calling an aggressive pressure game as usual, watched as Manitoba made mistakes. Both Meakin and Ryan crashed on consecutive shots in the eighth.

Nedohin's off-wing double in the fourth to take away a Manitoba steal was what Burtnyk called the turning point.

Ferbey had twice tried to convince Nedohin to draw, but he finally gave in and allowed his last rock thrower to try the shot.

"What a phenomenal shot under the circumstances," said Ferbey. "We were going to be two down, maybe three down. Dave liked throwing that rock all day, and when the guy throwing last rock is confident throwing it, you just let him."

All three first-time Brier members of the rink curled 90% in the final. Ferbey came in at 67%.

"The key to this game is to make all the right shots, and Randy made all the right shots," said Nedohin.

The 8–4 win was a game to remember. But despite all of the above, the 2001 Brier would be remembered by the team for Nedohin almost missing the biggest moment of his curling career because, perhaps inspired by the pigeon, he decided he couldn't wait to go potty before playing the final end.

Before Burtnyk delivered his last rock, Nedohin headed for the bathroom.

"Somebody came running back to the washroom and said they were shaking hands," said Nedohin. "I said 'What?' I must have mowed down four or five people trying to get out there."

The first person who extended his hand once he got back on the ice was childhood hero Burtnyk.

"I saw Kerry coming up to me and it was just an amazing, amazing feeling to have him come up and shake my hand after winning the Brier. The whole team came up and wished us well at the Worlds," said Nedohin who won the Hec Gervais Award as Most Valuable Player.

"I can't even explain it. We came into the final wanting to have a solid performance. We knew we were good enough to play with all these teams but to come in and expect to win the Brier...that might sound somewhat arrogant to do," said Nedohin.

Pfeifer was going to his third world championship. His first two were as a junior. This one put him over the moon.

"At first I couldn't even believe we were at the Brier, and now we've won it. It's an amazing thrill," he said.

Ferbey said Pfeifer was a key.

In their first Brier the front end of the rink didn't get much notice from the media. But Pfeifer, unlike his teammates, made it as a second-team Brier all-star.

"He played just fantastic," said Ferbey. "He played as well as anybody out there. The guy is a phenomenal talent. He'll be back to this thing for years to come. He, Dave and Marcel, if they so choose."

Rocque, who pulled out a picture of his daughter Gabriella and had a good look at it during the fifth-end break, said being part of a Brier-winning team was wonderful.

"To play with such a great team is an honour, let alone to go to the Brier together and win it. It's just unbelievable. To stand on the same ice as Burtnyk is just an honour. Ever since I was 11 or 12 years old, when he first won, well, that's when I set my own goals. Here I am playing against some of my own idols. I've always wanted to go to the Worlds and here I am."

Meanwhile, Ferbey's retirement was on hold.

"It might be unfair for me to leave the team at this point. Right now, I'll have to say I'm sticking around for another year. Unfortunately, I can't get out. But don't worry. I'll be out before long."

When they returned home, the rink couldn't believe their profile, Ferbey included. When Ferbey returned to his Sherwood Park home, there were 35 messages on his answering machine.

"The crazy thing about it was that about 25 of those were from people I didn't have a clue as to who they were. It was overwhelming. I was shocked by the number of people who follow curling. It was on the streets, in the malls, at work, all the events we'd been asked to attend. In Edmonton, everybody follows the game."

Ferbey found out that it was entirely different than when he was part of Ryan's Express and when Pat Ryan won the Brier in 1988 and returned to win it again and go on to win the Worlds in 1989.

"It's bigger than it was in '88, that's for sure. The newspaper coverage, the TV coverage...I was amazed at the response. We were at a function where the whole place stood up and gave us a round of applause. The room was full of movers and shakers in the city. It wasn't like 'Who's that and what are they doing?' They knew. They were all commenting about what happened at different ends of different games."

After their first Brier win, they were honoured at events throughout the city—at the race track, at a charity function in support of the Inner-City Foundation, as guest bartenders at Mo's, and at an Edmonton Oilers game against the Philadelphia Flyers, they were invited into the dressing room to meet the players.

Curlers have an inferiority complex in the world of sports. They often view themselves as "just curlers."

But the team found out fast that winning a Brier made them more than that.

"The Oilers were enthused," reported Ferbey from his visit to the NHL team dressing room. "They followed us. They know about curling. People knew the game when I won with Pat Ryan in '88 and '89, but it's much more widespread now. I don't personally remember getting anywhere near this much attention. I don't think Dave, Marcel and Scott realize yet what they've accomplished here. They're still in awe of what they've won, but they don't realize the magnitude of the whole thing."

They would, soon enough.

CHAPTER 8

Champs to Chumps

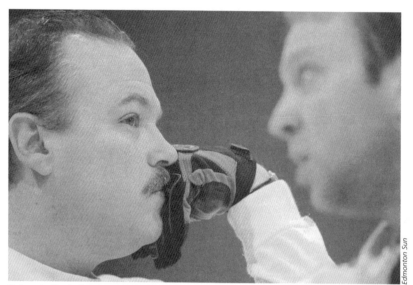

Edmonton Sun

Return to Earth: Ferbey and Rocque are left stunned at Worlds.

Lausanne is a lovely location on the Swiss shores of Lac Léman, better known as Lake Geneva. The home of the International Olympic Committee and Olympic Museum, it features an old town with tiers of steep narrow streets leading to a cathedral. The city spreads as far as Ouchy, a famous resort that became Lausanne's waterfront with a square featuring fountains and giant chessboards.

It's a nice place to visit, but you wouldn't want to curl there.

Randy Ferbey had been there once already at the World Curling Championship in 1988 when he won his first Brier curling with Pat Ryan's Edmonton Express.

That didn't go so well.

Actually it went great until the end.

Ryan, Ferbey, Don Walchuk and Don McKenzie ran the table in the round-robin and had a 9–0 record with scores of 8–4, 8–3, 8–4, 6–2, 7–4, 8–1 and 8–2 until the scores started getting a little closer with a 4–3 win over Daniel Model of Switzerland and a 6–5 win over Doug Jones of the U.S.A. to finish the regular round.

To that point, Ferbey had really enjoyed his first trip to Lausanne. His only complaint was the price of a drink.

"We went to a place and the cover charge was $20. Then it cost $20 each for our first beer. But we couldn't complain too much about the prices. We went bar-hopping with the rock group, Supertramp. That was a great experience."

The guys on the rink told all sorts of stories about the culture shock involved, although Ryan did point out "the crowds were about triple the size they were at the Brier in Chicoutimi."

The Chicoutimi Brier drew 45,225, about a quarter of a million fewer than one in which Ferbey would play down the line.

Ferbey said curling against Europeans at the Worlds the first time was an experience in itself.

"It's like curling against guys from another planet. It's really weird. These rinks are wearing a lot of wild get-ups—jump suits tight at the ankles. Baggy pants. They're quite colourful and I guess that's good for the game. They're certainly beyond Canadian curling fashion," he told me on long-distance telephone back then.

"You never know what the heck they're saying out there. You don't know if they're yelling hurry or whoa."

He said he saw two sights he'd tell his grandchildren about.

"The Swiss team beat Finland, which wasn't a big deal because this was the first time Finland had been in the championships, but the skip threw his broom high in the air. I mean real high in the air, about 60 or 70 feet in the air. The broom came down, handle first, and landed on the second's head. It's really a miracle it didn't kill him. If the angle of the handle had been straight down it would have gone right into his skull. As it was the poor guy needed a bunch of stitches."

The other sight was just as unbelievable but not as spectacular.

"It was an extra end between the U.S. and Denmark and the Danish second tripped and fell on the last rock. He tripped and fell over it but he wouldn't admit to it. He ran away! He was gone! They gave the game to Denmark!

"The guy came back out and claimed he didn't know what they were talking about.

"It's weird over here. They let anybody and his dog on the ice. I'm not kidding. You have cameramen everywhere and guys walking around drinking coffee. And I'm not exaggerating about the dogs."

Canada won the semi-final 4–2 against the Swiss to set up the final against Eigil Ramsfjell of Norway, the guy they laid the 8–1 licking on in the round-robin.

That left them with 26 consecutive victories including the provincials and the Brier.

And then it happened. They lost. In the final.

"I'm not going to let there be a cloud over my head," said Ferbey, the team spokesman on the phone back home after the 5–4 loss.

"There were 8,000 rinks trying to get somewhere at the start of the year and we lost the final at the Worlds. I don't care if it's darts or sewing quilts, it's the world championships and to have been in the final was remarkable."

Now, 13 years later, Ferbey was back.

Ferbey and rink had been invited to Switzerland for a bonspiel in 2000 prior to winning the Ottawa Brier and that didn't work out well, either. They didn't even qualify for the playoff round.

"Point out that I wasn't there for that one," said Marcel Rocque. "I always bring that up. One event I miss in all these years and they can't even qualify."

That time they didn't have a big red maple leaf on their back. This time they did. They'd find out soon enough that big red maple leaf looks a lot like a bull's-eye to the rest of the curling world.

"We went into the Ottawa Brier as a bit of an under-dog," said Nedohin. "There were so many top rinks there that we weren't looked at much and we really didn't have much pressure other than the pressure we put on ourselves.

"All of a sudden we're at the Worlds and everything had changed. The team was the same as it was a month earlier. But then, all of a sudden, because we're curling for Canada, there was added pressure to win.

"We knew there were good teams over there. You look at some of the great teams that have come over there and haven't won..."

It's a long list.

Terry Braunstein in 1965, Alf Phillips in 1967, Harvey Mazinke in 1973, Hec Gervais in 1974, Bill Tetley in 1975, Ed Lukowich in 1978, Barry Fry in 1979, Kerry Burtnyk in 1981, Mike Riley in 1984, Pat Ryan in 1988, Kevin Martin in 1991, Vic Peters in 1992, Kevin Martin again in 1997 and Jeff Stoughton in 1999 all failed to bring home gold. Phillips, in '67, Gervais in '74, Riley in '84 and Martin in '97 all managed to fail to even manufacture a medal.

This time Ferbey was back in Lausanne with a chance to personally become a two-time world champion. But he refused to make much of it.

"It's not a 'me' thing, it's a 'we' thing," he said. "Becoming a two-time world champion...well, every-body knows I'm not big on those trophy and ring things.

"One of the biggest things our team has going for it is its attitude. I've never known a team that hates losing as much as this team does. It's not that we're *bad* los-ers, in one sense of the term, but whether we're play-ing for a toaster in Tofield or whatever, we treat it almost as the world championships. We don't like losing."

Ferbey, with his return to Lausanne, said he'd learned a lot with his trip to the Worlds there in '88.

"We went undefeated the whole year and lost the final to Eigil Ramsfjell. You can never say you're going to win. You try your best and see what happens. All these teams deserve to be here. It's not like European teams are incompetent. They're very capable and have good work ethics. You still have to make your shots. If you're waiting for them to miss, it's not going to happen."

Peter Lindholm of Sweden, Andreas Schwaller of Switzerland, Markku Uusipaavalniemi of Finland, Andy Kapp of Germany, Dominique Dupont-Roc of France, Jason Larway of the U.S.A., Dan Mustapic of New Zealand and Johnny Frederiksen of Denmark were in the field. Also a big, troll-looking, likeable lout named Pal Trulsen of Norway, a guy who would begin his run as a Canadian killer right from the start.

Trulsen welcomed the Ferbey rink to the Worlds with a wild and crazy 13–9 victory in which the Canadians gave up a four-ender, the first at the event since Russ Howard managed to do the same against Australia at the 1993 Worlds in Geneva, Switzerland.

"We got out-played, I guess," said Nedohin, who *Edmonton Sun* curling writer Con Griwkowsky described from the scene as having "a hint of bewil-derment and a touch of panic in his voice."

Ferbey spent 15 minutes after the game in a meeting with team coach Brian Moore and Canadian Curling Association coach Jim Waite, trying to figure out what went wrong.

"We couldn't figure the ice out," Nedohin told the Canadian media while the skip and coaches had their talk. "Draw weight seemed to change from shot to shot. One rock would run straight and one would curl. We'd better have it figured out for the next game."

It took a little longer than that.

They won their next one, against Johnny Frederiksen of Denmark. But Canada had to steal on an extra end to win it 11–9.

Finally, in Game 3, they got it going, scoring a 9–3 win over Andreas Schwaller of Switzerland who shook hands after the seventh end.

Ferbey said he knew there would be a learning curve with his guys.

"They're young. Success came to these guys pretty quick," he said of Nedohin, Pfeifer and Rocque. "It all came together in three years, and there we are playing before 50 fans at the world championships, and maybe not really realizing where we were at and who we're representing. It's a tough situation for anybody."

IOC head Juan Antonio Samaranch made an appearance at the event on opening weekend and Nedohin had no idea who he was.

It was with great delight that the rest of the rink took to teasing him about that.

"Scooby Doo is probably all he knows," joked Ferbey.

"With temperatures outside the Malley Ice Centre approaching 23° C, memories of their slow start were starting to melt like the snow on the upper reaches of the nearby Alps," Griwkowsky wrote the next day when they slapped Jason Larway of the U.S.A 10–3 in eight ends and battled to win 7–5 against Andy Kapp of Germany.

But then they got beat 8–2 by "M-15," the nickname (count the letters) of Markku Uusipaavalniemi of Finland, a country that at that moment had four outdoor two-sheet surfaces protected by a tent.

It was the first time Finland had defeated Canada. It was also the most lopsided loss suffered by a Canadian team since Ed Werenich was drubbed 10–3 by the U.S.A. in 1983.

Uusipaavalniemi didn't exactly take it in stride.

"We've had unlucky games against Canada the last couple of times," he said. "Against this team we had better possibilities than against teams like Wayne Middaugh or Kevin Martin. These guys lack a little bit because they don't have that bullet-like shot, so it is easier for us."

Ferbey, who had brushed past reporters for a self-imposed 15-minute cool-down period, heated right back up again when he was told of Uusipaavalniemi's quote.

"That's his opinion," said The Ferbs. "When you're down 3–0, you don't try and throw high heaters. How can he make a statement like that? You've got to get up to hit. They didn't see what we were like there at all. That was one of our worst efforts in four years. It's just one of those games to forget about in a hurry because if it escalates, we're going to be out of this thing. They played extremely well. They hit as well as any team I've ever seen."

Uusipaavalniemi made a spectacular triple take-out in the second end for a steal of two. Then he recorded an end to tell his grandchildren about, hitting Ferbey not just for four but a steal of four.

When the Ferbey Four left the rink, a thought had occurred to them. Only one Canadian team had ever missed the playoffs at the World Championships, and with another couple of games like the one against M-15, they could put themselves in a position to do just that.

"You can't imagine," said Ferbey. "You come to these things and people back home take it for granted. They think it's a cakewalk. It's not."

Ferbey was getting feedback from everywhere after that one.

"Whether it was the throwing, the sightseeing, having not been here before or the ice...everybody has a different opinion on us," he said.

A 9–5 win over Dominique Dupont-Roc of France and an 8–3 victory over Dan Mustapic's rink from New Zealand put the Canucks back on track. They'd moved back into a tie for first with Norway and Sweden at 6–2.

Canada's last game before the playoffs was against Peter Lindholm of Sweden. When Lindholm won 7–2 to finish first, Griwkowsky reported that "Randy Ferbey lost his game and then he almost lost his mind trying to figure it out."

What happened was that Ferbey, Norway's Trulsen and Schwaller of Switzerland all finished with 6–3 records in a three-way tie for the second, third and fourth, the final three playoff positions.

In Canada there are sane ways to decide such things involving internal wins and losses and points for and against. However, the World Curling Federation called for a shootout to determine which team finished second, third and fourth.

When in Rome...the Ferbeys went with the flow. Each member of the team hit the button with their shots. That gave them second place, guaranteed.

Then the fun began.

The Swiss put their first rock in the house then sailed the rest through. Not to be outdone, the Norwegians blasted all their rocks through the house.

The idea was to avoid playing Canada.

Switzerland, because they'd put that first rock in the house, ended up third.

After going through all of that, they decided to flip coins for hammer, last rock advantage.

Switzerland won hammer.

"Interesting," said Nedohin. "To us, it would seem logical that the team that finished second after the shootout would get hammer. But, whatever..."

Ferbey found it amusing. "The shootouts, the ties, nobody gets last rock unless it's clear-cut. It's just a few things that can happen over here. Am I irritated? No. Not at all."

It was nothing compared to what was about to happen.

Curling, as the sport was attempting to win full Olympic status, added a few things to try to make itself look more worthy or something. One was officials. There didn't used to be any. Officials decided they had to make calls. And somehow Randy Ferbey, with his not exactly textbook style of throwing, became their "go-to guy."

Regularly Ferbey was called for hog-line violations. But this was the semi-final of the Ford World Curling Championships and what the world would watch was beyond belief.

Three times the Swiss officials pulled Ferbey rocks in the game against Switzerland's Schwaller. After the seventh end and the third pulled rock, Ferbey lit into the head official when television replays showed clearly that he'd released the rock in time.

But the major memory to the members of the rink was Nedohin lying on the ice, his hands behind his head, staring at the ceiling, after missing one that he makes 99% of the time.

It resulted in a steal of one and a 6–5 win for Schwaller.

As soon as he watched it roll out, Nedohin realized it was a shot that would haunt him for a really long time.

"I'd like to take it back. Unfortunately, I can't. I can't explain it. I just missed. It had nothing to do with me being nervous or the pressure. The confidence was there. I never really thought about the consequences of it until it was over."

Four years later, before a match-up against the same Schwaller at the Worlds in Victoria, the Ferbey Four were still talking about it.

So were members of the media who were there in Switzerland and couldn't help noticing, as Allen Cameron of the *Calgary Herald* noted, "the sharp-eyed hog-line judge celebrating with Swiss team officials and the media."

"Obviously, we lost a game to them that we shouldn't have lost," said Ferbey four years later when Cameron, working that week for the *Tankard Times*, jumped all over that angle with Schwaller back to another Worlds for another go against Ferbey.

"Or, we got cheated out of a game, I guess you could say," Ferbey continued. "Schwaller's team was pretty rah-rah-rah about it and what not. But that's the way Europeans are."

Those who were there would remember Ferbey swearing a blue streak at the hog-line judge. Actually, you didn't have to be there. That was telecast from coast to coast. Canadian coach Jim Waite was also seen arguing with Swiss head official Hans-Uli Sommer.

So much was made of the hog-line calls that over the next few years it was the calls and not Nedohin's wide open hit-and-stay to win the game on the 10th end which would be most remembered by the curling world.

"It could have been a lot easier," said Ferbey. "It was an easy shot. But without that officiating it might not have come down to that shot. That was always the point."

TV replays proved Ferbey right.

Waite, four years later, said he'd never been more infuriated about a curling call. But what made him even more incensed was the celebration by Schwaller.

"David missed his last shot and the Swiss were all jumping around and high-fiving and the Swiss crowd was going nuts. OK, you can accept that from the crowd. But…

"I thought this team was really jobbed over there.

"Let me tell you a story from that night. At the closing dinner, David stood up at our table to propose a toast to the guys and apologize for missing the shot. Marcel said, 'Sit down and shut up. We win as a team and we lose as a team.' And right there they committed, that night, to going back and winning Alberta, winning Canada and winning the Worlds the next year."

If losing that game wasn't bad enough, they lost the bronze medal game 10–9 to Pal Trulsen of Norway the next day to become only the fifth Canadian team in the 42-year history of the event to fail to return home with a medal.

"I don't know what to say," said Ferbey when it was over. "We all wanted to win. We got a couple of bad breaks. The whole week wasn't a real solid week for us. That's the frustrating part. We showed signs all week of being outstanding and we also showed signs of being a very mediocre team. All I know is that we tried our best. This whole week, we tried our damnedest. There's a lot of expectations to make the medals. If we let people down, believe me, we let nobody down more than ourselves by not getting a medal. These guys are young and hungry and I know they'll want to get back. It might motivate them even more."

When they returned to Edmonton, Wes Montgomery had a column waiting for Nedohin in the *Edmonton Sun.*

Sports fans all across Canada cringed and felt sorry for this year's Brier champ as he came inside with his attempted wide-open hit and stay against Switzerland last weekend…a shot he would make nine times out of 10 with his eyes closed, a shot that followed a brilliant individual performance. But what the Hec.

Local curling legend Hec Gervais' storied career is spotted with easy last rocks he missed in attempts just to get to the Brier. Playing against Calgary's Ron Northcott in a late '60s provincial final at the old Corral in Cowtown (think 12-end games and corn brooms) Gervais, a former world champion himself, shook hands, walked out of the Corral in his curling shoes and wasn't seen for two days.

Montgomery also told of 1973 when Hector had the hammer at the provincials playing the 13th end when he had a hit on a lonely rock in the four-foot for a win and got "nothing but air."

The next year Gervais won the Brier again, returned to the Worlds and lost the semi-final to—you guessed it—Switzerland.

"So you see, Dave, it happens to the best of them, of which you are one, and they bounce right back. Hey, at least you came close. Hector's shots were toast as soon as they left his hand," wrote Montgomery.

When Ferbey returned he found some interesting information, too.

> **"David stood up at our table to propose a toast to the guys and apologize for missing the shot. Marcel said, 'sit down and shut up. We win as a team and we lose as a team.'"**
>
> **—Jim Waite**

There was news of the development of an electronic hog-line detection device that had been under study by a group of University of Saskatchewan engineering graduates. The Canadian Curling Association was ready to give it a go in a year.

"Hopefully before that," said Ferbey, who quipped that he believed he already had the Brier record for hog-line violations.

"I hear it's almost foolproof, working on a heat transfer from the handle to hand theory."

Ferbey had been trying to add them all up and believed he'd been called 15 times during national and international events. He said if the detection device worked, it would prove his innocence by the lack of hog-line violations attributed to him in the future.

But Ferbey and his pulled rocks and Nedohin and his unbelievable miss needed to be dealt with before technology could come up with any cure.

Five years later Ferbey said the proof was in the pudding.

With five years of history playing with the electronic sensors inside the rock handles, which eliminated hog-line judges everywhere, Ferbey had been innocent every time he threw a rock.

"Since that game in Lausanne, I didn't have one hog-line violation. What does that tell you?"

Looking back, Pfeifer says the loss in Lausanne was what made this team.

"One loss has defined this team, the loss in the semi-final of the 2001 Worlds. To come back and pick up where we left off showed that we weren't going to let setbacks get in our way."

But another setback loomed.

When Ferbey won the Brier, it also came with a trip to the Olympic Curling Trials in Regina. Again, Ferbey had been there and done that.

It was back in 1988 when curling became a demonstration sport at the Calgary Olympic Winter Games.

"It was a little different back then," said Ferbey of those Olympic Trials as a member of Ryan's rink.

"It was a bit more low key. It wasn't quite as high on the priority list."

With the Nagano '98 Olympics, curling had become a full-fledged medal sport. All of a sudden the Olympics had become bigger than the Brier, bigger than the World Championships.

"Now just being a part of it is something special," said Ferbey. "It's even bigger than it was four years ago."

Qualifying rules insured the best over the four-year Olympic quadrennial would be involved. The field included Wayne Middaugh, Kerry Burtnyk, Kevin Martin, Bert Gretzinger, Jeff Stoughton, Kevin Park, John Morris, Russ Howard, Greg McAulay and Ferbey's Ottawa Brier-winning bunch. And the women's side wasn't much easier.

It's a difficult thing to get your head wrapped around the Olympic Trials. To most they are tougher to win than the Olympics themselves. Unlike any other event, provincials, Brier or World Championships, there's no free space on the bingo card.

"You have to put it in perspective," said Ferbey when he arrived in Regina.

"There are 20 teams here, and there will be 18 teams that go home with nothing. Eighteen *good* teams that go home with nothing," he said of the combined men's and women's event.

"Here an easy day might be Middaugh and Gretzinger," said Ferbey. "We're definitely not the favourite—I think there are four or five teams you'd favour ahead of us."

Martin would win it 7–6 and go on to win the event and represent Canada in the Salt Lake Olympics. Ferbey, who lost three straight before getting back on track too little too late, ended up with a 5–4 record in the round-robin.

For a few months at least, with Kevin Martin going to the 2002 Salt Lake Olympic Winter Games, Ferbey, Nedohin, Pfeifer and Rocque would go back to being second bananas on the Edmonton and national curling scene with a lot of people suspecting they were just another one-hit wonder at a Brier.

CHAPTER 9

My Wife Understands Me

Behind every successful curler: Team Ferbey wives Heather Nedohin, Raylene Rocque, Chantelle Pfeifer and Wendy Ferbey (top left to right), "fifth woman" Jodi Holowaychuk and Mrs. Coach Cheryl Moore (bottom).

Marcel, Scott and Dave, will you take Randy to be your lawful wedded skip, to love, honour, cherish and obey, to have and to hold, from this day forward, in sickness and in health…

"All of the wives have always joked that these guys are more like husbands and wives to each other than with us in some ways," says Chantelle Pfeifer.

"I mean it's crazy how well they get along."

There's been a common thread to all of the stories of Marcel Rocque, Scott Pfeifer, Randy Ferbey and Dave Nedohin.

They all met and married curlers.

"It's crazy how well we get along," says Heather Nedohin of the wives. "We have a blast together. There's never any bickering or anything like that. We really enjoy each other. The guys can go do what they have to do and we'll go off and have a great time together."

In there somewhere may be the secret to the team's success.

"I'm not sure we'd have accomplished what we had so far if it hadn't worked out that way. We certainly couldn't have done what we've done without our wives being as understanding about what's involved with this game," said Scott.

Chantelle was a schoolgirl at a curling club when Scott met her. He started dating her, ended up on her brother's rink and won the World Junior Curling Championship with him.

How's that for a love story?

Chantelle says all the wives take pride in the roles they play.

"I think it's helped a ton because we understand the magnitude of how amazing their team really is. When you're a curler yourself, you understand how hard it is to get the right combination to succeed.

"When they're gone for 25 days out of the month curling, it can get a little tense. But we've been there. We can understand."

By this point it has become crystal clear to the team that they had something together, really had something together and not just on the ice but off. Not just in the winter, but the summer.

It's tough to keep a team together in this sport. But this team has discovered the secret to success.

Their wives understand them.

Exactly, says Randy. "I think it's huge, the understanding that's involved. Curling has never been an issue. We don't have to make excuses."

Randy met his wife Wendy at the curling rink. "Ottewell Curling Club. She wouldn't leave me alone," he jokes.

"Actually, I did ask him out," said Wendy. "If I hadn't asked him out, nobody else ever would have.

"It was 1981 and it was the Ottewell's Grey Cup party. I asked him to my Christmas party after that and it's been happy, happy, happy ever since, I guess."

They even curled together. Twice they made it to the Canadian Mixed Championships together, the last time losing in the final. The other members of their rink were Pat and Penny Ryan.

"I think we signed a prenuptial agreement that curling was our life," said Wendy.

While the skip is big on being involved with sons Cody and Spencer in baseball and daughter Taylor in soccer in the summers, it's been mom who has spent the last decade or so getting the two teenage boys and one daughter to Saturday morning curling.

"They had no choice," she said. "My kids were going to curl."

Wendy is willing to take her share of credit for the success of her husband and the rink. "Our kids have grown up expecting their dad to leave in September and get back in time for Christmas. They've grown up expecting their dad to win everything, too."

What they didn't see, she says, was the years between the two Brier wins with Pat Ryan in 1988 and 1989 and this remarkable run with the Ferbey Four.

"He was in a drought for 11 years and thought it was all over until he met this young crew and it started all over for him," says Wendy. "They're Randy's boys, too.

"But it's been a long haul and I don't know how many women would put up with it."

Take her share of credit? Absolutely!

"I had to quit five years ago. When I quit, Randy started winning again.

"We needed some balance in our lives. One of us was always on one side of the country and the other on the other side of the country. Our kids had a lot of babysitters," she said.

"Yeah, I had to quit so he could start winning again. And I think I'm the better curler," she laughs.

Born in Calgary, Wendy Bain started curling at the age of 11.

"Both my mom, Ann, and my dad, Jim, were curlers. They introduced myself, my sister Sherry and my brother Rod to the Curl Canada program at the original Calgary Curling Club. But school sports took priority and I didn't return to curling until I was in Grade 10. That's when I was asked to join the rink of Trish Houston."

Trish is the sister of Neil Houston, manager of Championship Curling of the Canadian Curling Association, who won the Brier with Ed Lukowich.

"My family moved to Edmonton in 1979 where my mom and dad continued to curl and signed us up to play at the Derrick where I played junior with Lindsay Graves. We made it to Northerns in 1980 and provincials in 1981."

In the fall of '81 she joined Edmonton's famed Super League, which many believe is the reason so many top teams are produced out of the city.

"That's where I met Randy. I needed a date for my Christmas party so I asked him. It was a toss-up between Randy or Darren Fish at the time. Randy won the toss. While we first met at a Grey Cup party, my first date with him was on December 10. We attended Randy's company Christmas party that night and my company's Christmas party the next night."

Losing out in the Northerns with Val Hurlimeir in '84 and '85, Wendy began curling mixed events with Randy.

"I played mixed with Randy and my mom and dad in '84. We advanced to the Northern Alberta playdowns.

"Anybody who plays with his mother-in-law and his wife should get a purple heart and a gold star," laughs Randy.

Actually, they basically begged Wendy's mom and dad to join them.

"Lorne Barker and Cathy Will were curling with us that year and they couldn't make it. We had to pick somebody up. We had to find somebody who hadn't curled in any of the playdowns. We ended up going to mom and dad and asking them."

A year later she and Michelle Solinger convinced Randy and Don Bartlett to compete in the mixed and won the province and advanced to the Canadian Mixed Championship in Markham, Ontario, where they finished with a 5–6 record.

"That was the first nationals for Randy and me in any level of curling. It was a real fun week. We had all our parents there.

"It gave Randy a trivia question claim to fame when TSN ended up not being a rights holder for curling. For a year there, until TSN became a rights holder again the following season, he was the first and last guy to curl on TSN.

"That was the very first time TSN televised curling.

"It was also the first time Randy and I ever roomed together. And it was also the last time we ever roomed together at a curling championship because Randy says we didn't win because we roomed together.

"Actually, the guys have their own rooming situations and they stick with it. I either room with Raylene Rocque or Chantelle Pfeifer. Usually it's both. Chantelle usually comes at the start of the week and goes home. She prefers to watch the big games at the end at home on TV. And usually Raylene comes for the end. I'm the one who is usually there all week so I usually switch from one roommate to the other."

There was one other mixed scenario.

Still curling competitively in women's, Wendy failed to get out of the province, so in '86, she joined Randy and Pat and Penny Ryan to do the mixed thing again.

They rolled to a 9–2 record and made it to the final where they lost on last rock to Dave Vandine on a team with a guy by the name of Hugh Millikin. He'd later move to Australia from where he'd take teams to the World Curling Championships.

"I told Hugh losing to him in that event drove me out of mixed curling. The skip was yelling 'Whoa' and Hugh was sweeping the thing like crazy. If he hadn't kept sweeping that rock I think we would have won. All I can tell you is that it was my last game of mixed curling."

> **"All the wives have always joked that these guys are more like husbands and wives to each other than with us in some ways."**
> **—Chantelle Pfeifer**

A couple of months later, on May 24, Wendy married Randy in Edmonton.

"We had five groomsmen and five bridesmaids and about 450 people at the wedding. Many of our curling friends were there at this large Ukrainian event and I think I got caught up in the day. When I signed the marriage certificate I forgot to read the fine print: 'Be prepared to spend the rest of your life with a man who will be consumed by the sport of curling.'

"Our honeymoon was spent at the Morinville Curling Club playing in their summer bonspiel. It wasn't until 17 years later, in 2003, that we really took a honeymoon. For my 40th birthday Randy booked a trip to Las Vegas. That was the first time we took a trip together by ourselves."

Competing with Penny Ryan, Sandra Rippel and Helen Griwkowsky, wife of *Edmonton Sun* curling writer Con Griwkowsky, Wendy made it to the Northerns in '87. She did the same with Karen McCrady for the next five seasons and with Cindy Serna for three straight years and Faye White for three years after that.

But after three years with Rhonda Skillen, including one trip to the provincial finals, she called it quits in 2001 and explains:

"I'd always wanted to play in the Scott Tournament of Hearts but Randy and I had to make a decision. We needed to put balance in our lives. We were finding it very difficult to balance our family, work and part-time/full-time sport.

"We were finding it very difficult to get time off work, make enough money and bring up our family. Our three kids were beginning to wonder if their parents were Auntie Sherry or Grandma and Grandpa, Auntie Trudy or Baba and Gido.

"Randy was doing much better than I was in curling, he'd just won the Brier after all those years between the two he'd won before. He was bringing in more money from curling than I was.

"I decided it was time to see what he could really do. I hung up my shoes and began being an employed mom.

"It was also at that time that I began to really put time into my job at Sobeys where I was promoted to a management position. And I needed to be closer to home with the kids. They were growing up and getting involved in their own sporting activities as well.

"The year 2001 was the first year that our kids had their first Thanksgiving with their mom. I was always in Calgary at the Autumn Gold and Randy was either in Regina, Winnipeg or over in Europe.

"It hasn't been easy. In a lot of ways it's been like being a single parent. Thank goodness for the off-season. By the time the curling season is over, it's time for a marriage counselor. I bet we could get a discount as I know three other marriages that could use it, too.

"I joke that Randy became successful at this sport when I quit it, but there's a lot of truth in that, too. I know he felt more at ease when I was at home with the kids.

"Every Saturday morning during the winter you can find the kids and me at the Shamrock Curling Club. I have coffee with the gals and the kids are out on the ice trying to become a champion like their dad. They all like the sport and I'm sure it will become a part of their life as it has with ours.

"Randy and I have talked about when it is time for him to hang 'em up, too. But when you have a passion and it becomes your job, why should you give it up? Really, how many people ever get the chance to do what they really love and succeed at it?

"I feel he'll wind it down once he fulfills his final dream at becoming an Olympic champion. It's the only event he has not yet mastered. I believe in my heart he will conquer it before the will starts to fall away.

"I have been to all the Briers in which Randy has participated and to four of the six world championships. I regret not being at the Worlds in '88 and '89 but a baby was the reason for the first and the second was expense and motherly pride. My advice to wives and husbands is to support your spouse and go when you have the opportunity. It's an experience you can't get back."

Dave Nedohin credits much of the success of the rink to having the support of their wives, which would be hard to find if they'd married non-curlers. But he says the odds of all four of them having married curlers is… well, probably about the same as winning four Briers.

"The first time I saw Heather was on TV when she won the Junior Worlds and I still lived in Winnipeg.

"I thought 'Wow, maybe it would be cool to meet her.'

"And I did meet her. I found out she was a friend of Wendy Ferbey. But it wasn't until the middle of winter a year later when, sort of out-of-the-blue, I decided to get her phone number, call her up and ask her out."

So what's the real story?

"That's what happened," said the former Heather Godberson, who won Alberta, Canada and the Worlds when Dave was in Winnipeg.

"The first time we even met each other, he was competing at the barefoot nationals in waterskiing and they were held at Shalom Park here.

"My best friend, Rona Pasika, was curling with Wendy Ferbey. Wendy's team and Randy's team had a summer barbecue. Dave asked Rona to come out to watch him and I went with her.

"To be honest the first thing I thought was 'What a stupid sport.'

"Now, well, could you write that now I've come to appreciate it a bit more. I'm not saying that's totally true, but…"

Heather says she doesn't know if curling fans really know her husband.

"David's a very family-oriented guy. His parents just moved to Edmonton from Manitoba to be closer to our daughter Halle. We now have two children. But the way this rink works, the wives all have seven children.

"As a family, we really enjoy the off-season. We go out to Whitefish Lake, which is about a half hour south of

Lac La Biche, developing our lot. You can always find us in a park playing or riding our bikes.

"The hardest thing for David is being on the road and spending that time away from Halle. Thank goodness for our sponsorship from Bell Mobility Canada. All the phone calls for the guys on the rink are free. Dave phones four or five times a day. He reads Halle stories over the phone. They sing songs over the phone.

"With both of us curling, our calendar is pretty intense. My main responsibility now is Halle. But David's parents really help us out. David's dad is the coach of my team. He travelled with us in 2005. He's a level three certified coach. Grandpa comes with me. Grandma looks after Halle," she says of David's mom Kris.

"When it comes to Dave, my job is to keep him healthy, well fed and well dressed."

Two of three, she says, isn't bad.

"Keeping him well dressed is a challenge. Sometimes he's home for 24 hours and right back on the road again. It's tough keeping him in fresh clothes. And when it comes to the right belt, the right colour shoes and all that stuff, he's impossible."

Living with a last-rock thrower is not unlike living with a field-goal kicker.

If they make 'em, they're heroes. If they miss 'em, they're goats.

But when you're a last-rock thrower yourself...

"You win some and you lose some," says Heather. "Halle doesn't know and she doesn't care. She just says 'Are you coming home, dad?'

"David has made a lot of great ones and missed some opportunities. An elite athlete always rebounds from it. The loss in Lausanne at the world championships was humbling to David. Same with the Brier they lost in Saskatoon. After they lost that Brier... Well, it's traumatic to give up three on the last end. But it was OK. Dave rebounded. I always think he comes back stronger."

Born in Fort St. John, B.C., Heather grew up on a farm just north of town and was exposed to curling at a young age.

"First, I was helping my mom wash windows and take care of the Fort St. John curling rink," she remembers. "After I'd watched enough to learn the game, I decided to give it a go."

First she mastered the Fort St. John farmers league at the age of eight and went on to competitive curling at the age of 11. She competed in four British Columbia provincials before moving to Alberta to attend Grande Prairie Regional College (GPRC).

During her two years at GPRC, Heather won two Alberta College Athletic Association gold medals and was selected as all-star skip both seasons. She was also named as co-winner of the school's athlete of the year award.

In 1996 Heather Godberson and rink captured the attention of the province first, and then the nation.

That was the year she skipped a rink featuring Carmen Whyte of Tofield, Kristie Moore of Grande Prairie and Terelynn Bloor of Fort St. John, B.C. to the Alberta Junior title, then the Canadian Junior championship and finally the World Junior title.

Ah, yes. Take up curling and get to see the world.

"We never left the province!

"The Peace playoffs were in Grande Prairie. The provincials were in Calgary. The Canadian championships were in Edmonton. And the World Championships were in Red Deer."

The Kristie Moore on that team is Brian Moore's daughter.

"He was my coach before he was the boy's coach," says Heather. "Kristie is from Grand Prairie and Brian lives there to this day running his seed store and buffalo ranch. He's been great for curling up there, sorting out prospective players.

"We loved Brian as our coach. His son Chad played with Carter Rycroft," she said of Kevin Martin's former long-time second.

"He was our coach the year we won. He had a great way of bringing out the fun and taking away the pressure. There'd be times there was so much pressure they all wanted to throw up. He'd pull me aside and make light of the situation.

"He was our driver, too. And he'd have us all killing ourselves laughing in the car. He was pulling pranks all the time.

"I introduced Brian to David. David introduced Brian to the team as a potential coach."

Heather was honoured as the all-star skip at the Junior Canadians.

The following year she joined Cathy King (then Borst) as the third and ended up tied for fourth in the Olympic Trials to Sandra Schmirler's eventual Olympic gold medal champions.

> **"The first time we even met each other, he was competing at the barefoot nationals in water-skiing...to be honest the first thing I thought was 'What a stupid sport.'"**
> **—Heather Nedohin**

That spring, she made it to her first Scott Tournament of Hearts with Borst, where they finished fourth in Vancouver, losing the 3–4 game to Newfoundland.

"That was my first Scott. I was in awe of the whole thing. I walked in there and thought 'This is the dance! It can't get any better than this!' Then I noticed that the veteran players didn't feel quite the same way. I noticed there wasn't a crowd. It was only my family and a few other spectators. And it smelled in there. There was a farm show before we moved in. Me, not knowing any different, hadn't really noticed it wasn't up to par. The ice was perfect and that was all that mattered to me. I couldn't have been happier."

Until TSN put her game on TV.

"I got miked. It was my most embarrassing moment. I dropped the microphone in the toilet in the fifth-end break. Brenda Bohmer and Katie Horne howled about that.

"I was the second team all-star. My percentage was the highest during the week. I really admired Jan Betker, the third on Schmirlers' rink and I thought I had a chance to beat her out for first all-star. But they gave it to her. Damn. Damn. Damn."

In 1998 Heather and teammates won the Scott in Regina with a 10–1 record in the regular round (losing only to the Northwest Territories) before winning it all and punching their tickets for the Ford World Curling Championships.

"That was the year Sandra Schmirler and the girls came back from winning the gold medal at the Olympics in Nagano. To me, that was the best Scott ever and the best part didn't even involve us. When Sandra and her rink walked out in that rink, it was breathtaking. The crowd just roared. It was their first appearance since they returned. There were signs all over the rink, thanking them for bringing back the gold and making Saskatchewan so proud.

"They didn't have much left for the event, though. They were out of steam. They were jetlagged and just couldn't get back on top of their game. It was a thrill just to play against them that year and a real thrill for me to play against Jan as an Olympic champion. I always recognized her as the outstanding third in all of women's curling. To play against her in that situation was a big thing for me."

Get Heather talking about winning the Scott final over Anne Merklinger and, to this day, she still gets a lump in her throat.

"It was all like a whirlwind, standing in the house with Cathy, making the call, then letting it ride. It still gives me goosebumps thinking about it," she said of the shot that put it away.

"The thing I remember best is standing looking at each player's eyes. I re-live that moment every time the guys win a title. It doesn't have to be the Brier or the Worlds. I re-live it every time they win the provincials. I know how much work goes into it.

"I'd had a long run of placing third at the provincials and wonder if it would ever happen. When it does happen, live it and breathe it because it doesn't last long. The moment is over so fast.

"I always think of that when I watch the boys win. I see them out there and look sideways and see them taking the hacks out and tearing the signs down and everything. And I think the same thing every time. It

doesn't last long enough. The next thing you know you're back on the ice as just another club curler starting all over again.

"It's so, so sweet. But it doesn't last long enough. I think all of the wives know all of those things. We're all so proud of them. We understand the rush. We understand the bond they have together. We understand how you live for that moment. We live for them and through them."

Heather and the Borst rink would go to the world championships and come back with bronze.

"We travelled far again. Kamloops.

"Having seen David in Lausanne and Bismarck, I look at it differently now. I have nothing against 'out-of-Canada' Worlds. But having always been to one either in Alberta or in a province next to Alberta, I hadn't had that experience. Canada hosts a curling championship amazingly well. The crowds. The ice. The media. It doesn't get much better. And when it's in the neighbourhood your family can travel. I always had a bandwagon of family following us."

The rink lost the semi-final.

"That was heartbreaking. But we were determined to come back with a medal. We played Dordi Nordby of Norway for the bronze and we weren't going to lose."

The following February the rink found themselves in Nagano at something they called the Olympic Commemorative Championship.

"It was the year after the Olympics and they'd invited all the rinks to go back to Nagano for a special bonspiel. Sandra Schmirler and her rink were asked to go back but they turned it down. Because we were the reigning Canadian champions, they asked us to go as their replacement."

It was, to the day, exactly one year after the Olympics and it was awesome.

"We stood up on the Olympic podium one year too late."

To this point, Heather was the big winner in the relationship and David was her significant other.

"I made it to the show before he did. But even back then we were both feeding off each other. We're both so competitive in all aspects of life. If we go out for a casual bike ride, it usually turns into a race. Being competitive is our nature.

"But it really is inspiring to watch David evolve so much as a player. I saw him when he wasn't successful and then watched him finally break through. I watched David when he first started playing with Randy and where he is now. He's taken advice from me, coaches, books, and now he's making shots that I can't believe. I see them and say 'Where the hell did that come from?' He's really raised his game from the mental aspect.

"I watched him lose the provincial final in Grande Prairie in 1999 and not get to the Edmonton Brier. I felt it. It was heartbreaking. We both could have gone to the big show in the same year."

In 1999, Heather and rink went back to the Scott as Team Canada. At least it was a bit of a trip. It was in Charlottetown, P.E.I. this time.

"I was very ill. I missed out on the Hot Shots event, the practice session and the opening banquet."

They lost the final to Colleen Jones' rink, which would win five of six through 2004.

This time Heather was selected the all-star third in the Scott.

On August 28, 1999 Heather Godberson was joined in marriage to David Nedohin and, not long later, reunited with her former world junior championship team with her new name, Heather Nedohin, on the rink.

"Kristie Moore was 16 when we won the world championship. That year was the first year she was no longer a junior.

"I decided to give it a try. But it was so tough leaving Cathy, Brenda and Kate. It was at the 1999 Brier and we were all sitting around when I was asked 'Are you in or out.' I said 'out' and we all started bawling."

Reuniting with the girls she won her Worlds with in junior was made extra special when the team, which was the pride of the Peace, went back to Grande Prairie and won the provincials to go to the Scott.

"Back when we were together in '96, Grande Prairie took us as their own. I was from Fort St. John, B.C., but they adopted me. Kristie was living in Grande Prairie and Brian was coaching us. Kristie's mom was the manager of the curling club. We were back home in 2000, but we had company. Renee Handfield was the rink from the Peace we ended up tied with after the round-robin.

"We were down for eight ends but ended up winning, without the hammer, coming home tied. The crowd went crazy."

Off to the nationals again...

"Another big trip," Heather laughs. "The Scott Tournament of Hearts was in Prince George, B.C."

Finishing fifth at the Scott that year, Heather hasn't been back.

"At least I made it to the dance floor once as Heather Nedohin. "It's the family joke that when I stopped going, David started going. We seem to have a family rule that only one of us goes to the championships every year and I keep letting it be his turn. Har. Har."

It's actually a whale of a statistic.

Starting with the 1996 world junior title, Heather followed with trips to the Scott in 1997, '98, '99 and 2000. David has been to the Brier in 2001, '02, '03, '04 and '05. Heather also won the 2006 Alberta mixed to advance to the 2007 Canadian championships.

"It was so great that Raylene made it to the Scott in 2005 and Marcel back to the Brier," said Heather.

Curling, by now you are beginning to get the idea, is a small, small world.

When Scott Pfeifer hooked up with Colin Davison to win the province, Canada and then the World Junior, he was also well on his way to winning the heart of Davison's sister Chantelle—who would eventually become his wife.

"I was 17 when I hooked up with Colin and won the world championships in '94. But I started dating Chantelle when I was 16 and she was 15. Before I curled with him, I met up with her."

Of course, they met at the curling rink.

"I wasn't scouting for a player for my brother's curling rink," she laughs. "We met before Scott started curling with my brother. It just worked out that way."

Scott remembers the time and place.

"Chantelle and I met in 1992 at a local junior bonspiel in St. Albert in November. After courting each other on the phone for a while, we ended up dating in January 1993. She was 15. I had just turned 16.

"We both went to provincials in the Crowsnest Pass that year," he said of where they started going steady.

"After dating for eight years, we finally got married on September 16, 2000. Marlow Vincent Pfeifer, 'MVP,' was born premature on December 15, 2001, only five

Sex Symbols: Chantelle, Wendy, Heather and Raylene pose for fun photo in Las Vegas.

Cashman Photo Enterprise of Nevada, Inc.

days after we got back from the Olympic Trials. Dominic 'Torino' Pfeifer was born July 14, 2003."

Scott says when you share your life with another curler the thrill of victory and the agony of defeat can conflict. "In the same year I won my second provincial title, Chantelle was playing with Renee Keane and they ended up losing their final two sheets over from where we were winning ours at the Crestwood Curling Club."

Not for a lack of trying, Chantelle never made it to the Canadians during her junior career. She teamed up with several lesser known teams in women's, also playing with Deb Santos, Tara Weaver and Diane Dealy one year.

In 2000 she was the fifth player for Heather Nedohin's team at the Scott Tournament of Hearts.

In Chantelle's final year of curling, before she started to stay home to look after MVP and Torino, she played a year with Raylene Rocque.

"You'd think somewhere in there she'd have played with Wendy Ferbey," said Scott.

Happily a stay-at-home mom now, Chantelle says she's able to handle the time her husband puts into the sport and sometimes being gone 25 days out of the month in the winter, because she was a curler and gets the gig.

She says she's amazed, in her everyday life in Sherwood Park where the two live (as do teammates Dave Nedohin and Randy Ferbey), how sort of semifamous he's become.

"The team isn't going to last forever. They can only ride this wave so long. But as long as they're riding it and being so committed, I think all of the wives are going to be very understanding.

"All I can tell you is that when Scott comes home, he does the dishes; he's a husband and a dad and that's all that matters to me. That's what I really like. He curls as much as he does, but when he comes home, he's such a good husband and such a good dad."

She looks at her husband as he relates to the team.

"They all have such different personalities, so very different. I think Scott is kind of the mediator on the team. He's the even-tempered one."

For Raylene Rocque, it was not love at first sight—with either Marcel or curling.

"I basically grew up in a curling rink. Both my parents curled. So I swore I'd never curl myself," laughs Raylene. "My mom and dad dragged me down, by my ears practically, to join the junior curling league in Spruce Grove. I was 12 years old.

"They said 'Just try it. If you don't like it, then quit. But just try it.'

"I tried it. I loved it. It snowballed from there. I was hooked."

She curled all her junior years and six years of ladies with LaDawn and Laurelle Funk.

Twice junior provincial champion and twice runners-up with the rink skipped by LaDawn, she stayed with her Spruce Grove mates for six seasons on the trail to the Scott Tournament of Hearts but never made it.

"We had two very heartbreaking years, in 1993 and 1994 where we lost the provincial final both years. In 1994 we had a wide open takeout to win. I actually felt devastated for LaDawn," she said of the former world junior champion.

"I always wanted to get back together with LaDawn Funk in ladies but I could never convince her to forget the ghosts and get back into the swing in curling."

Raylene went on to play with several other well-known skips including Deb Santos, Jackie Rae Greening, Cindy Serna and Shannon Orsini, and currently curls with former Scott winner Cathy King who represented Canada with Heather Nedohin throwing third rocks back in '98.

"I love my new team. We connect awesome on and off the ice. We won $43,000 in 2005 on the cash circuit and missed out on an Olympic Trials spot by a half point. It makes me sick to think about that."

On the other hand, it did provide for a pretty interesting role reversal. Normally Raylene is the wife at the Brier. But at the 2005 and 2006 Scott Tournament of Hearts, Marcel was the wife at *her* Briers.

"I went to the Scotts in 1999 as a fifth for Renée Handfield," said Raylene of the soon-to-be Renée Sonnenberg, who was set to marry Les Sonnenberg, one of those excellent Alberta curlers who couldn't get to the Brier because the Ferbey Four kept knocking them out.

In 1999, Handfield was the Alberta rink in the same event as the soon-to-be Heather Nedohin who was curling in the event as Team Canada that year.

"In doing that, as well as watching Marcel, it made my passion even greater to get to the Scotts. And I believe I was prepared for the big show.

"I really enjoyed being a fifth, although being in the stands almost made me crazy because I wanted to be out on the ice so bad. They did ask me to come in for the last game but I felt they needed to win their last game as a team, so I declined.

"I wrote lots of things down to take with me because I knew in my heart that one day I would be back and on the ice competing.

"With our roles reversed at the Scott and Marcel sitting in the stands watching me, I certainly found it easier to be out on the ice than in the stands. Out on the ice you can do something. Sitting in the stands you feel helpless. I felt I was paying Marcel back for all the anguish he put me through. However, after several rum and Cokes, he seemed to settle down."

Marcel says if he wasn't married to a curler he'd probably have had to pack it in by now.

"If I had to explain this to a non-curler wife, it would be almost impossible.

"Raylene had to get pregnant around the curling schedule. We had our two kids around the curling season.

"My daughter Gabriella was five on March 9 at the 2005 Edmonton Brier. That was the first year I was home for her birthday since she was born. I've never been at any of her birthdays. I've always been at the Brier."

Raylene remembers the first time she set eyes on the guy who didn't hit her right off as her prize.

"The first time I met Marcel was at an Olympic curling camp in 1994. He was curling with Don Walchuk and I was curling with LaDawn Funk. There were definitely no sparks the first time I met him. I

actually didn't think highly of him, if you want to know the truth.

"We were sitting in on the nutrition session and he and his team were talking about their preparation, and let's just say I didn't agree with it. I was also in a serious relationship with someone else at the time and so was he.

"The next time I met him it was strange. It was almost like instant love for the both of us. I guess timing is the key.

"The rest is history. We both curl hard and work hard. We have two kids and a dog and try very hard to find a balance in all of that. We could not do what we do without my sister Cyndy Jones. She is a big part of the key to our success. She comes in and lives with our kids. She's also a huge fan."

With Raylene it's not necessarily over when curling season is over.

She's spent two off-seasons training and competing in two full marathons.

"I honestly think we're both addicted to being busy. But you know what? I've never been happier.

"I am so proud of Marcel's successes. I suppose, in a way, by living vicariously through his successes, it has made my desire to win myself much greater."

But it's not so easy to watch him.

"I'm a nervous wreck sometimes watching my man curl. The world championships in Victoria in 2005 were very tough to watch but I always try and stay positive because I know he can sense negativity.

"I do end up questioning some of their calls. Then they end up killing the other team with a five-ender. Then I think, well, I guess that's why they're the best team in the damn world."

CHAPTER 10

The Shot That Rocked the Rockies

Hot shot: Nedohin makes some great ones.

Because of the great Brier boycott, Calgary 2002 was supposed to feature a field of forgettables.

Because Kelley Law and Kevin Martin had crashed and burned and returned home without a gold for Canada from the Salt Lake Winter Olympic Games, it was also supposed to be soiled and spoiled by a dramatic drop in interest.

It didn't work out that way. It proved to be one of the most ballistic Briers of all time.

It was proof that the Brier is bigger than the names the Brier made but also proof that the new Brier Kings, the

Ferbey Four, had a special sizzle that made a marvelous marriage to the great Canadian rock concert.

It was the first year of the Grand Slam curling war. While Martin wouldn't have been able to enter the Brier playdowns anyway owing to winning the Olympic berth, several other curlers who had their curling names created by the Brier—Wayne Middaugh, Kerry Burtnyk and Jeff Stoughton in particular—headlined the list of curlers who signed up for the World Curling Players Association Grand Slam.

Defending Brier champion Randy Ferbey didn't join them. Neither did Guy Hemmings, arguably the most popular player in the game. Nor did Russ Howard—old "Hurry Hard!"—the curler who went to the Brier every year when all his golf pro friends went to Florida.

The Grand Slam, it was announced, would hold four events for prize money of $450,000.

"I like the idea of playing for bigger money but any time you go up against the biggest curling event ever, I have a problem with that," said Ferbey.

For his rink to go, being Brier champions, it would involve an even bigger sacrifice being that they'd qualified for Sport Canada funding and overseas bonspiel appearances. But that wasn't it, said Ferbey.

"I'm a traditionalist and I think we should leave an event of the Brier's stature alone. Why would anybody want to harm the biggest event ever to happen in curling and one of the biggest events in the history of sports in Canada? Why do you want to jeopardize that? I don't understand it."

Ferbey, Hemmings and Howard were suspended for three years from playing in the Grand Slam events.

"That's the problem," said Ferbey. "You ban the Brier champion, you ban the most popular curler in Canada and now you ban the biggest name curler who's probably done more for curling than anybody in the last 20 years. It's totally ridiculous."

The idea was to have the top teams sign contracts agreeing not to enter the Brier playdowns so the four Grand Slam spiels would be the only events featuring top teams.

With Kevin Martin heading the Grand Slam group as president, the defending Brier champions and the team that came home from Salt Lake with a silver medal found themselves on opposite sides of a curling war.

"There has to be another way to go about this without hurting curling," said Ferbey as he began the playdowns.

"One official asked me a few weeks ago why I didn't at least vocally support them. Hey, I've supported it ever since it started and would love to see it thrive and would love to be playing on it. But because we decided to defend our Brier championship, they suspended us for three years. How do they expect me to say nice things about them? Unfortunately, some of their decisions seem to be drawing a line between some of the country's top curlers."

Immediately, the Grand Slam curlers suggested it wouldn't be much of a Brier in 2002 without their involvement. This was lost on the sports fans of Calgary who had set a record crowd of 223,322 for Martin's Brier win in 1997 and were buying tickets at a record rate.

Ferbey made it through the Edmonton-area playdowns, from where 11 of the past 12 Alberta champs had emerged, with an 8–7 win over Rob Bucholz after spotting him a four-rock lead.

At the Northerns in Camrose, Rick Snethun, a Wainwright area farmer, sent Ferbey to "B" event with an 8–3 upset over the defending Brier champs. But the Fab Four, all sporting goatees, managed to work their way through "B" event to make it to Dawson Creek, B.C., the Peace Zone host of the only out-of-province provincials in Canada.

"The goatees helped us two years earlier when we won five straight bonspiels," said Ferbey. "My wife wasn't happy about the goatees, but it worked before so we decided to do it again."

Pfeifer was the go-to-guy when it came to the goatees.

"It takes me longer to grow it so I started first," said the second. "A little bit of superstition never hurts. We decided to keep them for the provincials."

With the hairs on their chinny-chin-chins a little longer, they became the second team in provincials history to go 7–0 when they scored a 6–5 win over Adrian Bakker of Calgary.

It was a game they had to win twice.

On the seventh end, Dave Nedohin had just delivered his last rock for two and a 7–3 lead. The Velcro had been ripped on the gloves and the handshakes were about to be exchanged when…

A hog-line violation was called!

Now it was 5–4 for Bakker.

"I'd never won a game twice before," said Nedohin.

This was the year before Ferbey set some sort of world record for hog-line violation calls. But this call was on Nedohin.

He said it was ridiculous. "Not a chance. Not even close."

Ferbey rolled his eyes.

"Those officials are always on the ball, so I have no doubt he was over. It just takes the fun out of the game when they do something like that. I still contend a person slides the same all the time. He doesn't slide over the hog line one out of 30 times. He's either going to be over the hog line all the time or never."

The next day the Ferbey Four put the return trip to the Brier away with a 6–5 win over Mike Vavrek of Sexsmith in a great game, as so many Alberta finals have been over the years.

"Unbelievable game. Both Dave Nedohin and Kurt Balderston put on a performance," Ferbey said of the last-rock throwers.

"I can't say enough about the guy who throws last rocks for me. I wouldn't want anybody else right now. Kurt made a game of it in the eighth end. He made a couple of shots that were just phenomenal to tie the game. They're a good team. But I can't say enough about my team. We've got patience. We've got perseverance. And we're going back to the Brier."

Nedohin shot 91% in the final.

"It ranks among my best games," said Nedohin. "This last week, in my mind, is the best curling I've ever done. To be able to throw last rock and win the game is just a wonderful feeling. That was just a great final to have and I'm just excited to be on the top end of it.

"We're finally at the level we wanted to be at. We've been fine tuning it ever since the Olympic Trials. I know we're going to the Brier with no hesitation in our minds that we can win it.

"After the win last year, Randy told us we didn't realize what we'd done. Believe me, I realize it now. Before the game even started, I knew exactly what he meant when he said we didn't realize how big it was. I'm truly just ecstatic about it right now."

Ferbey, who seldom shows much, had wet eyes. It was his fifth purple heart. And suddenly he had a chance to do what nobody had done before.

"Things are very similar to the years I won back-to-back Briers with Pat Ryan," he said.

"It would be a fantastic accomplishment to match that. The neat thing would be that in 20 years, I guess I'd be the first guy to be able to say he did it twice.

"The first year we lost the World Championships. They were in Switzerland. The next year we won the

World Championships. They were in the U.S., in Milwaukee. Last year with this team we lost the World Championships in Switzerland. This year the World Championships are in the U.S., in Bismarck, North Dakota."

Ferbey having a chance to duplicate his history from 1988 and 1989 with Ryan's Express was an interesting enough angle. But to make it even better, Ryan qualified out of B.C.

Ferbey saw it coming all the way, but until they stepped on the ice for practice prior to the first day of competition in Calgary, it really hadn't hit them that for the first time as a rink, they had a shot at some history.

"If we could win this thing again it would put us in an elite category," said Nedohin. "To me, I think the big motivation isn't so much winning it twice as to get back to the World Championships. We have some unfinished business there."

But first there was big business to be done in the Saddledome. Tickets had sold well all year despite the Brier boycott and then sold even better when, one by one, the provincial championships were won.

Two-time Brier champs Russ Howard and Pat Ryan headlined the field, which also included names such as Mark Noseworthy and Shawn Adams as well as John Morris, the two-time world junior champion who won Ontario.

"This field is really good and compares with other fields in the past. Going into this Brier it doesn't look to us like it's going to be any easier than last year. I notice a lot of people aren't picking us to win," said Nedohin.

Howard went even further.

"I think it's a better field than last year," he said. "Even if it wasn't, a lot of Briers are no-name Briers until the Briers are over.

"I was in the 1980 Brier in Calgary. This one is a nostalgic one for me. My first Brier was in Calgary. I was 23. Now I'm 46. I've been in three Briers in the last four years and this is the toughest field.

"Every year you get older and the teams get better. I won the Worlds with my team in 1987 and I don't think that team would have made the playoffs here.

"In 1980 when I came to Calgary, nobody knew me. Nobody knew another guy there—a guy named Al Hackner. Nobody knew Mark Noseworthy. This is what a few people are forgetting. The curlers didn't make the Brier. The Brier made us. We can't forget that."

It was obvious before the first rock had been thrown that there wasn't going to be any drop-off in interest whatsoever from the Olympics.

"I don't think it will be a downer at all. I think it will work the other way," said Nedohin. "And judging from ticket sales…"

There was every indication that an all-time Brier attendance record might be set.

"The Brier is an entity all by itself," said Ferbey. "People have been going to these for 50 years. They watch the team from their province and often don't care who that might be. I'm a big believer in the Brier. I'm a big believer in representing Canada. The number one thing is that we want to represent our country again. We want that maple leaf on our back again. You can't put a dollar figure on that. Money isn't everything. The Brier has been good to me. Why would I want to walk away from something like that? It's going to be phenomenal to march into the Saddledome as defending champions in front of

Media scrum: Scott Pfeifer's son Marlow gets some early media training.

16,000 people cheering for us as Albertans. And I think this is going to be one of the best Briers ever."

Despite an Edmonton rink representing Alberta at a Brier in their rival city, Calgary, yet again, the fans cheered for the Ferbey Four. What was amazing is that after a few ends of their first game, they didn't boo the way they were curling.

It was a marquee match-up for openers. The defending Brier champions against two-time Brier winner Russ Howard, curling in a record 11th Brier as a skip.

It was 10–2. For Howard.

"Let's go to the Brier Patch and get a table," said Ferbey after getting hammered by old "Hurry Hard" who scored a record 86th Brier victory.

The Albertans even had last-rock advantage.

Howard stole four on the fifth end. Stole. Howard said it wasn't a personal record. "I think I stole six once."

He did steal four at the 1994 Red Deer Brier against Noseworthy.

After the 10–2 loss to Howard for openers, the defending champs turned it around. Maybe it was Nedohin getting up in the morning and shaving off his goatee. But they were good to go again.

"I needed a change," said Nedohin. "I grew it when we first started the playdowns. When we lost that first one 10–2…"

The Ferbey Four scored a 10–3 win over Nova Scotia's Adams and then rolled to a 9–2 win with the last rock left unthrown against Scott Bitz of Saskatchewan.

"It seems like every game we play is first-team-to-10-wins," said Ferbey. Three games in and they'd only played $18^7/_8$ ends.

"Hey, it was a good day. It was a lot better than yesterday," said Ferbey. "We've been in a lot of tough games and if we let a loss like the one we started with here bother us then we're not representing Alberta very well."

On Monday morning, Ferbey scored two on the first end against Francois Roberge of Quebec and won the match 7–5 and set-up the first sizzle game of the event since the Ferbey–Howard opener, which turned out to have about as much sizzle as a steak in the freezer.

With three straight wins, the rink from Wild Rose Country had a record of 3–1. The pack was, surprisingly, led out of the gate by Tim Phillips of Northern Ontario at 4–0, and the next match was a late-night date against Phillips' Moose Men.

It was a 7–5 Alberta win which the participants were proud of co-authoring.

"I'm drained. That was one helluva game," said Ferbey. "I don't know that we can play any better. We talked after the game and agreed that's probably the best we've played, ever. That was just a wonderful curling game in which to be involved and the best part of it is that we won and we control our own destiny now."

With Alberta and Northern Ontario, along with young Morris from Ontario, at 4–1, they were being chased by three 3–2 teams including Ryan and Howard.

Scoring an 8–4 win over the Territories and a 9–4 win over Manitoba on Brier Tuesday created another sizzle game on the horizon as the Ontario and Alberta rinks headed into "moving day," the second last day of the round-robin, atop the standings at 6–1.

"Anytime you can win six games in a row at the Brier it's a pretty good run, especially to start the week off," said Ferbey of recovering from that 10–2 lid-lifter.

Alberta ran the record to 7–1 with a 9–3 win over John Likely's Spud Islanders highlighted by a steal of three on the fourth end after scoring two on the third.

Then Huff & Puff kicked in.

The front end of curling teams don't generally generate headlines. But at the Calgary Brier, Scott Pfeifer and Marcel Rocque began to get famous.

Up to this point of their Brier history, Randy Ferbey and Dave Nedohin had been getting all the ink. But it was Marcel Rocque and Scott Pfeifer who put Alberta in a prime position to win their second-straight Brier by making like a couple of Harry Potters with their magic brooms, and it wasn't lost on anybody.

Men With Brooms was the title of a bad movie playing theatres at the time and the name of arguably the greatest end and the biggest win of the Brier in 2002.

The two sweepers, particularly Rocque, set some sort of record for perspiring in public in this usually not-so-sweaty sport as they created a five-ender and spanked Morris 9–3.

"Our sweepers showed they were superior, big time," said Ferbey of the rink, which suddenly found itself alone in first place with eight straight wins after that opening game loss to Howard.

"I've never swept three rocks harder, pillar to post in my life," admitted Pfeifer, the guy with his picture on the Olympic stamp but who couldn't have licked it at the end of the eighth end.

"My adrenalin is so pumped after that, I'm ready to go out and play another game right now," added Pfeifer, 10 minutes after leaving the ice.

Rocque didn't feel the same way at all. He was soaking wet with perspiration and in desperate need of a shower.

"Maybe I've sweated like that before, but definitely not in front of this many people," laughed Rocque. "We definitely put everything we had into it. We don't always make all the shots, but we earn our keep as a front end with our brushing. We make a lot of shots for Randy and Dave.

"We learned from guys like Don Walchuk," he said of the Olympic silver-medal winning third from Kevin Martin's team. "When you have teachers like that, you come through."

For a guy who just got his Ontari-air-e-air-e-o handed to him, Morris was surprisingly full of bravado after the loss.

"You know what? I'll tell you what. I'm just itching to play these guys again. I know they're a good team, but I'd love to at least show them that we have great players on our team. I'm just looking forward to another match-up.

"I really want another crack at those guys. I know our team can play a lot better than it did and we're gonna want to prove that," said Morris.

"Good," said Nedohin.

The Albertans lost to Noseworthy's Newfies 8–3 the next afternoon in a game over after eight, a sobering experience in that it meant they had to bounce back and win the next one or blow finishing first.

For his last game of the round-robin, Ferbey was up against his old skip Pat Ryan of B.C.

Scoring two on the seventh and three on the ninth, a 4–4 tie became a 9–6 win and Alberta finished at 9–2, Ontario at 8–3, Saskatchewan's Scott Bitz and New Brunswick's Howard at 7–4 progressed to the playoff, but Ryan's Lotus Landers headed home at 6–5.

"We weren't totally focussed but we came through in the end," said Ferbey. "I feel bad about knocking Pat out, but there's nothing we could do about it. Honestly, it wasn't our best game, but tomorrow will be totally different hype and a totally different focus."

Indeed.

Morris got his rematch with a 1–2 Page playoff system match-up against the Albertans who had curled 84% in the round-robin with Rocque leading the way at 88%, Pfeifer at 86%, Ferbey at 83% and Nedohin at 81%.

"Morris said a few things and I'd be disappointed if he didn't come out and play any better," said Ferbey.

Morris had decided not to add more fuel to the fire.

"I'm sure they have enough motivation already," he said.

> ## "I've never swept three rocks harder, pillar to post in my life."
> ## —Scott Pfeifer

Before they threw a rock in the 1–2 game in the Page playoff system, you could identify the moment curling fans fell for the Ferbey Four.

The time and place was The Great Tricycle Race.

It might have even been where Ferbey's rink won this one.

While Morris was getting outta-sight uptight for the big battle about an hour before game time, Pfeifer and Nedohin were racing around the carpet beside the sheets of ice on a couple of tricycles.

"I grabbed the early lead," enthused Pfeifer after it was over and photographers bounced into the press room with the curling pictures of the year.

"I had the lead. But my gripper fell off. That's when Dave took the lead."

The first of the 13,412 to watch the game were drifting into the Saddledome seats expecting to see the Albertans dialed up for a grudge match, not racing around the rink on tricycles.

Morris had been making so much noise about how itchy he was to play Ferbey again, the Alberta skip had finally been moved to ask the question: "Who does he think we are, chumps?"

The answer this day would come back "champs" as Ferbey put himself in position to be the first to win back-to-back Briers since he did it with Ryan in '88–'89.

And it really did seem like it started with The Great Tricycle Race.

It was Ferbey who gave them the green light when they found the two tricycles in the bowels of the building where they were being kept for Sun Stunts at Calgary Flames NHL games.

"I told them to get out there," said Ferbey. "That's Scott Pfeifer. He loves doing stuff like that."

Nedohin was up for the challenge and said being loose, like the tricycle race left them, was the key to winning the game to send them to their second straight Brier final.

"We were loose. When we're loose we play our best. We were relaxed. It was like last year at the Brier when we put on Guy Hemmings jackets after the fifth end," said Nedohin.

"If you asked me if we'd come to the Brier and do this sort of stuff, I'd say you're crazy. And when we jumped on them for a 3–0 lead and had them 4–1 after the fifth-end break, you could see the frustration in their body language, you really could."

At the break, Rocque entertained the crowd with a solo dance.

"Cotton Eyed Joe," he said.

"I teach it to my kids in school. Karla Tritten and I teach a social dance class at Riverbend Junior High in Edmonton. I've been teaching it for four of five years. The kids know I'm a goofy guy.

"We were talking behind the house before the game. This is not life or death. We all have kids and families. We go home Monday and go to work. We're regular Joes. You have to have fun and relax. And we play better that way."

The Ferbey Four won 9–3 in the end, out-curling Morris and men 89% to 67% with Nedohin hitting 92% to Morris' 69% in the last-rock throwing match-up.

With the win in the 1–2 game, Ferbey and mates had the Saturday off to watch the semi-final, practice and contemplate what was at stake.

It was at this point that I discovered that for a guy on the edge of curling immortality, Ferbey wasn't very well versed on the idea.

> ## "Maybe I've sweated like that before, but definitely not in front of this many people."
> ### —Marcel Rocque

I gave him a snap quiz on the subject.

"Name the three Richardsons," I asked of the three men the Alberta skip would go into the history books with, should he win his fourth Brier title the following afternoon.

"Well, there's Sammy. I met him here this year. And there's Ernie. He was the skip. I met him a few years ago. But I don't know about the other brother."

Name was Arnold. And he was a cousin.

"Arnold, huh?"

Arnold. Cousin.

"The Richardsons were out of the game when I came along. I grew up with Hector Gervais and Ron Northcott. But I know the Richardsons and what they've done. To be mentioned in the same breath with those guys is pretty amazing."

Ferbey, who had never seen himself as a Gervais or a Northcott, much less a Richardson, suggested three Richardsons and a Ferbey sharing the same record, to him, was like "what's wrong with this picture?"

Ferbey said a chance to get into the history books is nothing to scoff at. But…

"If it happened, I'm sure it's something that 20 or 30 years from now it would really mean something to me. But not now. Personally, at this point, records just aren't that important to me."

Nedohin swore then and there that, while everybody else on the rink was not sure they'd be able to say the same thing in the same situation, it was true.

"We want the records for Randy more than he does. It would be incredible to have Randy included with some of the greats like the Richardsons.

"I remember watching Randy and Pat Ryan play together. It was pretty exciting for me when Randy asked me to join his rink. I've relished every minute of it. Without Randy last year there is no way we'd have done as well as we did."

Ferbey said what he wanted more than to say he was personally one of the four four-time Brier champs was just one thing.

"To get back to the Worlds. I won the world championship with Pat in 1989 after we'd lost it the year before. I want to get back and finish off what we didn't do last year, like we did with the Ryan rink. We'd love another chance to get back and redeem ourselves, represent Alberta and change all that."

Morris, the son of Earle Morris, the man who holds the record for skipping teams in the Brier for the most different provinces (three), had done a lot of yapping going into the 1–2 Page playoff game and ended up

getting clobbered. After the loss Morris stomped around in a miserable mood, sulking like a grounded teenager.

"I don't know what to say. They might be too good for us," said the Ontario skip. "Who knows? I'm surprised they lost two games because if they played anywhere close to the way they played against us, I don't think they're beatable."

He even apologized.

"It was a pretty boring game and I apologize to the fans because I wouldn't have wanted to watch that. It wasn't too much fun."

Morris bounced back to beat Russ Howard 9–5 and make it a Ferbey–Morris final.

"It took a while to get over it," said the 23-year-old after the loss in the 1–2 game. "It was tough. They're tough. We can just go out there and play our guts out and see what happens. One thing for sure, we've got to play smarter. And Joe Frans and I really have to pick it up," he said of his third who, three Briers later would become the first curler to fail an in-competition drug test, curling for Wayne Middaugh's Ontario rink.

Nedohin out-curled Morris 89% to 67% in the regular round game and 92% to 69% in the 1–2 game. Ferbey out-curled Frans 88% to 66% in the regular round and 88% to 81% in the 1–2 game in the battle of third rocks.

"We're confident. I'm expecting a good game. To beat a team three times is difficult. But I like our chances," said Ferbey.

> ## "Who does he think we are, chumps?"
> ### —Randy Ferbey

In the end the Ferbey Four gave the curling world anything but a forgettable Brier final with an NHL hockey rink full of 15,466 fans in the stands and another 770,000 watching on TV.

In one shot, Dave Nedohin helped erase Kelley Law's fourth-end flub in the Olympic semi-final and Kevin Martin's wrong-turn, too-heavy draw to the four-foot in the Olympic final.

It was the shot that rocked the Rockies and unlocked the record book.

Nedohin's runback double take-out circus shot for four in the fifth end was the grand-slam home run, which made Ferbey a certified Brier legend and carved a special place in Canadian curling history for the four.

It was one of the greatest shots in Brier final history and the knockout punch put John Morris down for the third time in the tournament against the Albertans.

"I don't know where it ranks. All I know is that one is going to be up there. They'll be playing that shot over and over 20 years from now," said Ferbey.

Nine-time Brier competitor Pat Ryan watched Ferbey make history by winning back-to-back Briers with him in '88–'89 and watched him do it again this day.

"It was unbelievable," he said. "I didn't think that shot was there. The only thing wrong with it was that it wasn't in the 10th end and didn't have much drama leading up to it. But it was amazing."

Eleven-time Brier skip Russ Howard was sitting in the stands on the other side of the Saddledome as he watched Nedohin win his second Hec Gervais MVP Trophy and Shot of the Week honours on the spot.

"I thought they were going for two there. But that's their style. Two isn't good enough. They went for the really big one and made it. And they deserve it. They were the best team here all week. If that had been a life-or-death shot on the 10th end like Al Hackner's was in '85…"

Why wait for the 10th end?

"That was the ball game," said Morris.

The rink joined the Richardsons ('59–'60 and again in '62–'63), Gord Hudson of Manitoba ('28–'29), Matt Baldwin of Alberta ('57–'58), Ron Northcott of Alberta ('68–'69), Don Duguid of Manitoba ('70–'71) and Pat Ryan ('88–'89) as the only rinks in Brier history to win back-to-back.

And Ferbey joined Ernie, Sam and Arnold as the only two-time back-to-back winners and only four-time Brier champs.

"I guess it's pretty good," said Ferbey. "I guess it's an amazing accomplishment. For me these individual accomplishments don't mean much in this game."

Nedohin seemed to know exactly what he'd done with his shot of shots.

"Maybe Randy doesn't really know what happened to him right now but he will in a while," said Nedohin. "Ten years from now, I guarantee you, he'll know how special it was."

Ferbey was more interested in digging out an Alberta pin from under the ice.

At the Olympics, ice-maker Trent Evans of Edmonton buried a Canadian loonie under the ice in Salt Lake where Canada won the first Olympic gold medal in hockey in 50 years.

"See this," Ferbey said, producing the provincial pin? "It was under the ice all week."

CHAPTER 11

On Top of the World

Read All About It: Ferbey autographs front page of *Sun*.

North Dakota is not featured in most tourist guides. Nobody ever did a movie along the lines of "If this is Tuesday, this must be Bismarck."

The city of 60,000 is the beginning of the "Follow The Legends Trail" where Lewis and Clark, George Custer, Sitting Bull and Theodore Roosevelt lived out larger-than-life adventures. Bismarck is the home of the Dakota Zoo, the Double Ditch Indian Village Historic Site, the Lewis and Clark Riverboat and the Theodore Roosevelt Rough Rider Hall of Fame.

Not exactly Lausanne, Switzerland, where the Ford World Curling Championships had been held the previous year.

Bismarck was a chance for a do-over for the Ferbey Four, a rink which not only failed to bring back a gold medal from the 2001 Worlds, but failed to bring home a medal, period.

"We have a second chance, which most teams in Canada don't get. We have to make the most of it," said Ferbey before the team departed on a much shorter expedition than the year before and did so with expectations more than a little uncertain about their ability to put Canada back on top of the world.

Alberta, to this point, you understand, wasn't the province most curling fans in Canada necessarily wanted to carry the maple leaf internationally.

Before they won the right to represent Canada for a second straight year at the Worlds, Pat Doyle wrote in Larry Wood's Brier daily bugle, *The Tankard Times:*

"Look it up. 1991, 1992, 1997, 1998, 2001, 2002. Outfits from 'Saudi Alberta' wore the maple leaf on the international stage in each of those years at the world championships and Olympics and came home with zero titles. That's right, zip. Zilch. Nada. The ol' horse collar."

Understand, these curling writers from Manitoba keep track of such things.

Kevin Martin came home without a medal from the Albertville Olympic Winter Games, where curling was a demonstration sport, and with a silver from the just-completed Salt Lake five-ring circus. Martin was also 0–2 at the world championships. Edmonton's Cathy King went to the Worlds and lost in 1998. And Randy Ferbey & Co. had gone to Lausanne and didn't even manage to get a medal.

All those rinks just happened to be from the provincial capital, which had those City of Champions signs outside of town, and that didn't help matters either.

So what would make this year different than any of those other "Saudi Alberta" years?

"Experience," said Ferbey who had enough on his own with his fourth trip to the world championships. His boys had just won back-to-back Briers. And Bismarck wasn't on the other side of the world, but a mere five-hour drive south of Winnipeg.

"Dave Nedohin is a year older. He's more mature. He's a more confident curler now. What people in sports have to do is prove they are capable, prove it to themselves and to everybody else. I think he's done that. He believes in himself. He believes he can make anything."

Nedohin said losing the year before had left them in a strange space. In 2002, the Brier wasn't the "be all and the end all."

"We wanted to get back to the Worlds to redeem ourselves," he said.

Canada has trouble, sometimes, believing our curlers can be convinced anything is bigger than the Brier, the event which draws higher TV numbers and more people in the pews than any other event in the curling universe. And maybe that's been part of the problem in the past. But it wasn't that way with this team the year after they went to Lausanne. The goal was not so much to win the Brier as to get back to the world championships.

"To win the Brier two straight years really proves to each of us that we're one of the best teams in the country and we didn't just get lucky or something," continued Nedohin.

"Last year we had Randy's experience. This year we have the experience of the whole team that can carry us through. We're not going there wondering what it will be like. There's different rules, a different atmosphere and, as we found out in Lausanne, different officiating from the Brier.

"The teams have a different style of curling. You watch them and you think 'Well, they're not going to make that shot.' Then they do. It's just that their style is different. We know all of this going in. Nothing is really going to open up our eyes wide this time. We know the teams are good. We know what to expect from the media and the fans. We know nobody wants us to win—except the rest of Canada."

Nedohin said the rink was not only more mature but more professional.

"We were on a bit more of a roller coaster. It seemed like we never had time to settle down and relax. This time we've organized ourselves much better. And we're a lot more relaxed."

In 2002, the team went to Bismarck telling themselves it was going to be a home Worlds. With Bismarck within driving distance of Dave Nedohin's old hometown, he was convinced that Canada would have more fans cheering for them than Paul Pustovar and his American team.

"We'll have a lot of family and friends coming down. We've heard a lot of Canadian supporters will be going this year like they would any year the Worlds are in Canada. It's not that far from Winnipeg. It'll be like home ice advantage in some ways," Nedohin said.

Taking the temperature of the town was Con Griwkowsky's first assignment when he arrived to cover the event for the *Edmonton Sun.*

"As near as any stranger can reckon, the beer here is cold and the folks are prairie-town friendly," he wrote.

"Not many people in the stands yesterday for opening day of the Ford World Curling Championships. Might be planning some other huge stunt like they did a couple of weeks back. The wire photos showed the residents of this town bucking for a spot in the *Guinness World Book of Records* for most people carving out snow angels flapping their arms in the rolling countryside."

So much for the idea of bringing the Worlds to Bismarck to get all that publicity and inspire tourism.

"There won't be quite as much to do as there was in Lausanne," guessed Ferbey before taking the ice for the opener.

Ferbey's personal plan was to pretend it was Milwaukee. Back in 1988, when Ferbey won the Brier with Pat Ryan, the rink went to Lausanne and failed to win the Worlds. The next year they won the Brier again and became world champions in Milwaukee.

Wisconsin. North Dakota. Close enough.

The field featured Pal Trulsen, the Olympic gold medal winner of only a few weeks earlier and familiar international names such as Markku Uusipaavalniemi of Finland, Per Carlsen of Sweden and Patrick Hurlimann of Switzerland.

The Canadians didn't exactly look like world beaters for openers, giving up a couple of steals early and having to battle back against Alois Kreidl of Austria for the win.

Nedohin, after the two steals, switched rocks with Marcel Rocque.

"Everyone was probably expecting us to come out and kick Austria's butt," said Ferbey.

Well, yes.

That wasn't quite the case against Carlsen of Sweden in the next one. Then again…

When Carlsen scored a pair on the 10th end to beat Canada 5–4, all the sirens were going off again. Struggling against Austria and giving away a game to Sweden was not the start they had envisioned.

Saudi Alberta again?

"Wait 'til we get used to the ice," said Ferbey.

It was tough to read much into a 9–2 win over Japan's Hiroaki Kashiwagi the next day.

"We're not as good as we can be, but it's coming," was Ferbey's analysis.

"We're a little more confident now. We know we can do it. We're not going to worry about what the other teams are doing. We just have to put the rocks where we want them. My job is to make sure they end up in the right spots."

The next day they were spot on. And they were able to leave the rink telling themselves they'd just accomplished something that nobody else in the history of curling could claim.

"We beat two Olympic gold medal winners on the same day."

Indeed.

Patrick Hurlimann of Switzerland was the winner of the 1998 Nagano Olympic Winter Games. Pal Trulsen was the winner of the 2002 Salt Lake Winter Olympics. These were the only two full-medal Olympics for curling to that point.

"We came into it looking at playing two previous Olympic champions and told ourselves it was really important for us to be on our game today," said Nedohin.

"Those two rinks have proved themselves. You can't argue with an Olympic gold medal.

"To come out the way we did today sends a message. We played two good games against two gold medalists. Trulsen had our number last year. For our team to score 23 points against two very good teams that will probably be in the playoffs at the end of the week, is something you have to be happy about," said Ferbey of going to 4–1.

"I think we're starting to feel like we're playing as a real team again," said Nedohin.

The game against Hurlimann wasn't even a game. It was an 11–4 blowout. As a rink the Ferbey Four shot 93%, all four over the 90% mark. Nedohin hit 95%.

Hurlimann announced following the game that, after 20 years of curling, he had decided to retire.

If that win wasn't impressive enough, the Canadians followed it with a 12–4 licking of Trulsen in a game that featured a six-ender in the fifth.

"It's not every day you get a six-ender at the world championships," said Pfeifer.

It's not every day you beat Trulsen.

"Pal beat Kevin Martin in the Olympics and beat us twice at the world championships," added Pfeifer of the Canadian killer from the previous year.

All wasn't perfect, however.

Rocque wasn't sure what was concerning him most, the condition of his right arm, which was requiring physiotherapy, or the condition of the ice.

"It isn't the same kind of sweeper's ice as it is at the Brier in the sense that you can make the difference in the game. At the Brier you can really pound them home. Here, you can throw it really, really light on some ice and drag it forever and it doesn't show."

Home ice advantage it wasn't, at least in terms of the ice. And the next day Pustovar's Team U.S.A. used the great equalizer that bad ice can be to score an 8–7 extra-end win.

"In the immortal words of John Morris, 'bring 'em on, bring 'em back.' They aren't that good," said Ferbey, proving he still had his sense of humour.

Nedohin called the ice "crap."

"I struggled today," said Nedohin, admitting the obvious when he hit the mixed zone.

"I thought the ice was crap but I didn't adjust to it and Paul did. He made every draw he could and I didn't adjust to the draw weight changing. What that game came down to was whoever drew better won. Paul had his draw weight and I didn't have mine."

Ferbey tried to shift the focus off his last-rock thrower and went on a post-game tirade at World Curling Federation officials, who allowed the host country to provide icemakers.

"You have to get the best icemakers in the world here, not the guys who just think they're good. They're not good enough. There have to be standards. Just because a guy may be the best icemaker in the United States doesn't mean he's one of the best icemakers in the world. This is the world championship. It is supposed to be the biggest show in curling. So get the best here. There's only a handful of people in the world who can make it properly. Bring them in."

Ferbey said he took advantage of the situation to editorialize about the ice. But he admitted the next day that it was a bit of a misdirection play, too.

"Dave knew he had a bad game, so the three of us got together and decided we'd kick him off the team if he had another game like that," joked Ferbey.

"We kind of let him deal with it on his own," levelled the skip about his last-rock thrower after Canada bounced back to have a 2–0 day the next day with an 8–5 win over Denmark's Ulrik Schmidt and a 7–6 win over Finland's Markku Uusipaavalniemi in a game that would have made the crowd go wild if there had been one.

The two wins guaranteed Canada a playoff spot and no worse than the fourth place finish from the year before.

"The most important thing is that we now have the chance to make amends for not winning a medal last year," said Nedohin.

"It really doesn't matter how we did it. We've fought hard here all week long. We've had our ups and downs. We've played great games and we've played poor games. Bottom line is that we're in the playoffs and go from here."

Whatever confidence level they had on site wasn't necessarily transferred back home when they lost their final game of the round-robin 6–5 to Warwick Smith of Scotland, which left Smith in first place and Canada with a nothing-to-write-home-about 6–3 record to finish third, drawing Paul Pustovar of the U.S.A. in their semi-final.

Their 6–3 record was the same as the year before in Lausanne. And it was déjà vu in the same semi-final spot, drawing the home team in the semi.

Nedohin went out of his way the next day to put out the call to Winnipeg fans to make the trip down for the final weekend to make them the home team and several of them did.

While Rocque and Pfeifer played tourist in Lausanne the year before on the last day before the playoffs, Rocque claimed the most interesting time, buying $750 worth of parts for his Harley.

Ferbey and Nedohin handled the playoff preview media requests.

"It's been 13 years since I've stood on the World's podium," Ferbey told the assembled scribes. "It's about time I won this stupid thing again and put it behind us.

"We have another chance. If we don't win this thing we'll be disappointed. That's still our goal and that's still the way we're thinking. Nothing has changed from three weeks ago.

"You'll see a different team out there," promised Ferbey of the team that lost their last game and lost to the Americans in an extra end earlier in the event.

"We're happy to play the U.S.A. In our round-robin game against them we didn't play our best game and Paul played exceptional. All we can do is the same in the semi-final and hope we can finish it off.

"We're going to be very aggressive against them. We're going to take it to them."

Nedohin said they may have finished third but in effect the result was that they'd finished second. According to the weird World Championship rules, a coin-toss decided last rock. Ferbey won it.

Ferbey pumped his rink up.

"I like our chances to be honest with you," Ferbey told reporters before they left the rink that night. "We're still the best team out there, I think. If we play as well as we can, we'll win."

And win they did.

But it wasn't easy.

Despite having the hammer, the Ferbey Four found themselves down 4–2 and the Americans were shooting the lights out.

It was Nedohin who finally punched their ticket to the final with a draw to the four-foot to score two in the ninth for what would turn out to be a 10–6 win.

"Randy and I kind of took our turns in the first five ends. If it wasn't one of us, it was the other. But our front end played great from start to finish and gave us the chance to win," said Nedohin.

Both Pfeifer and Rocque shot 91%.

"We settled down and started making some real good shots. We put a lot of pressure on them in the second half of the game. When it came down to it, we made the ones we needed to make."

Ferbey credited Pustovar for rising to the occasion and giving them a test which wasn't really reflected in the final score.

Old Guys Need Naps: Randy Ferbey caught sleeping with Scott Pfeifer.

Team Photo

"That team, I can honestly say, I didn't expect to play so well. We had to grind that one out—that was a grind from the git-go! We were given full credit for that victory. All four of us dug down deep for that one. About the fifth end I turned to these guys and said 'We don't want to get up in the morning and play that bronze medal game.' "

Just getting to the gold medal game, considering what happened to them the year before, was more relief than thrill.

"If you lose, you have to play the bronze medal game and then watch the final," said Pfeifer.

"That was the most nervous I've been for a game all year. We didn't want to leave here the same way we left Lausanne and be stuck in a rut when it came to the world championships."

The good news was that they were in the final. The bad news was that Pal Trulsen won the other semi-final, 5–4 over Scotland's Warwick Smith, to make the final a match the world would want to watch.

Less than two months earlier Trulsen had defeated Kevin Martin to win the Olympic gold medal. And if there was one guy on the planet Ferbey had trouble with, it was The Troll's Norwegians.

In Lausanne they lost the bronze medal game to Trulsen.

"We're going to have to have our, 'A' game from start to finish to beat Pal," said Nedohin. "In my mind we owe him one."

Trulsen was going into the game hoping to do what country-mate Eigil Ramsfjell did when he won the gold the first time curling was in the Olympics as a demonstration sport in Calgary 1988 and followed through to win the World Curling Championships six weeks later.

Trulsen, who went golf-ing on his off-day prior to the playoffs, said he was amazed just to be playing, much less in the Olympic final and the World final.

"When I started this season I was in hospi-tal," he said of two sep-arate operations to his left knee that left him limping throughout the season.

"I like to limp because it makes people feel sorry for me," he joked.

Not having to say they were sorry like last year was the entire focus for Ferbey.

"I'm not going to say we wouldn't be able to get our-selves up for the bronze medal game, because we came home without a medal last year and we'd be up for that game again if we have to play it. But you know the makeup of this team. We didn't come to Bismarck to win the bronze. We came to win gold and now we have the opportunity to do that."

They didn't give Trulsen a chance to have another great day at the expense of Canada.

There was little drama in the 10–5 win which made the Ferbey Four world champions for the first time, Ferbey a world champion for the second time and Pfeifer a world champion as both a junior and senior curler.

Pfeifer, who shot a remarkable 94% in the game, said the idea wasn't so much to get Ferbey and himself back on the top of a world podium as to get Nedohin and Rocque up there for the first time.

"That's what we'd been gunning for all year. Randy and I had experienced it before. It's good for them to witness the raising of the flag and the play-ing of the national an-them. Any time you can represent your country and win a world championship, you do your country proud and it feels good. This is very special be-cause I enjoy this team."

It was Rocque who best described it all.

Tears started welling up in his eyes in the 10th end and continued after the deal was sealed.

"After last year, who would have thought we'd get a second chance at it? Any step I've ever done, Zones, Northerns, Provincials or Briers, I kept telling myself there was nothing to get excited about. But I'm so happy I got to play with three friends and finally have a chance to celebrate. I've reached the pinnacle. After 20 years of hard work, my dream came true and I fi-nally got to release it all," he said unashamedly.

"The only thing better would have been to have had my wife and daughter here."

> "It's not every day you get a six-ender at the world championships."
> —Scott Pfeifer

Raylene was back in Edmonton awaiting the delivery of their second child.

Ending up with the hammer as a result of another coin flip, Canada scored one on the first end, gave up two on the second but scored two of their own in the third. Giving up one in the fourth, the Edmonton rink out-scored Norway 7–2 the rest of the way.

"By the end of the week Marcel and I knew that if we set the table Randy and Dave would come through at the end," said Pfeifer.

Pfeifer's 94% left him with an 86% record for the tournament. Rocque's 88% left him at 89% for the Worlds. Ferbey hit 85% in the final for an 83% week. And Nedohin was 79% in the final for a 78% week.

As a team they out-curled Trulsen 87% to 75% in the final, the Norwegian skip himself limping in at 69%.

So ended the Saudi Alberta story, the succession of City of Champions rinks that had failed on the international stage representing Canada.

"This team was built from scratch. That's what makes it much better from my perspective," said Ferbey.

"It's an unbelievable feeling. It was years of hard work—five years of hard work. To come to a climax and win the ultimate game in curling is a pretty good feeling."

Ferbey said he was also able to bury the idea that he didn't really "win" the world championship the first time with Pat Ryan as Patrick Hurlimann of Switzerland lost it on a last-rock miss.

"There's always been doubters out there because we stole the title," he said. "We didn't win it in true Canadian fashion where we kicked the other team.

"This time we made a great statement with a dominating win. To beat the Olympic gold medal winner is also a great accomplishment. Pal's had an exceptional year and to beat him is a great feeling."

Nedohin said it was, from start to finish, a team on a mission.

"We set our goals coming into the season to get another shot at the world championships. To expect a Canadian team to win every year has become a completely unrealistic expectation. There are so many good teams in Europe right now. In my mind Pal Trulsen was the best team. We knew we'd been playing well enough and we knew we had a good chance of being there at the end of the week to get it right. No matter what happened in the past, right now we're the world champions. Nobody can take that away from us and it feels great."

Nedohin, today, gives Bismarck its final review.

"Bismarck is not the first place on the entire planet we would have chosen to have our second attempt at winning the Worlds. Other than the hospitality, which was first rate, the city was pretty bland. An example was our CCA dinner night. In Lausanne we went to a beautiful restaurant on a peninsula on the coast of Lake Geneva. We had a fantastic four-course meal at a spectacular setting, as was the case with subsequent World Championships. In Bismarck, our best meal of the entire time there was a pan-fried steak with grits. But dessert was the largest ice cream sundae you have ever seen!

"The fans were not overly knowledgeable. The ice was, to put it kindly, marginal for a good part of the week. And their version of the Brier Patch was empty for the first five days.

"But looking back…Bismarck has a special place in our hearts for a lot of reasons.

"Unlike the fabulous city of Lausanne, the curling did grow on the people of Bismarck exponentially throughout the event. Lausanne went from absolutely empty to very, very few people in the arena. In Bismarck, the arena began to fill, their version of the Brier Patch began to hop and by the end of the week, the arena was exceptionally noisy, thanks in large part to the Canadians who showed up toward the end of the event.

"Our drivers, Hal and Sheila Peterson, were right up there with the most excited drivers and hosts we have ever had and did absolutely everything we asked for and plenty we didn't ask for during our time there. They even went so far as to come to Winnipeg to cheer us there. Our true American fans!

"By the end, our problems with the ice seemed like small problems. They were fixed by the end of the week. In the end the atmosphere was like that of a Canadian city.

"Our finish, of course, made it the most memorable for us. We beat the man whom we lost the bronze medal to the year before. We'd have many more classic battles with Trulsen over the next few years but in Bismarck we all discovered for once and for all that he is a true gentleman of the game and somebody I enjoy playing every time. If there is ever anyone you don't mind losing to it is Pal and his pals.

"I hope that after the Worlds not only did we leave with a little piece of Bismarck but perhaps we left a little of us in Bismarck, too. The people there certainly had more influence on us than we ever dreamed.

"Marcel said 'If we win this thing, I'll take my holidays here.' I have yet to see that. But I know he will."

It's like that with a place where you win. Ask any Olympian about the place where they won their gold medal. It'll always be special.

And coming back from winning their first world championship was when they realized the City of Champions was a special place.

"After the win, the celebration seemed a little surreal for us the next few days," said Nedohin.

"To win it, I think our predominant feeling wasn't one of elation so much as euphoria. Because we'd lost the year before in Lausanne, it was a relief to us not having lost again. It just felt all the way through like we had no other option than to win. I think the big excitement is much more immediate when you aren't expected to win. The reaction after Bismarck worked the other way. It sort of grew and grew when we returned to Edmonton and grew some more over the summer.

"Our 'stardom,' if you want to call it that, really began to increase after that."

CHAPTER 12

A Shore Thing in Halifax

Team Meal: Nedohin and Ferbey at Lobster Feast.

Back to back. But don't get back.

Sounds like a tune to go with a yackety-yak saxophone. For Matt Baldwin, Ron Northcott, Don Duguid, Pat Ryan and the Richardsons, it was better suited to the violin. They all knew the feeling.

In addition to Gordon Hudson in the '20s, they were the only rinks ever to win two Briers in a row. And they all recall the feeling of what it was like to win back-to-back and then not get back to attempt to three-peat.

Nobody had ever won three Briers in a row. To do it, first you have to get there.

Edmonton's Baldwin won in '57 and '58 but didn't get back.

"What happened to us should never happen to anybody. We got blindsided by two five-enders," remembered Baldwin. "We made it to both the 'A' and 'B' finals of the format we used back then and both games were against Herbie Olson. Herbie made two of the most spectacular shots I've ever witnessed and both were for five-enders. It wasn't a fluke he beat us. He had a good rink. They took the Richardsons to a play-off that year at the Brier."

The Richardsons won in '59 and '60. But they weren't there in '61.

"We didn't even get out of Regina," remembered Sammy Richardson.

"Big Bill Clark beat us. He played for the Saskatchewan Roughriders. Remember him? We didn't even get to Moose Jaw to the Southern Saskatchewan playdowns."

Calgary's Northcott put together back-to-backs in '68 and '69.

"We got back to the provincial final in '70 and went to the last rock of the last game. But we were playing Hector Gervais that year. And he beat us," remembers Northcott.

Gervais, The Friendly Giant, went to the Brier instead.

Duguid won the Brier out of Manitoba in '70 and '71. But it was Orest Meleschuk who won the province in '72.

"After I won the second one, I retired from curling," said Duguid. "Now, after all these years, I wish I had stayed around one more year. I wish I'd stayed around to find out if we could have won three in a row. I'll never know."

Ryan's Edmonton Express was the last, winning the Brier in '88 and '89. But Harold Breckenridge of Calgary came out of nowhere to win in '90.

Ferbey was third for Ryan's rink. Like Duguid, he's always wondered what might have happened if they'd had the chance.

"That was the year Pat moved to B.C. He took a job in Kelowna. We didn't even get to attempt to do it."

You get the idea.

While Hudson, Baldwin, Northcott, Duguid, Ryan and the Richardsons all won two-in-a-row and didn't get there the next time, the Richardsons did win two in a row a second time. Then they got there—the only rink to get to the Brier to go for three in a row.

"After we lost to Big Bill Clark, everybody was saying 'These guys had their shot at it.' But we got back and won two in a row again and made it back to the Brier to go for the three in a row," remembered Sammy.

"I thought we were going to do it, too. We won our first six. We were just flying. But the good Lord turned the tap off on us and Lyle Dagg ended up winning it.

"I'm going to Halifax expecting this Ferbey bunch to get there. If they do, I'm going to tell them about the lobsters. We went out one night and tried to eat every lobster in Charlottetown. We couldn't curl worth a damn the next day."

Ferbey, now tied with three of the Richardsons (Ernie, Arnold and Sam) with four wins each, had a chance to do what no curler had ever done before— win five.

"Wouldn't it be great if they did it? We're cheering for them," says Sammy. "I know Ernie feels the same way I do. Our records have been there a long time. I like this team and I like it a lot."

Ferbey said it was too soon for the lobster lesson and they didn't need the history lesson.

"We know the history. The history is motivating us. It's actually helped. It's easy to become complacent. You know, the 'been there, done that' thing. But we know that nobody has been there and won three in a row before. To do that would be unbelievable."

This year there was no getting around it. History was going to be their story line whether they liked it or not. And when they made it to the provincial final against Jamie King's Edmonton rink, they went to bed the night before knowing that the game the next day would be bigger than a breadbasket.

Bigger than any other game they've ever played before? Bigger than the Brier? Bigger than the Worlds?

"I'd say so," said lead Marcel Rocque.

"It's the biggest because it's a game we can never play again. We can play in another provincial final. We can play in another Brier. We can go to the world championships again. But we can only play in one to put ourselves in position to be able to be the first team in history to win three straight Briers."

Even Ferbey wasn't trying to downplay it.

"Up to this point, for sure. It's our biggest game. It wouldn't be if we hadn't won the last two Briers. But we did. How does it get much bigger?"

Second Scott Pfeifer seconded the motion.

"It's as big—bigger—than the last two Brier finals. If we win this game, the hoopla and the pressure in Halifax and all the attention with a chance to be the first to win three in a row will be quite distracting. But I'd sure like to find out how distracting. We've done all we can. We've won all our games. We've got to the final. We have choice of rocks. We have the hammer."

One game.

"Having choice of rocks and the hammer means a lot. I think having the experience we have is going to mean a lot. We're going to be aggressive on the first end. We want to take advantage of somebody's nervousness," said Ferbey.

"We wanted to make sure we were playing as good as we could play so we could take momentum into the final. There's no question having a chance to make history will be in our mind," said Nedohin, who led all last-rock throwers in percentage in the round-robin.

One game.

"We've won 18 straight games at the provincial finals. We were 7–0 last year and 7–0 this year in the round-robins. People get tired seeing the same team winning time after time. But I'm sure we'll have some people cheering for us. They know we have a chance to make history here," said Ferbey.

One game.

"It's going to be a nervous night trying to sleep," said Rocque. "It's like I told my sister. If I don't have a nervous sleep tonight, I'll wake up being afraid."

He slept nervously. And woke up calm.

By the end of the day he was living a dream.

"I'm living out a dream that never ends. Hopefully it rolls right on into history," said Rocque after rolling over King like a penny on the railway track to win Alberta.

After the 10–3 win, the back-to-the-Brier bunch said they didn't know where that train was going, but they did know it was picking up steam.

"We're a way better team now than when we won the first Brier," said Ferbey. "It's not even close. We're more confident. We're more patient. Dave Nedohin is so much better…in all eight games of the provincials he didn't miss a draw once. I don't even know if he knows that. I didn't want to tell him.

"We're a complete team. We're now an experienced team. Experience is a big thing. And we have very high standards."

Nedohin said they'd been able to tell they'd been getting better and better, and if the record $235,233 they made on the cash circuit, despite not being allowed to play the Grand Slam event games, didn't tell them that, the way they went 8–0 through provincials, playing with precision, did.

"We're way better, no question. We're at the point where we know if we play our best, we'll win. And that's the way we're going to the Brier. People have been talking about a three-peat and now it's within our grasp. Until we won this, the three-peat meant nothing. We want it and we're going to get it."

Ferbey was all over the idea of becoming the first team to win three Briers but didn't even want to discuss the idea of himself becoming the first curler to win five.

"This isn't about five for me. This is about three for us. I do not put myself in the same class as the Richardsons or a lot of those great curlers in history. Period."

But his rink…

That'd be different, he said. As a team, this would rank them right up there if they pulled it off, he said.

"This is special. It's never been done. And I have a good feeling. We feel the Nokia Brier is ours. This is the third Nokia Brier. Nobody else has ever won one."

Rocque left the Granite Curling Club that night a very emotional winner.

"I'm no curling superstar," he said. "I play with a big heart and give it all I have to give. This is something special. We have so much respect for each other. We've made some amazing money this year. But this isn't about money. It's a chance to make history."

For the second year in a row, despite the Brier boycott, the field was first rate.

Popular Guy Hemmings, after missing the year before, was back for his fourth in five years. Russ Howard, when he set foot on the ice for the 2003 Brier would equal Bernie Sparkes' record for 12 Brier appearances and Howard would become the only curler to do a dozen as a skip. He'd become the first curler to win 100 Brier games. Pat Ryan had made it back for his 10th Brier, validating his ticket by beating two-

time Brier winner Rick Folk in the B.C. final. Mark Dacey qualified out of Nova Scotia and was given a serious shot along with former world junior champion Brad Gushue, who beat Mark Noseworthy in the final in Newfoundland.

When Hemmings completed the field in the final provincial tournament, it gave Ferbey a chance to stand on a soapbox.

Kevin Martin, Jeff Stoughton, Wayne Middaugh, Kerry Burtnyk and the Grand Slam curlers boycotting the Brier had gone out of their way to, either whispering or shouting, suggest Ferbey's Brier wins ought to have an asterisk because they weren't there.

"For two years that's all I've heard," said Ferbey.

"Some have come right out and said it. They've said our Brier wins should have an asterisk because they aren't there. They say our Brier wins are tainted. They say they are the best curlers in the world. Well, the field has been set for the Brier again. Tell me whoever wins this should have an asterisk. Tell me it would be tainted.

"There's no guarantee getting to the Brier. None at all. That's what makes the Brier. Four guys can get a rink together and try to get a Brier and maybe play the world champions along the way. And when you get there, they're not cheering for Ryan vs Ferbey, they're cheering for B.C. vs Alberta."

When Ferbey arrived in Halifax, he found himself posing for pictures with Sammy Richardson, a couple of lobsters and the original Brier trophy Sammy won four times.

A few minutes later Richardson took Ferbey, his rink and the lobsters aside, and offered a little lecture.

He said this one was going to be different. This one is going to be crazy. And if Ferbey was going to win it, there's more to beat here than 11 other rinks. And that includes the lobsters.

"You have to be able to handle it. We didn't," said Sammy. "I know if it had been a normal year, we'd have won that Brier. But it wasn't a normal Brier. We were going for history. And we got out of our routine.

"Every team here is going to play harder. Everybody is going to want a piece of this team. And the media is going to devour this team. The media really picked on Ernie that year. He used to pretty much like to spend the Brier in his hotel room. That year Ernie was hardly ever in his hotel room. He was over at the TV station or over at the newspaper or over at this deal or that deal," he said of his skip. "I think he got tired."

Then there were the lobsters.

"We were rolling through that '64 Brier in Charlottetown. Won our first six. And then we were invited by our driver out to a lobster feed at his place.

"Our rink used to have a real focus. We had rules. I'm one of those guys who loves my beer. But during the Brier, I got to have one beer back in my hotel room. That was it. One. Except the time I made a great shot on the last end to turn a game around and Ernie told me 'Tonight you can have two.'

"But this night, we had a few and a lot of lobsters. We got home with a belly full and the next morning we weren't sharp.

"I talked to Randy and I think he'll be able to handle it. I think he understands that they're going to be living in a fish bowl and it isn't going to be easy."

The trick, says Ferbey, is to have the right attitude about the attention. "We're going to treat this the same way we've treated everything," he said.

"We're going to enjoy it. This is something that's not going to be with us forever. It won't last. And we know when to say 'enough is enough' and walk away."

Winning their second was pretty good training for this, said Pfeifer. "Last year was in Calgary and we were the home province favourites. This is more about chasing history. But that situation last year wasn't exactly normal, either."

Pfeifer said having Sammy talk to them was an inspiration. "He's a great guy and he's a real supporter of this team. It's amazing. He's a legend in this game. These are his records and he wants us to win."

Richardson joked that Ferbey couldn't beat his record in Halifax even if he won. "I won five. I was Jack MacDuff's driver at the Regina Brier 28 years ago. I count that one, too," he said.

"I went to get the driver assignments for that Brier in Regina and they told me 'Sam, you probably thought you were going to get a good rink. But you've won enough. We're giving you Newfoundland.' I picked them up at the airport and their goal was to win four games because that would be the Newfoundland record at the Brier. But Jack said 'Sam, I want this rink run like the Richardsons.' And that's what I did. Newfoundland curlers always had 50 people drinking in their room. I kicked them out and kept them out."

MacDuff testified at the dinner that preceded the Halifax Brier. "I will absolutely, unequivocally, say we'd never have won that Brier if we hadn't had Sammy Richardson as our driver. He kept us focussed and made us do the things we had to do to win."

In advancing the Brier upon arrival in Halifax, it set up easy:

It's a Shore Thing. But is Randy Ferbey a sure thing?

You can "Get Your Nose Blued" here. But this was one of the most star-studded fields in Brier history about to get black and blue as Ferbey and his Alberta rink attempts the first-ever Brier three-peat and Ferbey himself attempts to be the first-ever five-time Brier winner.

You could make a case that there were seven or eight rinks in Halifax capable of being in the playoffs. But was there only one rink that could win?

There were an unheard of 83 purple hearts in the 2003 Brier. That's a lot of trips to the Canadian classic—more than 900 games of Brier experience.

When it began here it was "Ferbey vs the Field." But what a field.

Russ Howard probably said it best, however. "If you sat down and tried to pick the best representative for each province, you'd probably have picked just about everyone who got here. It's incredible. This field is as strong as it can get and Randy Ferbey has the best team in the world. He'll have to play great to win this thing and he probably will."

Pat Ryan put it another way. "Ferbey is definitely the team to beat. I don't know if there's ever been this much experience in a Brier before. There are lots of teams here who can make the playoffs. Eight anyway."

Hemmings said Ferbey could say one thing few other rinks at this Brier could. "Those guys can say they keep getting better and better."

Hemmings made another point. "When I went to my first Brier in Winnipeg, they called it a no-name Brier.

> **"I could just fall over. I've never felt this drained. This has been the most grueling event we've ever been in... seven wins, but only one hour in the Brier Patch."**
>
> **—Dave Nedohin**

There were nine rookie skips. I think there are nine skips here who have been in more than one Brier."

And so it began.

Advancing this Brier was more interesting than covering it in the beginning.

The "big" story the first day was that somebody stole Rocque's broom after practice.

"I went out there today thinking, 'I hope this isn't a bad omen—somebody took something that belongs to us.'"

But Nova Scotia's Mark Dacey lost 10–4 for openers to the Albertans, who had found out the year before what it is like to be clobbered in their first game in a home-province Brier, losing 10–2 to Howard in Calgary.

The Ferbey Four was more concerned with trying to get a handle on Halifax than on the rink from the Halifax Mayflower Curling Club.

The Edmonton rink was the first of all the teams to arrive in town because they'd learned a bit about dealing with time zones from three trips to Europe during the season. And the exceptionally social rink didn't even go out and sample the famous Halifax nightlife upon arrival.

"The bars are open until 4 AM," said Nedohin. "We could have easily talked ourselves into that since that's only 1 AM back in Alberta."

But not only could they read a clock, they could read a schedule. Three of the next four days they'd play in the morning draw, have the afternoon off, curl, get home after midnight and get up five hours later to go back to the rink and do the same routine all over again.

"It's not the most pleasant schedule in the history of curling," said Nedohin. "We like to go out to the Brier Patch at night. We think it's important to be there and celebrate the Brier a bit with the fans. But they won't be seeing much of us there for the first three or four days."

Instead of going to the bars, they went to buy groceries.

"We figured if we could put together our own breakfast in our rooms, that would give us an extra half hour of sleep," reported Rocque.

"None of us slept worth a damn. Every single one of us had a bad sleep. The whole night, all of us were restless," said Ferbey of an 8–7 win against Howard.

A smart-ass reporter asked about the poor people who had to get up at 6 AM back home to watch them.

"All they have to do is wake up, roll over and turn on the TV," said Ferbey.

It was not pretty. Nedohin was curling 63% after seven ends before he finally made a shot.

"Finally he woke up. He made two great shots in the eighth," said Ferbey.

Howard raved. "That was a wonderful come-around by Nedohin on eight."

In Alberta's 10–4 opener, Nedohin cracked a five-ender on eight and ended up curling 78%. He was 73% against Howard.

A 9–3 win over John Bubbs of Manitoba in the nightcap left them at 3–0 and heading back to the rink the next morning to play Gushue and back for the night game against Hemmings.

They took Gushue 5–3 in a battle and Hemmings 9–7 in a high-wire act. When Hemmings let go of his last rock there were seven seconds left on the clock. Nedohin made another circus shot—a double takeout with Hemmings up by one and the game on the line.

The Albertans were 5–0 and the standings said they were dominating, but the rink was hardly feeling like they were dominant.

The next night, after scoring an 8–4 win over old teammate Ryan in the morning and en route to winning the nightcap 8–6 over Doug Harcourt of Saskatchewan, Ferbey leaned on his broom in the ninth end and looked like he was falling asleep.

"I felt like it," he said. "I'm totally exhausted. The way I feel, it's like we're 3–4, not 7–0. I don't know what it means to have gone 7–0 to this point in normal terms, but I think it's an accomplishment considering what we've had to go through. Three straight draws in the morning following late-night games the night before, really takes a toll on you. Add three time zones and it's something to go through. All we've done is curl and sleep and we've curled a lot more than we've slept."

Nedohin, who had another brilliant day, was done at the end of it, too. "I could just fall over," he said. "I've never felt this drained. This has been the most gruelling event we've ever been in, that's for sure."

The last-rock thrower said this was different than his first two Briers. "Seven wins, but only one hour in the Brier Patch."

Ferbey said they were so tired it was getting silly. "We were getting giddy out there. The guys were saying stupid things. And I couldn't even get mad at them.

I've never felt this wiped. Or this thirsty. I'm down big time when it comes to Brier beers."

Thirst quenched that evening and a schedule that allowed them to sleep in the next morning, the Ferbey Four was back at the rink. And Ferbey was saying that the only way they could be beaten at this Brier was by a bad break or a lucky shot.

Ferbey made the comment after his first game of the day, a 7–3 win over whistle-blowing Bryan Cochrane of Ontario. "I don't know anyone who can play it straight up and down with us the way we're playing," he said.

Only a few hours later one almost did.

The voice came out of the stands as Nedohin delivered his last rock with the next game on the line.

"Miss!"

He made it.

Alberta escaped with an 8–7 win.

Over the Territories!

"Is there a full moon out there or what?" said Ferbey.

In the end, the sun, the moon and all the stars were aligned. The Ferbey Four put away Scott Henderson of Northern Ontario 8–4 without Rocque.

Ferbey benched his lead. Went to the bullpen and brought in Holowaychuk.

"In three years we never had a chance to get him in," said Rocque of their fifth man at the Briers.

"And he played great."

Holowaychuk shot 96% replacing Rocque at lead.

"He's going to end up the highest career shooter in Brier history," laughed Pfeifer. "Who is ever going to beat 96%?"

The vote to put Holowaychuk in was unanimous.

"We talked about it," said Huff of Huff & Puff. "I said I could use the rest. We thought about me taking the first five ends off and going in for Scott and then moving me to second for the last five ends. But I didn't want to go in cold when we've got an unbeaten streak going."

Robert Campbell of Prince Edward Island was last up on their schedule. Who would have guessed the two teams to give Alberta the closest games would be the Territories and Prince Edward Island?

It was a 9–8 win to finish it off.

They'd run the table.

This was a team that had won the last three games of the Calgary Brier and went 8–0 at the Safeway Select provincials and won two straight at the Northerns before that as well.

Ferbey needed last-rock draws to beat the Polar Bears and Spud Islanders on the last two evening draws of the regular round, but that didn't worry him at all.

"Somebody would have to be curling extremely well and get breaks. That's the only way they're going to beat us," he said. "Eleven-and-oh is pretty good. Everybody else has four losses. It would be a shame if we didn't win it."

With Ferbey at 11–0 and Ryan, Howard and Dacey all tied at 7–4, the Brier had another first-rate final four.

As game stories go, there wasn't a lot to write when it came to covering Ferbey at this Brier. Not that they didn't keep a columnist in copy or anything like that. They were a delight.

Completely comfortable with being Brier Kings now, the rink started to reveal more about themselves behind the scenes. Like the real key to their undefeated run through the round-robin, they insisted, was their routine.

Randy Ferbey had to sit in the front passenger seat of the Alberta van on the way to the rink. Nedohin had to sit behind the driver. Coach Brian Moore had to take the middle seat and Rocque the outside seat behind Ferbey. Pfeifer had to sit in the back left. And fifth man Dan Holowaychuk had to sit in the back right.

Pfeifer's Brier CD would be put in the player before driver Frank Carmichael of Dartmouth was allowed to begin his drive to the Metro Centre.

"Every year I make a CD for the Brier," Pfeifer explained. "It's part of the routine."

Carmichael was then forced to take the exact same route to the rink. Down Water Street parallel to Halifax Harbour. Left at Duke Street. Up Citadel Hill. Left at Argyle. Past old City Hall. Right on Carmichael Drive past the Liquor Dome. Park in front of the players' entrance.

"The CD has to be turned up real loud," reported the driver. "They're all motivational songs that really pump them up."

The driver also reported that they must then sit in the van until a specific song comes on.

It was titled "Who The Bleep Is Alice?"

"I really like that one," said the driver.

There was no knocking the results.

Nedohin curled 83% during the week, Ferbey 86%, Pfeifer 87%, Rocque 90% and the rink as a whole 87%.

In going 11–0, the story line had expanded to not only becoming the first rink to win three Briers in a row and Ferbey to become the first curler to win five, but the possibility of the rink making it even more memorable by going undefeated from start to finish.

The last team to do it, of course, was Ryan's Express at the 1988 Briar in Chicoutimi, Quebec with Ferbey on Pat Ryan's rink.

"If we go through the round-robin undefeated, we'd better win the Brier," said Pfeifer.

Going through undefeated is an Alberta thing. Prior to Ryan's Edmonton rink doing it in '88 in a playoff format, the previous two to do it back in the days of the round-robin standings with no playoffs were Ron Northcott (1969) and Matt Baldwin (1957), both going 10–0.

A couple of teams went 11–0 in the regular round only to crash and burn in the playoffs. Manitoba's Vic Peters did it at the 1997 Calgary Brier. And Ryan's rink in Moncton in 1985, back before Ferbey signed on, breezed through at 11–0 and lost 6–5 to Al Hackner of Northern Ontario in the final in an extra end.

"In '85 the way we went through the Brier we felt, 'No way are we going to lose this game.' We were playing so well that year," said Ryan. "But then we got to the final…"

Ryan decided to go in a different direction the next year.

"We came back from that and, well, let's put it this way. If we won we wouldn't have been looking to make a change. I wouldn't have ended up curling with Randy."

In this Brier Ryan ended up curling against Ferbey in the 1–2 game of the Page playoff system.

If there was a Society For The Prevention Of Cruelty To Curlers, it would have been called in during the 1–2 game.

Ferbey vs Ryan was inhumane.

The Albertans sent the crowd to the Brier Patch after the fourth end when Nedohin missed his shot and had to settle for three to give Ferbey the 5–1 lead over his old skip.

It was cruel and un-usual punishment.

On the fifth end Ferbey stole two. It was 7–1 at the break. Ryan gave up another steal for one in the sixth. In any other game, they would have been shaking hands. But this one, because of TV rules that said you had to play eight ends in the 1–2 game before you can quit, went on and on.

Finally, Neil Houston of the CCA got the word to B.C. third Bob Ursel that they could shake hands after seven.

"It was supposed to be eight but we cut them some slack," said Houston.

"But with the final it's 10 ends or until you are math-ematically eliminated by running out of rocks," Houston explained.

"You don't expect anything like that, even in club curling or at a bonspiel," said Ferbey.

Winning the 1–2 game gave the rink Saturday off to watch the semi-final between Ryan and Dacey.

Ferbey had a message for the winner. "People know they have to play well against us, otherwise they are fooling themselves," he said. "I like our chances."

Suddenly people were viewing Ferbey as getting cocky. But others figured it was calculated, taking a page out of the book authored by the guy he was there trying to replace in history.

"Ernie Richardson showed up at every Brier and with wins and words made people believe they couldn't beat him," said one curler from that era. "Ernie was up 2–0 before he took the ice."

Ryan couldn't recover from the loss to Ferbey, and Dacey's rink went to the final with a 9–6 win over the British Columbia rink in the semi. And suddenly there was another story line beyond the Ferbey Four chasing history.

At home in Halifax, Nova Scotia had made it to a Brier final!

The Bluenosers hadn't won a Brier since 1951. Only one guy from that Nova Scotia Brier-winning rink was still alive and that curler, Fred Dyke, was in the building to watch Dacey score the win over Ryan to make the match.

It was definitely overdog vs underdog.

Ferbey would go into the final with a 34–4 Brier re-cord over the last three years. Dacey had already lost four in this Brier.

Only one team in history managed to win a Brier with four losses in the regular round. Ironically it was

> **"Air fare $400. Brier Tickets $300. Night in the Patch $200. Winning a bonspiel $47. Watching Ferbey lose: PRICELESS."**
> *—Sign in Brier Patch*

the Al Hackner team who beat an undefeated Alberta team with Ferbey on it.

No team had ever come out of the 3–4 Page playoff game to win the Brier final either.

To this point, the Ferbey Four had been, for the most part, wearing the white hats. But suddenly, because of their string of success and because of the old underdog deal, they knew they'd switched to wearing black hats for this one.

There was also the verbal spanking that Ferbey gave Newfoundland's Gushue about being a curler who had won $47 in his career and hopefully learned something about deportment in this Brier.

Atlantic Canada tends to stick together.

If they didn't know that, a sign being held by a Newfoundland fan in the Brier Patch on Friday night gave them a clue: "Air fare $400. Brier Tickets $300. Night in the Patch $200. Winning a bonspiel $47. Watching Ferbey lose: PRICELESS."

Ferbey said it all made an interesting backdrop for what was about to happen, one way or the other.

"I think a lot of people will want to see if we can win and make history here," he said. "But most people cheer for the underdog. This is what sports is all about. If we win, I'd like to believe that would be great for the Brier. If Mark wins…maybe that would be great for the Brier, too.

"For all of us, I can tell you this is the biggest game we've ever played. We can't ever play it again. We're not likely to have a chance for three in a row again. You can only play this game once. That's what makes it different than any other Brier final."

Rocque said he felt that way back at the provincial final, but for some reason not here.

"I don't feel the same pressure at all. I just feel like all we have to do is take care of business and everything will turn out the way we hope it will turn out."

The first Brier final ever to be played in prime time drew a record audience of 1.77 million viewers. And for the longest time there, it looked like third Bruce Lohnes, the former mayor of Stewiacke, N.S., was going to be able to run for Premier of the province.

Lohnes was making circus shot after circus shot—raise double takeouts, double-double takeouts—to make 1951 happen again.

"We had a front row seat to watch some amazing shots," said Nedohin who curled 96% and played second banana to Lohnes.

After an almost flawless first five ends for Nova Scotia there was a miss here and a miss there and then a string of misses by skip Dacey. The jig was up on authoring the biggest upset since Newfoundland's Jack MacDuff became the last Atlantic rink to win the Brier back in 1976.

"We curled as well as we could," said Lohnes. "We were playing a great, great, great team and we gave them all they could handle."

Unlike Morris during the Calgary Brier or Gushue during this one, Dacey didn't whine that he wanted another crack at them—although he'd get one beyond belief soon enough.

"We're proud of what we did. We told them we'd come to play," said Dacey.

"We didn't win today but I think we really did something for men's curling in Nova Scotia," said Lohnes.

For Rocque, Pfeifer, Ferbey and Nedohin, well, they knew the drill.

Line up at the far end of the ice. March down the sheet side by side. Take their positions on top of the podium. Accept the medals. Accept their trophies. Pose for the photographers holding up three fingers this time in front of their Nokia Brier Tankard.

That said…

"I don't think these guys know what they've done," said Ferbey.

"I don't know if I really do," said Nedohin. "Maybe in 10 years we'll all know. We're just trying to accomplish all that we can and hopefully end up at more Briers."

Everything about this day turned out to be better than expected.

"That was the most electric crowd I've ever played in front of in my life," said Pfeifer. "It was a thrill to play in that game."

This Brier was supposed to belong more to Ferbey than anyone else on his rink as he took his place in history. But this was, more than any Brier before, Nedohin's Brier.

Ferbey sent Nedohin to the podium to deliver the acceptance speech on behalf of the team.

"He's the best thrower in the game today and he's only getting better," said Ferbey of giving Nedohin that honour in his ultimate moment. "He's only 29, which is young for a curler, and not much scares him."

To shoot 96% in a Brier final, even with the way Lohnes played, was good for a third straight Hec Gervais Award as Brier MVP for Nedohin.

Rocque shot 88% and Ferbey and Pfeifer each 86%.

"People may get tired of hearing this, but we're a team," said Ferbey. "That's why we won again."

Pfeifer said while the media concentrated on the three-peat and five-for-Ferbey story lines, the rink had a different perspective.

"We're happiest for Dave. Now we get to go to Winnipeg to defend our world championship. Winnipeg is where Dave grew up. He never mentioned it once, but this was about getting Dave back home for me. I was really excited about being able to do that."

CHAPTER 13

Nedohinipeg Or Bust

Larger than Life: Nedohin as Worlds Winnipeg billboard.

Randy Ferbey said it was like four kids on the eve of taking a trip to Disneyland.

"We can't wait to get to Nedohinipeg."

Winnipeg they'd been to before. But not Nedohinipeg. That's what the Manitoba capital was being called on the eve of the 2003 Ford World Curling Championships.

"Dave went in early. One hundred and fifty people showed up to watch him practice. Can you believe that?" said Ferbey.

Nedohin's picture was on the billboards and in the ads. He was featured in all the TV commercials. His face was on promotional cards on every table in every curling club in Winnipeg and most of Manitoba. He was everywhere. If there ever was a poster boy for a

Ford World Curling Championships it was David Nedohin.

In 2003 they were the Winnipeg Worlds, and Winnipeg's Nedohin, even if he had to be borrowed back from Edmonton and Alberta for the event, was the organizing committee's major promotional vehicle long before the Ferbey Four punched their ticket for Winnipeg's No. 1 ticket seller to get there.

"I remember during the summer after we won our first world championship in Bismarck talking with Heather and the guys about what an amazing opportunity it would be to have a chance to do it all over again in Canada," says Nedohin looking back.

"After playing two Worlds out of the country, we knew how special it would be to play on home ice. Although we accomplished everything we wanted to accomplish after losing in Lausanne by making it back and winning it all, for me Winnipeg was 'The Dream.'

"For me, to do it again in my home city, the city where I was born and raised and threw my first curling rocks down the ice, was it. I always believed nothing could be more special than playing a world championship in the city where you grew up.

"As a young curler growing up, I remember going to the 1991 Worlds in Winnipeg. I really found myself dreaming that the next time they had one there I'd be curling in it. I spent as much time as I could at that Worlds, ironically enough watching our now arch rival, Kevin Martin."

What David Nedohin never dreamed was that he'd be chosen to be the face of the event months before making the dream come true.

"At the end of the summer of 2002, I was invited by the host committee to be the so-called poster boy for the Winnipeg Worlds. Unbelievable!

"I guess they felt I was the closest thing they had to a homegrown champion in the last few years. This was probably the beginning of Winnipeg really re-adopting me as their own. Obviously with as many world-class curlers as Winnipeg had produced, they didn't need to use me. But I was so thrilled and so honoured when they asked me. It was really a special moment that was followed in short order when I went to Winnipeg in early September for their golf tournament and some promotions."

It had started.

The problem with being a poster boy is that it doesn't really work so well if you don't show up to perform in the event you're poster-boying. "As the fall went along we were working hard enough and playing well enough to wonder why it couldn't be us again," Nedohin looks back.

But it's sport. Stuff happens. Stuff had happened to humble the world's best last-rock thrower before. And as poster boys go, boy oh boy…

"I went back to Winnipeg for Christmas that year and spent one day at the Charleswood Curling Club doing a complete photo shoot on and off the ice. We filmed commercials as well as the pictures for the billboards, those tabletop triangle advertisement pieces and all sorts of stuff. One thing that stands out from that day was all the kids and the 'fillers' who were there for the commercial, they kept on telling me how they hoped we'd be at the Worlds for Canada. They were cheering for an Alberta curler! In Manitoba! Amazing!

"That really managed to get to me. When I told the rest of the rink, I think it really made our entire team motivated to give it everything we had to make it happen.

"We also had the extra pressure of being three-time Brier champions. During the provincial playdowns we really had to focus on the present. Miraculously we went through undefeated and I left the ice thinking about being 13 games from reaching a lot of our dreams and particularly a big one of mine."

Looking back, Nedohin says the Brier was weird that way, with Winnipeg always looming large.

"I think the Winnipeg Worlds and everything else involved with our rink going for our third-straight Brier win was why Randy Ferbey made some of his comments, as harmless as they were meant to be, about Brad Gushue and other things at the Brier in Halifax. Randy worked really hard there to take the focus off getting to Winnipeg for me. It worked. Somehow the Winnipeg connection faded a little as we continued to roll along."

Well, other than the larger-than-normal number of Winnipeg media members covering the Halifax Brier and using Nedohin as their go-to guy.

"You know, it's something I don't think people really seem to believe about our team, but is totally true," says Nedohin. "The incredible thing about this team is how much everybody wants to win for each other.

"At our first Brier, it seemed like we were all really happy for Randy getting back where he had been 12 years earlier. Here was a guy most fans probably figured was done, coming out of the dust and regaining control of curling supremacy. We all wanted to make that happen for him. In addition, Randy and Scott Pfeifer, who both had been world champions before, were really wanting to win for Marcel and me, since neither of us had ever been to a national championship, never mind a Worlds.

"At the second Worlds, in Bismarck, I really wanted to win for the rest of the team since I felt a little responsible for not finishing what we started in Lausanne.

"By the third Brier everybody wanted to win again for me because the Worlds were going to be played in my hometown. I really felt that.

"CBC asked me if I'd go back to the old club where I played junior to get some footage and all of a sudden there were more than 100 people out there. They got my dad holding the broom and had me trying some double takeout shots. I'd miss the first three and then make one and they'd all cheer like crazy.

"They had me go to the banquet for a junior bonspiel and a big media press conference. Winnipeg was just going crazy for it and it was the most excited I've ever been for an event. To represent our nation in the city where you grew up in the greatest curling country in the world…that's pretty phenomenal. I could hardly wait for it to start.

"I lived in Winnipeg for 24 years. I really still feel like it's home. Winnipeg obviously felt the same way about me.

"I had visions of being able to reminisce with old friends and family in the Brier Patch, have the odd visit outside the event, and overall, just be able to relish in a fantastic opportunity. Boy, was I kidding myself!

"What I received was what I believe to be the highest compliment an athlete can receive. And I remember thinking that there are some pro athletes who experience it and have to deal with it almost daily.

"I remember entering the Patch for the first time on the first Saturday night. After spending nearly two hours, I finally reached the table in the venue that was being held for our team. Two hours later I still had not been able to leave our table. I would not have believed that I was going to be mobbed with that kind of fan support.

"I never tried to go back to the Patch until the next weekend. As much as I wanted to do everything I could to give my gratitude to the fans, I was more than a little bit overwhelmed."

Nedohin always heard athletes like Wayne Gretzky talk about finding the escape from all of that sort of thing to be on the ice. He realized that's the space where he had to go no matter how special every moment of that scene would remain.

"My focus was to make sure I was ready to play and not be too tired from all the requests that were made on my time from the fans, the media and the event organizers. I had to shut myself off from the outside world and do whatever it was I needed to in order to play my best.

"Like every other time, my team was there to support me, taking as much of the load off me when they could."

If history was their story line in Halifax, they found some more motivation in the record books for the 2003 Worlds, too.

Shoeshine, Mr. Nedohin? Winnipeg native gets the treatment prior to Worlds.

"No team has won back-to-back world championships since Don Duguid in '70–'71," said Ferbey. "That was 31 years ago."

Duguid, of course, was from Nedohinipeg. Except it wasn't called that then.

When they hit Winnipeg there was no question about who would be the favourites. There seldom is at the Ford World Curling Championships. It's always Canada, no matter how many "surprises" there have been over the years.

Norway's Pal Trulsen was back and wasn't trying to convince anyone otherwise.

"It's Ferbey of course. The big favourite," he said. "We've beat them before. We might beat them again. I don't know. A miracle can strike twice maybe."

The field included Per Carlsen of Sweden, Ralph Stockli of Switzerland, Pete Fenson of the U.S.A., Ulrik Schmidt of Denmark, Andreas Lang of Germany, Dong Keun Lee of Korea and the Finland skip who had become known as M-15, Markku Uusipaavalniemi.

First up, and first down, was Lang of Germany. Ferbey stole two on the fifth end to take a 6–2 lead and eased to a 9–5 win.

Nedohin, who had been used to the mandatory stop in the interview area after every game for a couple of years now, knew he was going to be commenting on every game they played in the Winnipeg Worlds.

"Making sure that we got a win first off was good, just to feel comfortable out there," he said. "Overall we played pretty well. I think that's more important. If you play well even if you lose, you feel better than if you'd won and not played well. At the start it's more how you feel out there than anything."

But on the first day the media was more interested in what Nedohin thought of the scene in his old hometown.

"It was just sort of how I imagined it at the Winnipeg Arena with people coming out cheering and having fun. I really enjoyed it."

The Winnipeg schedule didn't waste any time getting to the meat of it.

On Day 2, the Canadians led off with Olympic champion Trulsen and followed with the Swiss, not exactly Team Ferbey's favourite curling nation after the Lausanne Worlds.

A crowd of 6,008 filled the old rink where the Winnipeg Jets used to play in the NHL and WHA to watch Nedohin and teammates bounce Trulsen 9–3.

"We respect each other's abilities and we've both been very successful over the last couple of years. But at the same time, we've become very good friends with them and we enjoy playing against them. We have a lot of laughs as well and I hope we play them again," Nedohin said in his second stop in the mixed zone.

Ferbey had a different thought.

"I think Trulsen is playing a little possum," he said. "If you remember last year's Worlds, we blew them out in the first game, too. But they weren't playing possum in the final."

He suggested the Norwegians, with all those trolls under the bridges, may know how to play possum pretty well.

"I don't know if Norway does this on purpose. In 1988 when I was with Pat Ryan at the world championships we played Eigil Ramsfjell of Norway in the round-robin and beat him in five ends. Then he came back to beat us. Now it's the same sort of thing.

"I've never done that. I like to go right after opponents. These guys might have a different theory. What I do know is that they're better than that."

Trulsen said there was no possum playing.

"We're all struggling," he said.

Trulsen curled 59%. His third, Lars Vagberg, was worse at 56%.

"You can't make mistakes against Ferbey's team. They are all good shot makers. If you make mistakes, you're dead."

Ferbey completed the first third of the 10-team round-robin with an 11–6 win over Stockli's Swiss squad.

With the women also involved in the Worlds, every second day was a one-game day and the 5,715 who showed up to watch Canada vs Finland's Uusipaavalniemi, if nothing else, thought they might be sitting in on a rare event this curling season—a Ferbey loss. But Nedohin made his last shot on the 10th end to win it 8–6 to make them 4–0 and 27–0 back to the start of the provincials.

"It's been a while," said Pfeifer.

Back to two games the next day, 4–0 became 6–0 for the Canadians, which was the same number of games Ferbey and mates managed to win in the previous two world championship round-robins.

Canada was wonky in a 9–7 win against Fenson's American team in the morning and bounced back to beat Warwick Smith of Scotland 7–4 in the nightcap.

"Right from the first end something wasn't right," said Ferbey of the game against the Americans. "The four of us weren't sort of talking the way we normally do. I guess you can't expect to be on the top of your game all the time. We did show a lot of patience, though. And we came through in the end."

While the scoreboard suggested it was an easier win against Scotland, Ferbey figured they might see them in the playoffs.

"I think that's a contending team," he said. "It was good to show them that we're here to play."

Nedohin bottom-lined the day. "We're assuming we're going to be in the playoffs now."

Smith wowed the crowd with a triple takeout in one end and Nedohin came back with a triple kill of his own on the next end.

"We were kind of kidding about that," laughed Nedohin. "We were saying that a triple isn't going to be the shot of the day anymore. You've got to do better than that. It was a lot of fun."

The next one was no fun at all.

When it finally happened, when the Ferbey Four finally lost a game, only 4,584 fans were there to watch it.

Denmark's Ulrik Schmidt finally figured out a way to cook Canada's goose and end a 29-game winning streak.

"We decided to give it all we had," said Schmidt. "We decided to go out and play their game. There's something to be said for going out and playing total offence. If you try and hit with them, they'll eat you up. The only way to go is right at them. Rocks in play right from the start. We knew we were gambling. We knew they'd get their chances. In the eighth end they had a great chance for five. If they made it, well, we gave it our best. But, for once, they didn't make it. I'd play it that same way if it was the championship for the world title."

The rest of the rinks weren't jumping up and down saying they'd discovered the magic formula. But when you lose 9–7 to Denmark, suddenly you have the other rinks thinking maybe…

"It's disappointing," said Ferbey. "But we won't let it carry over. We knew it was going to happen sooner or later. We just were starting to think it wasn't going to happen this year. It would have been nice to go undefeated throughout this whole thing."

Nedohin bounced back after an off game as Canada recovered with a 7–3 win over Sweden's Carlsen and finished up the round-robin with a victory over Korea's Lee by the same score in the final draw, where the focus of most of the 9,869 fans was on Trulsen defeating Uusipaavalniemi 7–2.

Trulsen scored four on the first end and couldn't resist taking a trip over to where Ferbey was standing behind the house in his game.

"He comes over to me and says 'Maybe Finland is playing possum now.' "

Trulsen's a great guy. But Ferbey said he hoped he wasn't an early riser.

The results of the final day meant Trulsen vs Ferbey at the ungodly hour of 7 AM in a semi-final.

"It doesn't make any sense to us," said Ferbey of the impossible-to-explain ways of the World Curling Federation, taking away any chance of a crowd for their most attractive game of the tournament prior to the final, killing the TV numbers in Canada and putting the teams in a position where they might not be as sharp as normal.

There certainly was a lot to sell with the match-up. Three straight years they'd met in the playoffs, one in each possible game, semi-final, bronze medal and gold medal. Who'd win the best-of-three series?

"Anything can happen," said Trulsen. "The Canadians are the favourites and they deserve to be because they've been the best team here this week. But they've been beaten too. Ferbey showed us he's able to lose a game against Denmark, so we probably have a chance to beat him" said Trulsen, who finished fourth at 6–3 to Canada's 8–1 with Finland's Uusipaavalniemi and Switzerland's Ralph Stockli both coming in at 7–2 to create the other semi-final.

"I'm hoping Denmark told him how to beat us," said Ferbey. "I hope he plays the same kind of game Denmark plays. Denmark called a lot of different shots against us that most teams don't and they got away with one."

The replay of the previous year's world championship, in which Ferbey won, and the do-over of the bronze medal game the year before, which Trulsen won, made for good advance copy.

First of all there was the matter of the Norway coach Ole Ingvaldsen "puttering around with the rocks with which the Canadian team had practiced" as Larry Wood reported it in the *Tankard Times*.

Ferbey said he didn't know what that was all about. "I don't know what they're looking at. If they think they can psychologically beat us because of the rocks they choose then…have at 'er, boys."

Nedohin noticed as well. "Maybe they feel we're pretty good judges of rocks and maybe they'll take the rocks we beat them with for the bronze medal game. But there's no rule against it. It's fine with me."

Nedohin chose the same two rocks he used against Trulsen in the round-robin.

"We found the rocks we liked," he said.

Nedohin was making more of the game than the rocks they'd use to play it. "We played him at the last two Worlds and I guess this is the grudge match," he said.

"They're a great team," said Rocque. "They're obviously one of the best teams in the world and they won the Olympic gold medal to prove it. We're going to have our hands full. But hopefully we'll give him as many fits as we've given him lately because we've had his number lately."

Nedohin figured, like so many games the Ferbey Four plays, the first one to 10 would win. He also said they were much more secure with themselves and the way they were playing this time around.

"We played a lot better this week than we did at the last two Worlds. This week we were pretty consistent throughout."

Trulsen offered a warning to Canada. "We won't be playing possum this time," he laughed, referring to Ferbey's suggestion when the Canadians had an easy go of it in the round-robin game.

There was no possum playing.

And the poster boy was put in the position of being the hero or the goat as the game came down to the last rock on the last end.

With the hammer in the 10th end, Nedohin made a difficult come-around tap-back for two and a 9–8

win with a surprising crowd of 8,765 getting themselves up early to watch.

"That was the biggest one I've ever thrown," Nedohin testified to the media mob when it was over and Canada had advanced to the final for a second straight year.

The last-rock thrower said the shot was the epitome of the way it works with this team.

"It was pretty exciting to see the guys work it at the end and Randy really pounding his broom for once to get it far enough back to get the two. Everybody did their part and it was a great shot.

"I just kept my fingers crossed. Obviously it was a weight shot. If it had the right weight, they didn't have to sweep it too much. But if you sweep it early, even for line, then you'll run it straight and totally miss it."

Ferbey said it was Nedohin in his element. "When Dave throws last rock he's an exceptional player and very seldom misses. It's almost like he gets geared up for these shots and, let's face it, it gives us confidence. It's like we're never out of it.

"There's always doubt in your mind. When you've got to play in any championship, you've always got to make that last shot, the putt or whatever in your sport. It's very difficult to make it when you have to make it. It's easier in the early rounds but to make it on the 18th hole to win the tournament, the fourth quarter, late in the third period or in overtime, whatever…that's different. That's what he did today."

Trulsen played a guard with his last rock not believing a Nedohin circus shot for two was there.

"I thought we had an extra end there," he said.

The crowd gave the Canadians a standing ovation.

"That was unbelievable," said Nedohin.

Ferbey wasn't born and raised in Winnipeg but liked it just as much.

"You heard the crowd out there. They're just as excited as we are. It's something we'll remember. That roar that went up there for those last two Nedohin shots was unbelievable."

Jim Bender, veteran curling writer of the *Winnipeg Sun*, wrote, "The Canadians reacted as if they had already grabbed the gold."

That was the feel.

"What we do know is that we would have lost the gold if he didn't make that great shot," said Pfeifer. "It's more of a relief than anything. That's not the game you want to lose."

The two sides had traded leads throughout the breakfast bout and Trulsen scored two in nine to set up the dramatic final end.

"Unreal," said Rocque. "If you could guarantee me that script every time, I'd say play it like that every time. It sure got exciting out there."

Canada scored two on the first end but had given up three on the third after a blank second end. The Canadians came back with two on four but gave two back to Norway on the fifth. Canada hit for three on the sixth and looked to finally be in control, but after trading singles on the seventh and eighth, Trulsen hit for another pair.

Watching the scoreboard was one thing. Watching the time clock was another.

Normally, the time clock doesn't come into play with the Ferbey Four. Normally, they're the rink with plenty of time, usually built up from early in the game and a minimum of time used up by the front end.

But at the end of this one their clock read 0:00.

Nedohin not only had to make an amazing shot, he had to make it in a hurry.

"I'd liked to have taken more time to discuss it," said Nedohin, who released the handle with 16 seconds remaining on the Canadian clock. "But we knew what we wanted to do. That's going to be a great memory for a long, long time."

Ferbey said the last shot, indeed, would be remembered for a long time. But Nedohin's second last shot, said the skip, was one that deserved to be remembered as well.

"The roar on those last two shots was unbelievable. That last end was something," said Ferbey in the media scrum. "You guys are talking about his last shot. But his first shot was just as good. It gave us the opportunity for the deuce."

Nedohin played an out-turn tap and roll, narrowly squeezing past a guard to establish second-shot rock behind cover.

Some were suggesting his last shot was a lucky shot ,and there was even the theory that the rock caught some debris, thereby explaining the late finish.

"We called the shot and made it," said Ferbey. "There's no luck in that. It was execution. That game was in doubt from the first rock of the first end to the last rock of the last end. That was a tough game."

Switzerland's Stockli crushed Finland's Uusipavalniemi 7–1 to create a Canada-Switzerland final. Trulsen would bounce back to claim a second world championship bronze medal with a 9–7 win over M-15.

Stockli's Swiss squad, coached by 1998 Olympic gold medal winner Patrick Hurlimann said playing Canada in a final in Canada would be an experience.

"We know there will be 10,000 fans cheering for Canada but we still have to play our best curling to win.

They have a lot of pressure on them. Everybody's watching them. This is the first time in the Worlds for us. Who ever heard of Stockli before?"

As the Canadians prepared to play the team from St. Gallen, Switzerland, Ferbey contemplated where they were as a result of Nedohin's shot.

"One more win and it will be the perfect ending to a really outstanding year. It's really been an unbelievable year," he said of winning $235,233 in prize money en route to their final game of the season, which included wins in the inaugural Canada Cup and inaugural Continental Cup.

"We're closing in on a world title. Obviously it's a bit different than a provincial or a Brier. Those are very special because they are just as difficult to attain but to become a two-time world champion in this thing is a pretty good carrot."

Ferbey was referring to the rink. He was going for his fourth world title. So, too, was former world junior champ Pfeifer.

When it was over, Bender wrote the paragraphs that captured it completely in the *Winnipeg Sun*: "Time to take down that statue atop the Manitoba Legislature and paint the lad's picture on its face. Winnipeg's David Nedohin has become our Golden Boy of the roarin' game even if he does throw the last brick for a team out of Alberta now."

With Don Duguid looking on, Nedohin and his Alberta buddies became the first team to win back-to-back world championships since Duguid back in '70–'71. Only Ernie Richardson and rink had done it before and that was in the days of the Scotch Cup, an end-of-the-year series between Canada and Scotland that evolved into the world championships.

"It was a dream capped off by a dream event," said Nedohin as he came off the ice.

"It's as good as it can possibly get in this sport. We've now experienced it and it's unbelievable," he said of winning the Worlds at home.

When the TV cameras panned the podium to Nedohin, the building exploded with a cheer for their native son and Nedohin responded with a great grin.

> **"The memories from Winnipeg, for me, are certainly once in a life-time and something I feel very special to have experienced."**
> **—Dave Nedohin**

"This has been a dream season and I don't know if we'll ever be able to equal it," he said. "I don't know. Maybe somebody will some day, but it's pretty special right now."

Two years later an opportunity would come along to win the Brier at home in Edmonton and to have another shot at a world championship on Canadian ice in Victoria, but who would know then?

Canada had the same start against Switzerland as against Norway. They scored two on the first but gave up three on the second, came back with two on the third and gave up two on the fourth. What made it a real game was when Switzerland stole one on five to go to the break up 6–5.

Nedohin didn't get off to a great start.

Or as *Winnipeg Sun* sports columnist Paul Friesen wrote: "He woke up with a slight case of the flu and for a while it looked like Dave Nedohin was going to throw up all over his world championship dream.

"I mean, when's the last time you've seen our hometown hero put up the kind of numbers he had early in the gold medal final? After four ends against Switzerland, Super Dave was shooting less than 50%, a number so pathetic his skip didn't even want him to know about it."

Ferbey was able to laugh about it after the game.

"He looked up at the scoreboard and asked 'What's my percentage?' I go 'I didn't notice. I missed it.' I didn't want to tell him he'd been that bad."

When it was over, Nedohin played down his bout with the virus.

His rink-mates didn't.

"He felt like throwing up in there," said Rocque of the pre-game dressing room.

"After the first end he really didn't look good either. I mean he was pretty pale. How the heck do you curl when you're feeling like that? We just kept telling him 'Just make it when it counts. Don't worry too much.' That's a team right? Sometimes you're gold and sometimes you're not. That's why you have three other guys to help you through it. Dave gave us a chance to play in this final game with his great shot in the semi-final. It was for him."

The Ferbey Four claimed the game, scoring one on six, stealing two on seven, stealing another on eight and stealing yet another two on the ninth to bring on the handshakes and to send the game into the books as a 10–6 win.

They'd won a record $235,233 during the season, but this one wasn't worth a dime and it didn't matter a damn.

"Nothing compares to this," said Nedohin. "I don't care about how much money it is. Right now, we're at the pinnacle of the sport. We're the world champions for a second year in a row and won it at home. We won more money than anybody else this year, but who will remember that five years down the road? They'll remember we were back-to-back world champions."

Looking back today, Nedohin says in the end it wasn't just him but the entire rink that would remember Winnipeg as a special time and place in their careers.

"Winnipeg showed their true colours with the support while we were on the ice. And with fans as knowledgeable as they are in Winnipeg, it was no surprise to any of us to see them cheering on every team, even the teams playing against us."

One moment beat them all, though.

"The moment I'll never forget was the last rock against Trulsen in the semi-finals and, with no time left, our team made that last-rock shot to win.

"There was a slim chance of making that shot but with a complete team effort it worked out—Randy calling the shot, Marcel and Scott sweeping it to utter perfection, and particularly Marcel making the perfect comments at the perfect time to give me confidence that we were going to win that game. With that win, I am not sure that I have ever heard a crowd that loud.

"The memories from Winnipeg, for me, are certainly once in a lifetime and something I feel very special to have experienced. I will always be truly thankful for Winnipeg and for my teammates for making it a reality."

CHAPTER 14

More Than a Rivalry

Arch Enemy: Kevin Martin watches Randy Ferbey's shot over Dave Nedohin's shoulder.

Who "detests" Kevin Martin most? And who "despised" him first?

"We were just walking off the ice from the M&M Skins Game after we beat Kevin," recalled Marcel Rocque. "It was a game when the ice got bad. We left him a shot on the outside that he had no chance to make. Kevin was standing there being interviewed and, as always, he wasn't giving us any credit for a victory.

"Randy Ferbey was walking off the ice and we both made a couple of comments about that. And somehow Randy and I started on about who despised Kevin most and who was first," Rocque continued. "Looking back, it was hilarious. As I remember it, it wasn't so hilarious at the time."

"Scott Pfeifer and David Nedohin were sitting there in the dressing room having to get us to calm down. There was a little intensity there," added Ferbey. "The original argument was who detested him first. I said I did. And I still think I'm right. Marcel said he disliked him first. And Marcel, when he thinks he's right…well, Marcel can get a little heated."

Pfeifer said they'll all sit back and laugh about it 20 years from now. "I specifically remember going up to them and saying 'Hey, take it easy,' " he said. "It was a funny conversation when you look back and when you know our team and the rivalry with Kevin Martin. So many things on our team turn into little competitions. Who is the best at this or that. But that one about Kevin Martin was an all-timer. It started with who detested Kevin Martin first."

Kevin Martin vs Randy Ferbey.

In the front end of the new millennium, it's been the greatest rivalry in the roaring game. Like any great rivalry, it involves best versus best. And in this case, and the thing that really revs it, is that it involves two teams from the same city.

Pal Trulsen of Norway, the curler who beat Martin in the gold medal game of the 2002 Salt Lake City Olympic Winter Games, is as good as anybody to make that point. "Randy Ferbey and Kevin Martin have the best two teams in curling," he said.

The Ferbey Four became the first team to make more than $200,000 in a year, an accomplishment Martin has achieved twice and Ferbey three times and a feat no other rink has been able to achieve more than once. Martin became the first skip to take teams to the million-dollar mark of prize money, most of it playing with Don Walchuk at third, Carter Rycroft at second and Don Bartlett at lead—a rink he would disband at the end of the 2005–06 season.

Like any great rivalry, the teams don't much like each other.

"He thinks he's God. He always will," is one quote from Nedohin that received pretty good play in the papers at one point along the way.

Ferbey's dislike of Martin goes back to the year after Pat Ryan moved to B.C. "After Pat left, Don Walchuk and I played together for one year. We were one game away from going to the provincials together," he said. "I heard Kevin was looking to form a new team and I told Don, 'Why don't we throw our services out to Kevin?' "

That's right. It was all Ferbey's idea in the first place.

"Don could see the potential problems. He said 'No! No! No!' I finally wore him down."

It was called a dream team.

"Just before Christmas, in 1991, Kevin made a call. He basically cut me. We'd lost three bonspiels in the semi-finals. We'd made about $60,000. But Kevin threw out that Don would move up to play third and I would play second, knowing I wasn't going to go for that considering what we'd been doing and his reasons for making a change.

"Kevin's reasoning was that we could win the city, we could win the Northerns and we could win the province but we were never going to beat Wayne Middaugh with me playing third. Wayne Middaugh!"

Like Ferbey, Rocque also once played with Martin.

"Don Bartlett was having back problems and they needed a lead for the tour championship. I went with them and we won it," Rocque said. "The following year Don Walchuk came up to me and said they needed a lead again and that Kevin had told him to find someone. I told him I'd check to see if I could get off work and he said he'd go back to Kevin and tell him he'd talked to me. Walchuk got back to me and told me 'Kevin said you're not good enough and to get someone else.' That's just Kevin. Every time I play against them, I think about that.

> **"Typical Kevin.
> It couldn't be him.
> It had to be the rocks. It's
> always something else.
> It's never Kevin Martin."**
>
> **—Marcel Rocque**

"I did have one claim to fame playing with Kevin in that tour championship. It was the last game of the round-robin against Guy Hemmings on the outside sheet at the event, which was held in Fort McMurray. In one game I threw rocks 1-2-3-4-5-6-7-8. One through eight. I couldn't believe that. In the ninth end I started again with one of my originals. I love to tell that story. It's the only time I've thrown all eight different rocks in one game."

Leads, of course, end up being forced to wrestle with rocks other players don't like.

"Typical Kevin. It couldn't be him. It had to be the rocks. It's always something else. It's never Kevin Martin," Rocque said

He noted it's pretty much the same with both he and Ferbey when it comes to Martin. "There's bad blood between Kevin and Randy over the whole breakup of that dream team. There's bad blood with me, too. When someone tells me I'm not good enough, I don't have time for him.

"I don't think he's ever given me or our team the same credit that we have granted him," he added.

Rocque says the Ferbey Four always give Martin his due. "As a player, he's absolutely outstanding. No one questions his ability. And he's elevated the game in Edmonton just like Pat Ryan did before him. Kevin raised the bar. Personally, however, he's not the type of guy I'm going to sit around and have drinks with."

The irony is that Kevin Martin is the man most responsible for Marcel Rocque being with the Ferbey Four. Martin stole Carter Rycroft from the Ferbey rink. Rocque was brought in to replace Rycroft. Ferbey and Nedohin had first paired up for the 1997–98 curling season and added Scott Pfeifer at second and Carter Rycroft at lead the following year to try to make it into the Edmonton 1999 Brier. They failed on a last-rock miracle shot by Ken Hunka.

Rycroft defected to join Martin the following season.

Looking back, Nedohin says it was a good move for Rycroft and a good move for their team. "It turned out to be win-win for everyone. Carter went on to a great career with Martin, winning a pile of money on tour, going to a Brier and winning a silver medal at the Olympics. As for our team, we were missing a piece of our puzzle in Marcel 'Shot' Rocque. He certainly became the glue on our team to take us to the next level."

That turned out to be true. But at the time, when Rycroft left, Ferbey was steamed.

"Rycroft leaving…that was tough," said the skip. "Kevin was looking for a new player. Again. I remember we were in Saskatoon at the time, and Kevin and I were talking when all of a sudden he tells me, 'Carter will be playing with me next year. I got the best guy on your team.'"

The season wasn't over yet. And Kevin had come to Carter to get him to switch teams.

"I went to Carter and he told me Kevin promised him all sorts of wonderful things with Kevin's sponsorship dollars. At that time, we didn't have sponsorship dollars which were even close," he said of the money, which reduces travel costs.

Rycroft ended up missing out on a whole bunch of Briers and world championships, but does have an Olympic experience and an Olympic silver medal to justify the move.

"To this day I laugh at Kevin about his 'Got the best guy on your team' line. Scott and Marcel have turned into the best front end in the world. Today everybody acknowledges that," Ferbey says. He adds that the team's overall distaste for Martin, however, has worked out great.

"Dumb as it may sound, we probably owe a lot of our success to Kevin Martin. He gave us so much negative stuff to deal with and to feed off that it made us a better team. Without him, without our rivalry with him, I don't think we'd have achieved everything we've achieved.

"We're probably 50–50 playing against him. I'm not sure our record would be that good in those games without all that ridiculous stuff. If we've played 20 times over the last five years, I'd bet it's 10 wins each. And maybe other than one game for either rink, the percentages have been in the high 80s, low 90s. We don't want to lose to them and they don't want to lose to us."

To this day, the sponsorship issue that played a part in taking Rycroft away is an interesting situation. A significant part of it has always come from Edmonton-based multimillionaire Bruce Saville. He's long backed Martin. But not the Ferbey Four.

"At a banquet once," Ferbey says, "I heard Bruce tell the audience that one of the stupidest things he'd ever done was turn us down."

There's no animosity with Saville. Nedohin has a relationship with Saville that was instrumental in setting up a new business. Raylene Rocque curls for Cathy King, Saville's significant other, on another of his sponsored rinks, which has in the past included Ed Werenich, John Morris and Brad Gushue.

"It's interesting Bruce has never sponsored us," said Nedohin. "I know Bruce is interested. But there seems to be too many potential conflicts with existing sponsors as well as the whole thing with Kevin's team. Bruce is certainly one of the great donors and sponsors in this sport and even though the Saville Group is not one of our sponsors directly, I would have no hesitation in promoting him or his efforts. We need more Bruce Savilles in this sport."

> "To this day I laugh at Kevin about his 'Got the best guy on your team' line. Scott and Marcel have turned into the best front end in the world. Today everybody acknowledges that."
>
> —Randy Ferbey

The rivalry with the teams is real and based on curling. But the rivalry with Martin is separate.

The dynamics involved with the rest of them are fascinating.

Ferbey and Walchuk won two Briers and a world championship together with Pat Ryan and both say they are each other's best friends. They've owned race horses together.

"Don Walchuk has been my best friend since 1986," Ferbey said. "We won two Briers and a world championship together. As a curler, he's just pure talent. He's one of the greatest curlers who ever played the game, regardless of position. Scott Pfeifer is the best second in the game right now and Don Walchuk was the best second to play in his time at that position."

Walchuk, he said, became the second after Ferbey fought to keep him on the team with Pat Ryan. "At one point Pat Ryan didn't want him on our team. I was the one who got him back on the team. Don is a great guy, a guy you can talk to about anything. I always try to get him going on the subject of Kevin, but at the end of the night we joke about it."

Rocque played with Walchuk for years, making it to the final at the provincials together in 1994 and losing to Ed Lukowich.

"I went to two provincials with Don as the skip, including the one in which we lost the final to Lukowich," said Rocque. "When I joined the Ferbey rink and we beat Don as a member of the Martin rink in the provincial final in 2001 in Stettler to go to our first Brier, Don gave me a little hug. I'll always remember that. I'll also remember early in my career when he told me I was going to do OK in this game because I had the heart of a lion.

"I had a lot of great times with Don. He's a great curler, he's a great competitor and he's a great person. I have nothing but the utmost respect for him. He taught me a lot about the game and he especially taught me a lot about the dedication to the game. Don gave me my first big opportunity. But he also set me on a path to develop into the best that I can be."

Pfeifer and Rycroft came up through juniors at the same time and played for a year together before Rycroft left to go to Martin.

"I remember after Carter went and joined Kevin we played them three times in a best of three finals at the World Open and beat them two out of three," says Pfeifer, who also says they won the first game the two teams played after the move. "It's been the same with this team since that first game."

But again, there's a solid friendship there.

"Carter and I are real good friends. Carter and I go way back to juniors. I played against him quite a bit. We had the stag for his wedding at Dave's house. We went paintballing together."

Kevin Martin is a different deal.

"I don't very often agree with the things he says or does. Put it that way," said Pfeifer.

Nedohin, the one guy without a previous tie to anybody on the other team, said he started out in the sport with Martin almost on a pedestal when he watched him represent Canada at the 1991 World Curling Championship in Winnipeg. But that changed.

"I really had no problem with the guy originally. I thought of him as having one of the greatest teams of the modern era and he was certainly someone I looked forward to play," Nedohin says. "When I moved to Alberta, he represented the bar everyone wanted to reach if they were going to go to the Brier. The road to being the best, no question, went through Kevin Martin.

"On one side, the rivalry could be looked at no differently than any two competitive teams within the same region butting their heads time after time. Certainly the battle continued off the ice and things were said in the media to fuel the fire. That's not uncommon. Many times it's not so much personal as it is simply the competitive nature of the players.

"Looking at the situation, Carter is a good friend of mine and a good friend of Scott's, while Walchuk is a great friend with Ferb. Marcel and Walchuk are friends. When you have that many friendships between the players, you know that a lot of the rivalry is jostling for position or playing small mental games. However, there are also the Kevin issues. Over the years that's the one that has gone a little further than our competitive nature.

"I would think that in both camps there have been things said and done that appear to have come out the wrong way or were said at the wrong time. However, the real issues have certainly developed since the boycott of the 18 teams in 2002.

"Our team, for our own reasons, did not agree with the boycott, especially given that we had 24 hours to make our decision. As much as we supported the initiative of the players' association fully to build the tour and attempt to win extra bonuses from the Canadian Curling Association at the Brier, we did not agree with the method at that time," said Nedohin.

"This was where Kevin crossed the line, in my mind. He was the leader in an initiative to have us banned from the tour completely. Our team had wholeheartedly supported and continued to support the tour. However, the 'decision' was no longer in our hands as we were given an ultimatum. Kevin continued to insist we turned our backs on the players when we were the ones who were being shunned.

"I saw it as a way to degrade the accomplishment of our team the season before when we beat Kevin in the final at provincials to go to the Brier and win it all. Kevin continued to diminish our accomplishments. He often forgot that in 2002–03 we were the top money winners in the world, leading even Kevin and breaking the $200,000 mark for the first time," Nedohin continued.

"Even after we'd won our third Brier, Kevin was quoted in the paper as not recognizing our accomplishments because 'we'd played nobody.' There were lots of nobodies out there who didn't agree. Ask Mark Dacey, who we played in the Brier finals two years in a row, one with the Slammers and one before he came back," he said of the term that had come into use to refer to the Grand Slam players slamming the teams that had stayed on the Brier trail.

"Ask John Morris, who we played in the final of the Canada Cup two years in a row, one with the Slammers and one without.

"We've never had a beef with the World Curling Players' Association. I even have a contract with the WCPA with my new company Statusfirm, Inc. But we've certainly had a problem with Kevin Martin," Nedohin concluded.

All of that set the scene for a game at 9:45 AM in Hinton, Alberta. That was the time and place when Ferbey and Martin would begin throwing granite in the direction of the Rocky Mountains.

Just 15 minutes outside of Jasper National Park, Hinton is a town of 9,405. The "Rumble In The Rockies" brought a Brier-sized media mob to the 820-seat Bill Thompson Arena with the initial story line, "Why In The World Are We Watching Randy Ferbey vs Kevin Martin Curl At 9:45 Wednesday Morning In Hinton?"

Alberta may have become the No. 1 province in curling, both by winning Briers and by attendance at Briers held in Edmonton and Calgary, but when it comes to the provincial championship…well, it was a sad state of affairs. Ferbey and Martin seldom agree on anything, but they did agree on that.

"We're opening with one of the biggest games in curling, in people's minds at least, at 9:45 AM on Wednesday," said Ferbey. "Somebody should have used a little common sense and changed it. It should be 7 PM on Friday night."

Martin agreed. He said, "If a marketing company was running this, no way would you have the top two teams playing each other at 9:30 AM in the first game. The top two should be scheduled for the centre sheet at 7 PM Friday night."

This match-up had enough hair on it to come down from the mountains as some sort of Abominable Snowman wearing a kilt, playing bagpipes and carrying a sign reading "asterisk."

The provincials used to be called the Safeway Select, but they lost the sponsor after awarding the event to two towns that didn't even have Safeway stores. So this one was the "Your Name Here" Provincial Curling Championship, out in bear country with no television.

What a waste.

"Great for Hinton, though," said Martin.

The hype was huge. And there was more involved than Ferbey vs Martin.

John Morris, who lost to Ferbey as skip of the Ontario rink in the 2002 Calgary Brier, loved Cowtown so much that he moved there and won a berth out of the south. And despite Martin leading the boycott boys, the calibre of curlers in a) Edmonton and b) Northern Alberta, was the equal of any other area in Canada.

"I'd say seven of the eight teams here would have been in the top eight of the '99 Brier," said Brent MacDonald, who was in that one as a third for Ken Hunka's Edmonton rink.

"It's really a mini-Brier to get to the Brier," said Nedohin.

"You have three teams here who rank in the top five in Canada," said Ferbey.

But those quotes were buried. First and foremost this was Ferbey vs Martin.

Walchuk went into it with the idea it would go to the rink that wanted it more. "It almost seems like it's going to come down to who is the hungriest. I know that when we lost to them in 2001, they were hungrier. I could see it coming a long time before that," he said. "Let's be honest. There's a bit of a grudge and a huge rivalry. We don't like to lose and they don't like to lose."

The night before, the two rinks were chirping at each other at practice, where the teams were required to draw to the button to decide which teams had hammer, last-rock advantage in the Ferbey–Martin opener hanging in the balance.

"It was a mix-up when we started throwing for the hammer," Nedohin reported. "Kevin said 'Let's start

Speak No Evil: Nedohin and Ferbey assume same pose as Martin calls shot.

now' and Don Bartlett threw to the back of the 12-foot. But Bartlett, Carter Rycroft and Don Walchuk said they hadn't heard Kevin say it was starting and… well, they took the rock away and Kevin said 'Do you think we're cheating?' It was something that should have been in the hands of the officials, not the curlers."

Martin ended up with last-rock advantage, but it was all behind them when they headed to the rink the next morning.

"We have lots of problems off the ice but we have a lot of respect on the ice," said Ferbey.

Fire marshalls locked the doors 20 minutes before the first stone was thrown. The main parking lot was full at 8 AM. But less than two hours later, when all the smoke had cleared—except for the stuff coming out of the pulp mill—it turned out it was a big buildup for a large letdown.

The team that had lost only seven games on the Brier trail in the last four seasons kicked the bejabers out of a team that had already lost six in their return to the playdowns in one season.

"It was wonderful," said Martin of the environment. "Too bad about the game."

The team that had won three Briers in a row thumped the two-time Brier champions and Olympic silver medalists 7–2.

"We waited years for this?" said Ferbey.

Ferbey and mates were enjoying the moment for all it was worth after all the asterisk talk from Martin and the Brier Boycott bunch. But they also portrayed it as just another win in their 21-game provincial winning streak that included Martin back when it started and also made mention that their record was 10–1 on the playdown path for the season and the loss dropped Martin to 15–6. They also made sure to let everybody know they weren't making much of it in terms of the big picture, that if Hinton was about validation, that wouldn't come until the final game on the Sunday.

"We don't have any illusions that this game did anything but get us off on the right foot," said Ferbey of the game in which Martin came up seriously short to allow Ferbey to steal one on the third end and send them on their way to a shake-hands-after-seven win.

The media mob stayed around for the rest of the week, but another Ferbey–Martin match failed to materialize.

Kurt Balderston beat Martin 5–4 in the semi-final to cancel the rematch the curling world most wanted to watch.

"I keep telling everybody, 'There's more than just one good team here. They just met one,' " Ferbey rubbed it in.

When it was over, Martin made the point. "I hate losing. But that was a great game. It's a crying shame that wasn't on TV."

It left the Ferbey Four contemplating the same scenario as the year before. The quotes sounded the same. All that changed was that this was Hinton instead of the Granite Curling Club in Edmonton, they were playing Kurt Balderston instead of Jamie King, and they were dealing with a new calendar.

Nedohin said the thing about the final is, if you lose it, the next time you get back to the game you're going for one in a row like they were back in 2001 against Martin in Stettler.

When you've won 26 straight, it doesn't seem fair that it could all blow up in your face if you lose one game.

"That's called sport," said Nedohin. "It doesn't matter if you win 'em all or lose a few, the idea is to get to the final game and win it. That's the Grey Cup. That's the Super Bowl. That's sport."

The best quote came from Rocque. "This is the biggest game we can ever play because we can never play it again. It's for all the marbles. The one difference is that every year they add more marbles."

The next day, with Martin and his rink back in Edmonton and not even able to watch the game on TV or listen on the radio, was the day the Ferbey four became the Ferbey Four.

Rocque, Pfeifer, Ferbey and Nedohin did more than knock off Kurt Balderston and mates 8–5 to take the title; they knocked off any asterisk Kevin Martin and friends wanted to put beside their names.

They matched Ron Northcott's Alberta record of four consecutive crowns and won the right to head to Saskatoon to try to match Ernie Richardson's record of four Brier titles and go where nobody had gone before by winning four in a row.

The rink, which became one Brier away from filing claim as the greatest team in curling history, refused to lose.

For the longest time the team that had now won 26 straight games at the Alberta Curling Championship, and extended their record to an equally mind-boggling 31–1 against the best from the toughest curling province in the country, looked like the odds had caught up to them.

"We couldn't help but wonder for a while there if our time was up," said Nedohin.

Despite going into the final with last-rock advantage, Ferbey's outfit found themselves down 3–1 after giving up steals on two consecutive ends.

Pfeifer was more graphic than that. "I was crapping my pants after four ends," he said.

Ferbey said experience ended up winning the day and another trip to the Brier.

"Randy kept saying 'Be patient. Being down two isn't the end of the world,' " said Nedohin.

Nedohin tapped back for three on the fifth end and the rink stole two in the sixth and ended up eventually running the Sexsmith rink out of rocks.

"That's as nervous as I've ever been before. I think we all felt it more than we ever have before at any provincials, any Brier or any World Championship," said Rocque. "It just felt so different in the change room before the game. We were a little tighter than ever before. We definitely had the nerves and jitters. And then we got down like that in the first four ends. We just didn't want to let it all go."

Pfeifer said the early slump just made the win all the more sweet. The tougher it is to win, the greater the accomplishment feels.

"It's an unbelievable feeling," said Ferbey. "It's amazing to do this again and again and again and again."

In the end, this team couldn't lose for winning. Rocque's wife Raylene won $1,606 in the 50–50 draw while her husband was throwing a rock in the ninth end.

But the best part of it all was that they'd won a provincials with Kevin Martin in the field and they were going to the Brier. Martin, Jeff Stoughton, Kerry Burtnyk, Wayne Middaugh and the rest of the Brier boycott bunch, who tried so hard to devalue their accomplishments while they were away, were not.

"I've been telling everybody that there are more than four rinks in Canada," said Ferbey.

"No one has a God-given right to get to the Brier," said Nedohin, looking back. "Hinton was sweet justice for all Martin's 'Nobodies.' Kurt Balderston was one of the 'nobodies' that we beat in a provincial final. After we beat Martin in the preliminaries, Kurt had his chance and took full advantage of it, knocking Kevin out of the provincials. We liked that a lot."

CHAPTER 15

Nedohin's Toon Town Meltdown

It's a Hero-Goat Game: Dave Nedohin knows the highs and lows.

Ernie Richardson was there, sitting in the crowd at Saskatchewan Place. There was almost the expectation that, if the Ferbey Four made it four in a row at the 2004 Saskatoon Brier, he'd emerge from the stands, tap a corn broom on each shoulder and anoint them as "the greatest" on the spot.

And yet Randy Ferbey and rink somehow managed to come to the Silver Anniversary Brier like they came to the first one, still excited about curling in front of 12,000 fans and very much in awe of how all of this had happened to them.

"It's blowing our minds," said Marcel Rocque as they arrived, watched Ferbey win the hot shots competition and a $34,935 Ford Escape XLT and heard the

Edmonton 2005 Brier Committee announce they'd already sold 80,598 tickets, a year in advance.

Rocque continued, "We can win as many Briers as Ernie Richardson if we win this one. Ernie Richardson! Not one of us ever dreamed we'd go to a Brier someday with a chance to do something like that, to equal a record set by a legend like that. It's an incredible honour and privilege just to be in a position to do it. It's unreal."

As the Alberta rink prepared to take to the ice they contemplated not just making history on the big picture, but in the Brier record book, which had them at 35–4 during their run and a record 16-consecutive game winning streak. The old record was 14 set by Pat

130

Ryan's Edmonton rink on which Ferbey played third. Three more and they'd tie the consecutive-game, consecutive-Brier winning streak by a province.

Manitoba, in a run from 1937–39, won 19 straight. But that record was put together by three different skips, not the same four guys.

The Albertans didn't know that.

There's also the Road To The Brier, the playdowns as they're usually referred to. And there's no record book to look that stuff up.

Showing up with the same kid-at-the-carnival attitude in which they arrive at the Brier every year, Scott Pfeifer worked it all out.

Over the last four years to this point, qualifying out of the Edmonton zone, they'd gone 18–2. Out of Northern Alberta they were 24–4. And at the provincials 31–1. Add in their 35–4 Brier record and that was 108–11. That's in the toughest city in the toughest zone in the toughest province in the toughest curling nation in the world. Not to mention four provincial titles, three straight Brier wins and back-to-back world championships.

"It'll come to an end," said Ferbey. "Sooner or later it will come to an end. Let's just hope it's later."

It would be sooner. But in the meantime they'd make a run for the last of the winning-streak records out there.

For openers, as was the case the year before when they played in Halifax and met the home-province rink skipped by Mark Dacey, they were scheduled to play Bruce Korte of Saskatchewan. But they could have been playing the man on the moon for all the Ferbey Four noticed. They weren't playing for the 11,445 fans in the stands, they were playing for Ernie and Sam Richardson, Matt Baldwin, Ron Northcott, Fred Storey, Bernie Sparkes, Pat Ryan, Don Walchuk and Rick

Lang. They were playing for the legends of the game, the other living curlers who had also won three Briers in their career and were sitting together up there, live and in person, brought to Saskatoon to celebrate the 75th anniversary of the Brier. The night before they'd given the rink the most amazing moment of their careers at the Brier banquet. Forget the fans, this game was for the greats.

Ferbey and mates made all the big shots in an 8–7 opening game win.

"We didn't want to go out on the ice and lose a game in front of all those greats no matter who we were playing or how hard the crowd was cheering for us to finally lose one," said Pfeifer.

Seventeen straight!

With an 8–7 win over Jay Peachey of British Columbia and a 9–3 win over Robbie Gordon of Northern Ontario, Ferbey's outfit made it out of the gate at 3–0.

Nineteen straight!

They'd tied the record of the three different Manitoba rinks spanning 1937–39, one that saw Spats Gowanlock go 9–0 in the middle year to make it possible.

Suddenly it wasn't the Nokia Tankard that was the trophy in play, it was Ferbey.

Up next was Mike Harris of Ontario.

Harris, as well as anybody, knew what it's like to be the answer to a trivia question. Until he made it to Saskatoon 2005, he was the answer to the question, "Name the curler who won an Olympic silver medal but never played in a Brier?"

"I'd like to be the answer to 'Who stopped Randy Ferbey's record winning streak at the Brier at 19?' " said the CBC colour commentator who had finally made it out of the TV booth and into a Brier. "I'd love to be the guy who stops it. We all want to be the guy."

Harris was the last chance to stop the Ferbey rink from registering the record outright. If Harris didn't get him, Brent Scales and the Buffalo Boys from Manitoba were on deck.

"I don't know if we want to beat him to stop the streak. But we definitely want to beat him just for confidence and what it would do for you from a mental point of view," said Scales. "For whatever reason, whoever does it is going to feel pretty good. In their situation, I'd be hoping I'd lose one here before they get to the playoffs. You don't want to go to the finals undefeated and have your luck run out there and lose that."

It looked like their number had come up against Saskatchewan in the Brier lid-lifter but Nedohin was making circus shots to save the day.

Against B.C., it worked the other way around. Nedohin missed four last-rock shots, two of them to provide steals and one to give up two.

He flashed on a wide-open takeout on the fourth end and bounced one off the boards in trying to clip out a biter in the ninth. On the other hand, Alberta's last-rock thrower drew for three in the eighth and drew to the pot with the last rock to win it in the 10th.

If they'd lost that one, it would have been written that Alberta wasn't defeated by B.C., but by Alberta.

"It's easy to win when you play great," said Manitoba's Scales. "The trick is to win when you don't. That's what they do."

Up next after Manitoba would be the, uh, Territories on Tuesday morning.

The Polar Bears, skipped by Brian Wasnea, a former Edmonton resident of 15 years, said he didn't come dreaming of beating the Edmonton rink in the final.

"I was playing second for Orest Peech at the Edmonton 1999 Brier when we went 0–11," he said. "But if you remember, we played Russ Howard in the last game of that Brier with Russ needing to beat us to make it to the playoffs and the crowd cheering like crazy for us to win one. We took them to an extra end."

Never say never.

Howard was set to play Ferbey the following day.

Setting a record for most Briers with 13 upon arrival, the New Brunswick skip opened with his record 101st, 102nd and 103rd Brier wins. So he was a guy who knew a bit about records.

"It's amazing to win that many games in a row. These are the top teams in Canada—the top teams in the world. Sure you want to be the team to stop the streak," said Howard.

Newfoundland's Brad Gushue was scheduled as the last guy to get Ferbey in the round-robin.

"I'd love the opportunity to be the team to do it," said Gushue. "Who doesn't want to beat the best team in the world?"

P.E.I. skip Mike Gaudet had his own take on beating Ferbey when his turn came.

"I couldn't care less about stopping their streak. I just want to be able to say I beat the three-time Brier champions, that I beat the back-to-back world champions."

Either way, the first rink to beat Ferbey at this Brier would become a pretty big story.

"And a trivia question," reminded Harris.

As Ferbey and Harris paraded behind the bagpipes for the occasion, the press bench was largely empty. It was trade deadline day in the NHL. And, while they somehow managed a 7–5 win over Harris to set the record and run the streak to 20, Ferbey came off the ice sounding like a general manager who was thinking of trading his best player.

"That was terrible," he said after the morning draw and yet another series of flashes by Nedohin, which turned an easy win into yet another high-wire act that came down to the last rock to win.

"We had pressure on those guys every single end. That game came down to last rock and it never had to happen. I haven't seen Dave miss that many shots in a whole week."

Ferbey took a deep breath after the team escaped with the win.

"But we're not going to trade him."

There was a little levity in the number of absolutely awful shots, complete misses of wide-open, close-your-eyes takeouts that Nedohin managed at that point in Saskatoon.

Confronted with a takeout against one of two rocks that were only 6 inches apart, when Nedohin sat in the hack to prepare to throw his rock, lead Marcel Rocque cracked "Well, you can't flash this one."

Nedohin said a couple ends later Rocque added "Well, the good news is that it can't get any worse."

> **"It's easy to win when you play great. The trick is to win when you don't. That's what they do."**
> **—Brent Scales**

Feted by the legends of the game as perhaps the greatest shot-maker of all time, Nedohin had indeed made a few circus shots. But he'd made many more that looked like something you'd see at the Newsman's Bonspiel, or the Boozeman's Nonspiel as it is more commonly called.

"It's a good thing I've made the last shots," he said of having to use the hammer three times in three games to win with a pressure shot with the final brick. "We'd be 1–3 if I'd missed those shots, too."

Several times in the game with Ontario, his teammates said Nedohin went from bad to worse and played almost as bad as the worst game he's ever curled at the Brier, the opener of Calgary 2002 when Russ Howard scored a 10–1 win in one of the only four games this rink had managed to lose during the run.

"Dave usually makes a shot in about the third or fourth end to put away guys. It's not happening here so far this year," said Ferbey.

Indeed, he had one opportunity to make a double takeout for five but missed and settled for two.

"Nedohin has had three bad games and they've still won those games," said Harris. "What does that tell you?"

Despite Nedohin's struggles at the most important position, the Alberta rink made it 21 straight with a

6–4 win over Scales' Manitoba outfit in the evening, leaving the three-in-a-row champions the only remaining undefeated rink in the event as Nedohin curled 82% —still the lowest on the team—in that game.

"He's been our worst curler," said Ferbey, more in amazement than anything.

With Rocque and Pfeifer curling in the low 90% range and leading all players at their positions and Ferbey up there with the third-rock throwers in the mid-to-high 80% range during the week, Nedohin dropped to eighth place with a 73% record.

"He's made too many shots in the last four years to get down on him," said Ferbey, adding that he wanted Nedohin shooting in the 90% range for the last three days of the Brier, not the first three days.

Brian Moore, listed as coach of the team, said Nedohin always starts slow at the Brier. "He's just taken one game longer than usual to get it going," he said. "He does this every year."

Ferbey says Nedohin is so used to shooting to near perfection, when he's not it tends to eat him up. "He's his own worst critic. When he misses a shot he gets so mad at himself."

Nedohin didn't want to blame the ice.

"The thing that's so baffling to me is that I'm missing the easy shots—the wide open takeouts. I'm making most of the difficult shots and the draws. I've never missed as many wide open shots in my life. Hopefully the guys aren't too worried. They are all playing so well. I'll come around. I'll be OK."

It looked like everything was OK the next day.

Guess who showed up at the Brier the day before?

The Nedohins. Heather. Halle. And David. Heather and daughter Halle arrived from Edmonton, David from wherever.

Russ Howard watched Nedohin get his game together to beat him 7–3 and said, "I knew it. I knew he'd get out of his grave. The rest of the rink had been playing great but Nedohin had struggled. I knew he'd climb out of his casket and curl 90% against us."

Actually it was 92%.

And another 92% game against the Territories went with it as the Ferbey Four ran their record to 7–0 and 23 consecutive wins at the Brier.

"Nedohin had a good day," said Ferbey. "When his family gets in, he has a good day."

But the next day it was over. Twenty-three skidoo. Times two.

Randy Ferbey was beaten. Huff & Puff couldn't blow the house down. Saskatoon native Mark Dacey and his Nova Scotia rink beat the three-in-a-row defending champions 8–7 to take the tournament into the last day with the same 8–1 record as the Albertans.

What made it 23 skidoo times two was the other winning streak Ferbey had going, 23 straight wins that season dating back to a loss in the Edmonton zones prior to running the table at the Northern Alberta and provincial championships.

"Maybe the curling gods decided to finally get back at us," said Ferbey. "It was not supposed to be that easy.

"The way it happened, I'm more bothered by the *way* we lost. We don't lose games when we're three points up. If Dave had made his last draw on the eighth end, we would be answering questions from you guys about going undefeated again.

"We're still here to win the Brier," he said of the rink which went 11–2 to win in 2001 in Ottawa, 11–2 in 2002 in Calgary and 13–0 the previous year in Halifax.

If you figured there might be some sense of relief to finally end the run, there was none.

"Not a chance," spat Nedohin, the Brier MVP for the previous three years. "I'm not happy about it, not one bit. I hate losing. It has nothing to do with the number of straight wins we had going. It could have been a two-game streak. It doesn't matter. The streak was just something for people to talk about."

Dacey said it tasted great and felt good…for the moment.

"We put their streak to an end and let the world know that they can actually lose a game at the Brier," he said. "It's kind of nice to be the team to do it.

"They're human beings. We don't play against them physically, just against their rocks. They're like playing Tiger Woods," said Dacey, the head professional at the Fox Harbour Golf Resort in Nova Scotia.

It occurred to Dacey that there could be a possible downside.

"Those guys will be even more motivated to kick our butts the next time. Dave missing both his shots on the last end is completely unusual."

Nedohin crashed on a guard with his first shot in the 10th and called out "forget it" to his sweepers half way down the ice on his second shot.

"Losing for the first time in a long time feels exactly what it is supposed to feel like," said Pfeifer. "I had a stinker. I didn't set things up like I had all week." Pfeifer curled 100% in one game and 99% in another and led all seconds all week until coming up with a 73% effort in that one.

"It always sucks to lose," said Rocque who shot 98% in vain in the game. "But we've said it all along. There are good curlers here. We didn't come here expecting to go undefeated again. This is the Brier. We're going into the final day of the round-robin with one loss. How bad is that?"

Before returning to the ice and scoring a 6–5 win over the Spud Islanders in the evening, Ferbey said one of the things about losing a game after winning 23 in a row at the Brier and 23 in a row on the playdown path is that it doesn't teach you anything about bouncing back from a loss.

"We don't know how to deal with it. We're going to have to look at some of the losers out there."

The Ferbey Four wouldn't have to wait long to get a rematch against the Blue Nosers. Both the Albertans and Nova Scotians finished off with two-win final days.

Alberta scored six on the first end against Dan Lafleur's Quebec rink and coasted to a 9–2 win, and scored a 10–3 win over Brad Gushue of Newfoundland.

So it was Ferbey–Dacey in the 1–2 game of the Page playoff system. But with a difference. In the previous three they'd played, the Albertans were the No. 1 team. This time they were the No. 2 team. No last-rock advantage.

"There will be so many rocks in play I don't think it'll make much of a difference," said Ferbey. "He's going to see a lot of granite."

Of that, said Dacey, he had no doubt. "We're going to have to come out with guns-ablazing. These guys just keep coming at you and wait for you to crack. Then they're all over you. The good thing about the 1–2 game is that the winner goes straight to the final and the loser gets a second chance through the semi-final. But you don't want to have to use it."

Certainly, he said, it wasn't likely to be like the regular-round game.

"Dave missed three shots in the last couple of ends," he said. "You don't see that often."

But having beaten them at the Brier two days earlier could go a long way.

"At this level you don't think anybody is unbeatable," said Dacey.

Maybe. But for the fourth straight Brier, Ferbey and gang went direct from the 1–2 game to the final.

It was an over-after-nine 10–6 win with Huff of the "Huff & Puff" front end curling 97%, his second best percentage of the Saskatoon event in which he not once curled under 90% and ended the regular round at 93%.

Dacey beat B.C.'s Jay Peachey 7–4 in the semi-final to make the rematch.

The final had more than the four-in-a-row story line for the Albertans. The rematch of the previous final, which drew a stunning 1.77 million viewers in prime time, was one thing. The only other time the same two teams met in back-to-back Brier finals was when Rick Folk and Russ Howard met in '93 and '94. Howard bounced back from losing a Brier final in '93 and won the next year. Folk, Al Hackner and Kevin Martin had also turned the same lose-the-final-one-year, win-it-the-next trick.

With Dacey ending the Ferbey streaks in the regular round and Ferbey bouncing back in the 1–2 game, it was the third game of a best of three series, too.

And there was also the twist of Dacey having home-ice advantage in back-to-back Briers, the first where he lives and curls in Halifax and the second where he was born and raised in Saskatoon.

"That's pretty unbelievable," said Dacey. "In the semifinal I heard a fan in the stands shout 'Go City Park.' That's my old high school. It's kinda neat that way. Just the chance to be in another Brier final is unbelievable."

But mostly it was "The Underdog" vs "History."

People love to cheer for the underdog but fans don't drool for dynasties.

Ferbey said the underdog thing he understood. But the dynasty thing he didn't.

"I think we've reached the point where more people are looking for us to lose than to win," said the skip of the team that went into the final with their Brier record up to 46–5 over the four years.

"We've been winning so long. I understand that. But we're going out there to do something that nobody has ever done. This is a special team. I'd think that decades from now people here would want to be able to say 'I watched that team make history.' I'd think a lot of people would want to go to the rink, hoping we'd win, to be able to say 'I was there watching that.' "

On the morning of the final at the Brier Brunch, for a second straight year, third-rock-thrower Ferbey, second Pfeifer and lead Rocque were named to the first all-star team by the Curling Reporters of Canada. The previous year, all four spots on the first team, for the only time in history, were all from the same rink. This time Nedohin, who also won first all-star status along with Pfeifer in 2002 in Calgary, wasn't even picked to the second team. But after seven ends of the final, Nedohin's name was on most ballots on the press bench as Brier MVP for the fourth straight year.

It was there. It was over. It was 8–4 with three ends to go. Four in a row was in hand. In the minds of just about everybody in the building and a near-record audience watching on CBC, the Alberta rink was off to the world championships to attempt to become the first team in history to win three in a row there.

All they had to do was close.

And they couldn't.

They didn't.

"I'm having a hard time looking the guys in the eyes right now," said Nedohin of gassing a game that was already won by missing shots on the eighth and 10th ends he'll have nightmares about for the rest of his life.

"I missed a couple of shots in the eighth— shots I'm supposed to make. If I make my shots, we win the game, we win the Brier again. I take the last shots. It's up to me to figure things out. It's my job to make those shots. I'm taking this on my shoulders. The guys played great."

> ## "We just beat the best team in the world. It's so amazing to be part of this."
> ## —Rob Harris

Traces of tears were in the eyes of Randy Ferbey, Dave Nedohin, Scott Pfeifer and Marcel Rocque as they were forced to stand there through a 25-minute closing ceremonies thinking about what happened to them here.

"Utter disbelief," said Pfeifer. "The game was in the bag. I feel for Dave. He's the reason we won the last three Briers."

Ferbey said obviously they gave the game away.

"You can't help but be confident when you are four up with three ends to go. It came down to poor execution. It came down to sitting in the hack and making the shots. We stopped making them and they started making them. I'm sure Dave is going to blame himself. But it's nothing to be embarrassed about. He's made a lot of shots. The thing that gets you is that we've never lost a game like that before."

The focus was on Ferbey's rink losing the game more than Dacey's rink winning it. Nobody has ever won a Brier like that before. Nobody.

"That has to be the greatest comeback in curling history and against one of the greatest teams in history," said Rob Harris of ending the three-in-a-row reign of the Ferbey Four.

"This is awesome. I guess it's time for somebody new," added the second for Mark Dacey's team, which came back to score three in the eighth and three more in the 10th end to beat the Albertans 10–9.

The 19 points is the highest combined score for a final, eclipsing the mark of 18 set in three previous Briers since the playoff format began in 1980.

"We just beat the best team in the world. It's so amazing to be part of this," said Harris.

"I stayed calm," said Dacey, who was a nervous Nellie in the early ends, but got it done with the adrenaline pumping in the end.

He drew for three with Nedohin sitting behind the house covering his face after missing a clutch shot to set it up.

"My guys believed in me. I believed in them. To come from behind like that is so unbelievable. It looked like a real cake-walk for those guys. But if you make your last six shots in the last three ends, things can happen."

This wouldn't go down in history as one team making shots, though. It would go down as a team, on the very verge of being anointed as the greatest in history, gagging.

Nedohin, the MVP winner of the last three Briers, was definitely the goat, setting the entire comeback up when he missed on his first shot.

"That's the one. If there's one we could have back it was Dave's first shot in the eighth," said Ferbey.

This looked like the same game as all the other Ferbey finals.

Against Manitoba's Kerry Burtnyk at Ottawa 2001 it was 3–3 at the fifth-end break. Ferbey scored two on the sixth, eighth and ninth. Game over.

Two years previous at Calgary 2002, John Morris thought he was going good in a 3–2 game when Ferbey hit him for four in the fifth. Game over.

The previous year at Halifax 2003, Nova Scotia led 4–3 after six ends and watched the Ferbey Four put up five points over the next three ends. Game over.

But not this time. Nedohin out-curled Dacey 84% to 75%. Ferbey out-curled third Bruce Lohnes 90% to 88%. Marcel Rocque out-curled lead Andrew Gibson 95% to 90%. Only Harris had an edge, 94% to 88% over second Pfeifer.

But this time, statistics were for losers.

It was a comeback nobody saw coming.

"We beat them! I won the Brier right here in Saskatoon—in my hometown," said the Nova Scotia skip who moved away from the heartland of the sport eight years earlier. He came back to register the most dramatic comeback in the 75-year history of the event and the first win by an Atlantic Canada team since Jack MacDuff's miracle win for Newfoundland in 1976 in Regina.

Late in the game a fan seated directly behind the house was heckling Nedohin when he was in the hack and during his delivery. The team asked the officials to do something, but nothing was done.

Whether the fan had anything to with what happened is open to debate. It was more obvious to the people at home watching TV than those in the building when Rocque, who was miked for the final, threatened to rearrange the fan's dentures if he didn't desist: "Once more and you're mine."

Like golfers in their backswing, Nedohin said it's something you don't expect to hear.

"I'm not using it as an excuse. But he was yelling my name during my delivery and I certainly did hear him. We had been fan-friendly throughout the game and joking back and forth with some people in the crowd that obviously had too much to drink. But this guy went too far."

In the end, the game was still there to win and they could only hang it on themselves.

"All the way through this, we've felt we were kind of a team of destiny. But when you look back at the week, they were the team of destiny," said Rocque.

"They beat us the same way earlier in the week. We let them back in with a big end in that one, too.

"What can you say? This is sport. That's why you play the games."

It's a game they'll be playing over and over again for the rest of their lives.

Maybe one day Nedohin would bump into Steve Smith, the Edmonton Oiler who scored on his own net to cost the last dynasty in hockey their third Stanley Cup in what could have been a five-in-a-row run.

Maybe someday they'd share the worst day of their careers. But the day after the defeat, misery wasn't looking for company. While his teammates flew home from Saskatoon on a flight full of Brier fans, Nedohin drove back with his wife and 20-month-old daughter.

"I didn't sleep," said the goat of the most colossal collapse in the history of making history at the Brier. "I kept thinking of what I could have done and should have done and about everything we missed out on because of the shots I missed."

As Nedohin drove through the two provinces back to his home in Sherwood Park, he thought about so many things.

"I thought about going into the history books, the Olympic funding we lost, the TSN Skins Game spot we didn't get. More than anything I'd love to wear the Maple Leaf on my back, and not being able to go to the world championships hurts the most," he said of a chance to go to Sweden and win three in a row of those, too.

Rocque said he could sum up his feelings coming home in one word.

"Numbness," he said.

"It's a situation almost unacceptable for us. We never give away games like that. And we did it to them twice. A couple of shots got away from us. Take back two shots, both on the eighth ends in those two games, and we run the table and are 13–0 two years in a row," he said.

Choke is the ugliest word in sport and dealing with that is the most difficult, said Rocque. "The thing that's hardest to swallow is that we gave it away. We beat ourselves. And it all is now starting to sink in what we gave away. It was more than one game."

Ferbey, when he returned to town, said there was no pretending that what happened didn't happen. "Under the circumstances, to lose the biggest game of curling the way we did is pretty tough to take. We're just going to have to find a way to deal with it. We're still in a state of disbelief. This game is going to take a long, long time before it goes away."

Rocque said they would live to win again.

"Maybe this had to happen to us. Something like this happened to us once before," he said of Nedohin missing a last-rock shot in the semis of their first Worlds in Switzerland.

"I think my team will keep me," said Nedohin.

CHAPTER 16

Pros and Cons of Being Pros

Looking like billboards: Ferbey Four assume new look to give sponsor more bang for their bucks

Randy Ferbey viewed it as being "temporarily unemployed."

Wayne Middaugh viewed it as "turning pro."

After losing the Saskatoon Brier, the Ferbey Four decided to put curling ahead of everything else in an attempt to get to the biggest Brier ever held, the 2005 Tim Hortons Brier in their own hometown, and to win a fourth title. They decided to put curling ahead of employment to follow it with a third World Curling Championship and to proceed to concentrate on the Olympic Trials in Halifax with hopes of going to Torino and becoming Canada's first men's curling team to win gold at the five-ring circus.

They would get to the Edmonton 2005 Brier, and after they beat Middaugh in a round-robin game, controversy broke out.

"They're pros," said the Ontario skip. "Randy's team is the only professional team here. They're head and shoulders above everybody else. He's a guy who plays 15 or 18 weeks a year and practices every day. He curls. I've got a full-time job. You can't take the New England Patriots and put them against a college team. They're professionals."

The members of the Ferbey rink laughed at Middaugh.

"I don't get it," said Rocque. "Wayne is a golf pro in the summer who curls all winter."

Ferbey, at first, had a puzzled look on his face when the media mob switched scrums to get a reaction.

"What does he mean?"

After a brief explanation Ferbey rolled his eyes.

"We all know Wayne. We've all known him for years," he added, suggesting he comes from the "whine" region of Ontario.

"Nothing changes. I don't want to go there. All I ask is give credit where credit is due."

Finally, Larry Wood of Calgary, covering his 44th Brier, his first dating back to when Ferbey was in diapers, pushed the right button.

"We beat Wayne when we were *un*professionals," responded Ferbey.

"Where's the controversy?" asked Nedohin. "He plays for money. We play for money. I don't think there's such a thing in curling as being professional. I don't know what a pro team would be. I don't think this is one.

"We're committed to doing what we're doing this year *like* pros. We're committed more than anybody."

That was the plan and exactly what the Canadian Olympic Committee wanted our potential medal winners to do in all sports.

But it wasn't all planned.

"Our devotion was put to the test," said Nedohin. "It was an interesting time on the whole scale of things. After our successes at the Brier and the Worlds, certainly our main goal had become the Olympics. And everything came to a head on several fronts.

"First, Marcel was told by his principal that he would no longer be able to take the time off for curling that he had in the past. Scott had graduated with his MBA and needed to make some career choices. And I was given an ultimatum by my business partners, from the business which I had started, to choose between curling and work.

"Everyone knew we needed to support our families and that was our first priority. It appeared we'd have to go through the next couple of years playing very little. I came back to the team and said if the whole team was on board to treat curling as our profession, I would be willing to leave my engineering business

and likely my career in pursuit of our goals for the Olympics.

"Marcel notified the school board that he would be taking a leave of absence for the curling season and Scott took a job in Edmonton that would allow him to curl even though it was possible for him to get a better job in the industry elsewhere.

"We made a commitment beyond anything that any other team has ever done, risking everything. This could not have happened without the four guys on this team being committed to each other and, most importantly, our families supporting our decision and believing in us. The level of commitment we've had likely surpasses that of most professional athletes."

Curling as a business, they all maintain, isn't the way to get rich quick. Or even slowly. Or even at all.

"People who think there is any money in this are delusional," is how Rocque phrases it.

"Right now there's no real future in it. We've had a real chance to look at it objectively. We've done about as well as you can do and we've made some pretty substantial sacrifices to do as well as we've done.

"I've replaced the money I lost teaching. But at the end of the day, I have lost pension and lost time. Whatever job you have, you hold yourself back with promotions and that sort of thing.

"There's a little money there. But you have to be doing it for the love of the game."

Each member of the rink has a slightly different slant on that.

Ferbey says when you ask if you make a living at curling, you're going to get a "yes and no" answer from most members of the Ferbey Four.

"We have to win our salary. You can do exceptionally well if you find the right four people, don't have any bad years and find some good sponsorship to cut down on the expenses.

"I remember talking with Ed Werenich once. It was at a time when there were a lot of new rinks coming on and people were talking about how well they were going to do. Ed referred to one of them and said 'Let's see how good this guy can play when he has two small children at home and a mortgage payment to make.'

"We pay our way. We pay entry fees. It's when you go home and come back with nothing, that's the test. That's when you have to look at your wife and kids. And at the same time you have to watch three other guys going through the same thing.

"You have to find four top curlers who also happen to be the right four guys to get along together and be able to go through all the same things at the same time.

"I'm convinced there are hundreds of curlers in Canada who, if they put the right four guys and the right situations together, conceivably could do pretty well."

Pfeifer says when you have a $200,000 year as a team, some people are going to see you as a professional curler.

"If we could continue at the pace we've had for the last few years, it would at least be possible. But even in a big year it doesn't totally add up. In 2004–05, I had to take nine weeks off work from the beginning of September until the end of April. There's just not enough money to turn pro and curl full-time. But there's enough money where a good rink with jobs who can take nine weeks off work, can do well. Those kinds of jobs are tough to find."

A golf pro, like Middaugh, he suggests, is one of them.

Ferbey has an interesting history of occupations.

Ferbey worked the mutuel windows part-time for a number of years at Northlands Park, and before that he worked full-time for Globe Envelopes, a job he lost because of a manager's concern about the time he was taking off to curl.

"The next one I kept for a while. I worked 21 years at the Northern Alberta Institute of Technology, the first 16 as a printer and the last five in the front office as an accountant. NAIT was very supportive of the curling and the time involved.

"I left NAIT to join an oil company, Tartan Controls, in the rental division. Again it was a company very supportive of curling. But the division I worked for dried up. I could see that I was going to be laid off and it happened just before we decided to dedicate more time to curling.

"You could say the decision to do what we did was easier for me than anybody, because of that. Absolutely. You could also say it was harder. I didn't have a job to go back to. If we didn't win at curling, how was I going to pay the mortgage?"

Ferbey ended up owning an Asham curling supplies franchise in the Ottewell Curling Club.

"I don't think you'll see me working a 9 to 5 job again."

Nedohin's situation was entirely different.

"For me it was either quit curling or sell my share of the consulting firm to my partners."

He sold.

"It was a tough thing to do."

Unable to restrict himself totally to throwing and sweeping, Nedohin did, however, use the year to begin a new business integrating video with computers involving web design and marketing.

"Three of us decided to take the year off, but I'm kind of back to working. But it's on my own terms. And my partner in this business understands the benefits of our curling success and how it could translate into the success of our new business.

"Because of our team's commitment, for the second time in my life I had to make a major decision between career/money and my curling dreams. This time, it was obviously a little more difficult than when I first moved to Edmonton because I now had a wife and a family to support.

"I knew my business partners at CT & Associates Engineering were not willing to support my dream. So I was not likely to last long with them in any event. Somehow there had been a reasonable level of support for the previous years. Suddenly that changed. It was difficult because I'd put in a lot of time on the road working as well as curling. In addition, the curling, I thought, added a significant amount to the marketing efforts of our company and securing some significant clients.

"When the ultimatum was given to me in the spring of 2004, it really sent a clear message that these were not the people I could continue working with, even though after the decision there was some discussion to try to change my mind. I'm not sure they ever believed I'd walk away."

In some ways Scott Pfeifer seemed out of step with the rest of the rink before Nedohin found himself back in business.

Pfeifer spent the previous years combining curling with university studies while his teammates juggled curling and employment.

"I graduated with an MBA from the University of Alberta and became employed as an electricity analyst," said Pfeifer. "It's ironic with the rest of the team taking a year away from their jobs that I was the one going to work. For the previous years I was the only one on the rink without a job. Then I became the only one on the rink with a job."

Pfeifer said his life in the real work-a-day world took a while to come together.

"I was a poor student from 1994 to 2000, getting my Bachelor of Science with a specialization in Environmental Earth Science from the University of Alberta. Between 2000 and 2004, I was employed as a hydrogeologist for a company based here in Edmonton. I worked there for the 2001 and 2002 seasons when we lost in Lausanne in the 2001 Worlds and won in Bismarck in the 2002 Worlds.

"I went back to the U of A from 2002 to 2004 to receive my Masters of Business Administration (MBA) in Natural Resources and Energy. We won the Worlds in 2003 and lost the Brier final in 2004 while pursuing my post-graduate degree."

Pfeifer says, yes, he could have had a more lucrative job.

"I didn't want to be in Calgary. And the point at this time of my life is that curling is a very high priority. I'll probably never be on a better team. As long as there's the Ferbey Four, I want to be one of the four. As long as I can curl with these guys and find out just how much we can accomplish together, curling is going to be a priority."

Rocque, while he was able to return at the end of the world championships and work a couple of months and do some set-up stuff with Riverbend Junior High School in the fall, had to not only give up work, he had to give up the kids.

"In the four years I spent juggling a full-time job and juggling everything involved with being part of this rink, it was the kids at school who made it all worthwhile at the end of the day.

"To me this is what being a role model is all about. I taught since '96 but none of the kids were really aware of curling until I won something. It was kinda neat having my students come up to me to talk about curling. They started to follow it. The staff started to follow it. When I was away, the staff would let the kids know what was going on. When we won, they'd have assemblies for me when I came back. It was great to be able to share experiences with the students."

Rocque, when he came to Edmonton from St. Paul to curl, planned on going to the U of A.

"I knew I wanted to continue curling. I liked kids and I liked sports, so I decided to be a physical education teacher. I figured if I graduated, I could at least substitute as a teacher when I wasn't curling."

He ended up with the job he loves at Riverbend. And it's at this late date that the original plan to be a substitute teacher kicked in.

It's always fun to look at the Brier or World media fact book and the incredible assortment of job combinations that come together on one rink. It really is butcher, baker and candlestick maker. The Ferbey Four illustrates that as well as any rink out there.

Nedohin is the head of finances for the Ferbey Four. He lays it all out.

"The top three or four teams can make enough, with a great season and good sponsorship, to support their families in a modest sort of way for that season. The difficulty lies in the fact that any one team will not likely be in the top three or four consistently year after year. And sponsorship is very hard to come by."

Nedohin offers this as an example of a weekend:

Entry:	$ 1,100.
Flights:	$ 2,000.
Hotels:	$ 800.
Food:	$ 1,100.
Incidentals:	$ 600.
Total:	$ 5,600.

That figure obviously fluctuates with location. The dollars change dramatically between an event in Newfoundland and an event close to home where no flights are involved.

"On the average weekend, our goal is the qualifying money. That's usually about $4,000 and means you're in the final eight of a 32-team event. Get that qualifying money covered and you'll end up doing OK."

Once you're qualified, the money in a good spiel usually breaks down to something like:

Final eight:	$ 4,000.
Final four:	$ 6,500.
Final two:	$10,000.
Winner:	$15,000.

"If we get to the final four it usually averages out that we've made $900, or $225 each. If we win the event it usually averages out to $9,400, or $2,350 each for the week of work. This is average since some spiels we enter have less prize money (maybe $10,000 for first) and some are more ($30,000 for first, like the Grand Slams).

"Really the only way to make any money worth talking about is through the Skins Games, the four Grand Slams and the Canadian Curling Association events—the Continental Cup, Canada Cup and the Brier."

Counting all of their sources of winnings, the Ferbey Four has earned over $200,000 three times in a single season. No other team has ever done that, and only Kevin Martin has reached that mark twice. Ironically, both teams did it the same years both times, 2002–03 and 2004–05. The Ferbey four team did it again in 2005–06.

"If you use the $5,600 per event and spread it over 18 weekends on the season, it would work out to about $100,000 in expenses," said Nedohin. "That leaves $100,000 to the team. We're talking $25,000 clear per player. If that still sounds OK, now factor in the time off work.

"Obviously, sponsorship money is not included in this, but it's all very tough to come by. Unless you are in the top five teams in the world, you're not very likely to get more than $20,000 per team in sponsorships.

"For us, we have also been fortunate as a result of winning the Brier to be carded athletes. This means we received some grant money from Sport Canada on a weekly basis to assist in our training and expenses. This was typically $1,100 a month per player but has recently been increased to $1,500 a month. Only the national champions are eligible for this money.

"Overall, we have been successful enough to have been able to pay the bills over the last two years, although we took a huge gamble to do so. If we didn't win as much as we did, we were all prepared to lose our shirts on this."

In round numbers, the team won $25,000 the first year Ferbey and Nedohin curled together in 1997–98, $30,000 the following year when Pfeifer hooked up, $70,000 in 1999–2000 when Rocque completed the team, $35,000 the first year they won the Brier, $45,000 the second year, $225,000 the third year, $125,000 the year they lost it in Saskatoon and they would go on to plateau at $232,561 in 2004–05.

"Only four of those years we actually made money," says Nedohin, of covering expenses.

Don't let your babies grow up to believe they're going to be professional curlers. Not that the money list isn't interesting. In 2005–06 it read like this:

1. Randy Ferbey, Edmonton $208,099
2. Kevin Martin, Edmonton $171,500
3. Glen Howard, Coldwater, Ont $135,262
4. John Morris, Calgary $87,500
5. Jeff Stoughton, Winnipeg $77,000
6. Wayne Middaugh, Ajax, Ont $70,000
7. J.M. Menard, Boucherville, Que $62,991
8. Pat Simmons, Moose Jaw $57,000
9. Bob Ursel, Kelowna $50,750
10. Pierre Charette, Buckingham, Que $47,456
11. Mark Dacey, Halifax $46,644
12. Mark Johnson, Edmonton $45,456

Everybody else was under $35,000. That doesn't include expenses. And it has to be divided four ways.

Sponsorship money isn't included in all that.

"From our sponsorship side mostly Marcel and I have made the major contacts and sealed the deals. But Randy is key," says Nedohin. "He's the guy who attracts all the attention."

Ferbey generates, with his name alone, the occasional commercial and plenty of appearance fees.

But he doesn't take the money from those deals himself.

"Everything this team receives financially is split four ways. If I do a speaking engagement worth $1,000, then that $1,000 is divided four ways," said Ferbey.

"I know teams out there that don't do that. I know Kevin Martin doesn't do that. With us, it's divided four ways."

Even Ferbey's commercial for Strauss Herb Company?

"Yup, I'm doing all the work there and they each get a quarter of the money," laughs Ferbey.

While they've since produced a new Strauss commercial featuring all the members of the rink, the curling world made a lot of fun of Ferbey for his solo commercial.

"We weren't sure we wanted 25% of that one," said Pfeifer. "Randy looked like a raccoon in that one. We forget how tanned he always gets in the summer. And the commercials run in the winter."

Nedohin says Strauss is a different deal. "Although we are not sponsored by them as such, we have been involved in promoting them through commercials. Everyone knows Randy's 'cheesy' commercials."

Ferbey and Nedohin made an appearance on the popular CTV sitcom *Corner Gas* and were paid $700 each for the 20-second cameos.

"We divided it up," said Ferbey. "Without all four individuals, you don't get these opportunities."

From the dozen years between Briers, nobody asked him to do any commercials or go on any TV shows.

"I owe it to them. That's the way I look at it. Besides, it's not something that started with me. I think that started with Pat Ryan. He had the idea that it was unfair for him to take something that was a result of the accomplishments of the team.

"It's all part of the concept of being a team. If you look at team in the dictionary, our picture should be in there. There are not many teams in curling. There are a lot of curling groups, but not many teams, *real* teams."

Sponsorship money makes it all so much easier. Depending on how a team wants to work it, it can cover how much they can afford to travel or how many entry fees they can pay to enter cashspiels. Or both. It can take away a big part of the downside.

"Sponsors are very difficult to come by in curling," says Nedohin. "For some reason it always seems that businessmen think because these are guys that work for a living that they don't need the same money as a figure skater.

"This always baffles me since curlers can provide way more advertising and promotional potential than many other sports simply because we are on television and in the newspapers with our on-ice clothing on a weekly basis throughout the winter."

When Ferbey and Nedohin hooked up the first year, they thought they did OK with sponsorship.

"Back in 1997 our team was ecstatic with our first sponsors of $2,000 to $3,000.

"We've been very fortunate over the years to have formed some wonderful relationships with some long-time sponsors such as Denmar Energy Services, JVC, Culligan of Canada and WestJet, the latter two of which are no longer with us. Our most current sponsorship additions include World Financial Group, Purdy's Chocolates, Purolator and Asham.

"Without the sponsors our team wouldn't have been as committed—there was no way we could have left our jobs, even for a year."

The teams aren't allowed to wear their sponsorship jackets and uniforms at the Brier, Worlds or Olympic trials. It makes it exceptionally difficult to get the sponsor the bang for his buck if you're not successful on the cashspiel circuit.

And while the Ferbey Four story is very much tied to the Briers and Worlds, they've had more than their fair share of TV time and newspaper coverage as a result of their successes in curling's "regular season."

The team won the '02 and '04 Continental Cup, the '03 and '04 Canada Cup, the '02 and '04 M&M Skins Game and the '02 TSN Skins Game. In '02 and '03 they also won the Bund Trophy in Switzerland and in '05 an invitational in Perth, Scotland. Runners-up in the Swiss Cup in '03, the team was also a semi-finalist in an event in Oslo, Norway, the same year.

Then there are the dozens of lesser cashspiels that they've won, which include Saskatoon, Edmonton Shamrock (twice), the Edmonton World Open, Vernon, Bonnyville (twice), Wainwright, Olds, Leduc and Jasper to include some of the ones closer to home.

When it came to sponsorship, the Ferbey Four became trail blazers in 2005–06.

"Our team took an approach that I don't believe any other team in the world took before. We became very professional about it," said Nedohin. "I don't mean professional in the terms Middaugh 'accused' us of being at the Brier in Edmonton. I mean from an organizational perspective. This includes meetings, on-ice and off-ice dress, media, marketing, promotion...."

"We decided we had a lot to offer. We believed if there was any curling team in the world that could add value to sponsors, it was our team. We took a page out of one of the most successful sponsorship-driven sports in the world—NASCAR. We used that as the model for how a team should look, act and promote themselves.

"We were fortunate enough to hook up with a few great sponsors and capitalized to a level no other team in the history of curling had ever done before. We chose on-ice jackets and branded them with our sponsors, title sponsor World Financial Group, Purdy's Chocoloates, Purolator Courier, Denmar Energy Services and JVC. The sponsors were prominent no matter where the TV camera or still photographers focussed.

"Other curlers teased us that we looked like billboards. We did. That was the idea. We were determined to show the world that curlers are marketable. With likely double the amount of sponsorship any team has ever seen before, we think we were successful."

While they'll debate whether or not there is any money in curling as a business, there's no debate about running it like a business.

When you've won two Briers and become world champions, as the rink did in 2002, it's more than just curling. People start demanding your time for dozens of appearances and worthwhile causes.

"As exciting as everything was for us in the summer of 2002, we knew we had to learn how to manage our time and our duties," said Nedohin. "We had to try and meet the needs of our sponsors, charities and promotional events along with balancing families and careers. The careers part of the equation is the thing that most other athletes don't have to worry about.

"Time management and scheduling was something our team had to learn, and we spent many hours scheduling from year to year. From that summer of 2002 on, we were almost as busy in the off-season as we were during the curling season. Scheduling travelling, deciding which events to enter, hotels, sponsors, cresting, clothing, speaking engagements, appearing in parades, celebrity golf tournaments and other charity functions became a major thing."

Ferbey says the longer they go on together and the more success they enjoy, the more all that sort of stuff grows.

"One unique thing about our team is that we basically talk every day, all year round. It almost never goes more than two days. It's just that there's so much going on. I get requests. The other guys get requests. We probably meet more in the summer than in the winter."

The positions on the business side of the Ferbey Four aren't exactly the same as on the ice.

"We have an agenda. Most times I'll be the one to prepare the agenda. Randy will be the one to chair the meeting," says Nedohin.

"Randy is always the first one to talk when something needs to be discussed. Our team meetings are a huge part of our continued success and communication. They are, in our minds, as important to the longevity of the team as the on-ice practice.

"Our team essentially works like a mini-business," says Nedohin. "And just like any business there are disagreements in how it should be run, who does what, etc.

"One thing about Randy, he's great at heading up a meeting where we have to talk about some difficult issues. Everyone has so much respect for him, that it's usually Randy who initiates the discussions.

"People may wonder how we settle problems without getting pissed off. The answer is we do get pissed off. If there is a problem with someone or something, if someone is doing or not doing something, we talk about it. On our team we take great pride in communication. It's the only reason that four strong-willed, bullheaded in some cases, people can stay together as long as we have.

"The perfect example was New Year's Day 2001," says Nedohin. "Things were not going the way they should have been going. We had come off a great season on the cashspiel circuit in 1999–2000. But we weren't going very well in the fall of 2000. Things were not quite right.

"It was at the point where small things start to fester and become bigger problems than they should. You could feel a little bit of the tension.

"A meeting was called at the last minute on New Year's Day. Our team met for the better part of the day to figure things out, point fingers and solve our issues.

"While every other team in the world was still busy stuffing their faces with turkey and desserts from the Christmas season, we were in a problem-solving mode. We all know the things that are said will piss you off, but they need to be brought up to improve our team. Six hours later we left the meeting rejuvenated. Re-energized. Re-focused."

Indeed, says Pfeifer.

"I guarantee you that we were the only team meeting on New Year's Day. We'd had a mediocre cashspiel season, and we were talking about what we had to do in the playdowns coming up. We weren't all on the same page. But we came out of that meeting shaking hands and really coming together as a team."

Nedohin says it was a turning point. Time and time again this team has turned negatives into positives.

"From there we went on to win our first Brier, which we had been written off before it even started. We all look back at New Year's Day 2001 as a key moment in our development as a team.

> **"Other curlers teased us that we looked like billboards. We did. That was the idea. We were determined to show the world that curlers are marketable."**
> **—Dave Nedohin**

"Keeping that in mind, we usually go through one or two of these meetings each year and, hard as it may be to believe, we almost look forward to them."

Again, all that starts with Ferbey.

"We get upset with each other. But we get it out. We'll do it in a hotel room or somewhere with the four of us. Then we'll leave with it all hashed out and it won't come up again," says Ferbey.

"If you don't like the way I'm doing something, let me know. Right now. Part of being successful is learning how to accept criticism and dealing with it."

Unlike NHL and CFL players, there's no massive support staff to arrange for travel and to handle equipment, baggage and all that other stuff.

Each player has various responsibilities.

Nedohin writes the cheques and enters the spiels.

Ferbey is the equipment manager. Being in the curling supplies business, he knows what to get, where to get it and, occasionally, how to get it for nothing.

While Nedohin usually books the practices, it's Ferbey who is in charge of them.

"Randy is very important during our practices," says Nedohin. "He makes sure everyone is working on what he wants to see. Without pointing fingers, or being too structured, he seems to always get what he wants out of the practice."

Ferbey says practice isn't about everybody throwing 40 rocks each and every day or anything like that with this rink.

"Everybody is different on our team. Dave needs 50 rocks. I might throw 10 or 15. I can't throw too many," says the old guy. "Scott, maybe 15 to 20. Marcel might throw 20 to 25. It depends. The big thing is to be there with your teammates."

Rocque says Ferbey is weird that way. He doesn't much like to practice himself. But he's big on practice. "When I first came to the team Randy didn't practice as much as he's practiced in the last few years. I don't think there's any magic in why Randy's numbers are higher now than they might have been at some stages of his career—he's working harder.

"Right from the start I felt I owed it to Dave to go practice with him. In the end there are not many teams out there who work as hard as this team," said Ferbey.

"A lot of teams tend to practice their favorite shots, the ones they're good at. My philosophy has always been to practice what you're bad at."

"I'm adamant that the team has to practice together. Dave and I disagree on that now and again. Sometimes he just wants to go out and practice on his own. I remember when Pat Ryan moved to B.C. and I was still curling with him. He phoned me one day and told me he was working on his out-turn and that he got it just perfect. He had a junior curler holding the broom for him, and the kid was telling him that he had it down just great. Somebody else holding the broom just doesn't know the delivery. Sure enough…"

Ryan, when Ferbey caught up to play with him again, had achieved something the opposite of perfection.

"I think the third and the skip should practice all the time just to learn the releases. It takes months and years to learn that."

Pfeifer says it's true from his point of view. "Without Randy there telling you what you're doing wrong with your release, you might as well be throwing rocks against a brick wall."

When it comes to practicing what you don't do well, Ferbey says that's just part of what separates the top curlers from the ones who don't get there.

"You have to be your own worst critic. You have to be honest with yourself. You have to know when you've thrown a bad one and not come back to the other end and pretend that you don't know what went wrong when you missed the broom by 6 inches."

One good thing about being the Ferbey Four is that they seldom have to pay for practice ice time.

"Generally we do not pay for ice, although we have paid for ice from time to time," says Nedohin. "Mostly the club is fine with us being there since it does bring some excitement to club members in a lot of cases, and our team has been very open to signing autographs or taking the time to talk to some of the club members."

There are a whole bunch of other duties involved that maybe you don't think about.

"I don't think we ever sat down and organized everyone into specific jobs," said Nedohin. "They just sort of evolved."

Like Pfeifer's job with the rocks.

He studies them. He charts them. He knows every rock the Canadian Curling Association uses for the Brier, World Championships in Canada, Canada Cup, Continental Cup, etc.

"Yeah, I'm the rock guy. It just kind of developed into my job because pretty much everybody trusted me. I'd say 'Throw these two. That's the best chance you have for a match.' To the other guys, a rock is a rock. Randy couldn't care less. I could give him a couple without handles and he wouldn't notice. Well, there is Marcel. He's always complaining because he always gets the worst ones."

Pfeifer, you could say, is the travelling secretary of the team, much like they have in baseball.

"Scott is the one to book all the travel," says Nedohin. "He's in charge of the flights, hotels…"

The entire rink is amazed the way Pfeifer can find pleasure with a map.

"I have a map fetish. I love travelling. Guilty as charged.

"Everyone on our team has a guilty pleasure. Marcel has chocolate. Randy has cigars. Dave likes the odd scotch. I like a map."

It can't be exaggerated, they all insist.

"Give Scott a map and some rail system in England or something and he can be thrilled for weeks on end," says Ferbey. "When we go to Europe, he's got it all prepared down to the minute. He knows what time the trains are leaving, how many blocks we have to walk to the train station…it's amazing.

"We never have to worry about airlines and hotels. It's booked. It's done. Most people get to Europe and look around with that 'Where am I? What do I do? Where do I go?' sort of look. Not Scott. He takes us marching right off."

Nedohin shakes his head.

"Map reading is Scott's favourite hobby. While most guys get excited about *Maxim*, Scott would really rather read a map. He is really interested in knowing any information he can about schedules, draws, teams, maps, locations, history, etc. He's our walking travel agent, but he's also the only one who has ever lost his wallet while travelling overseas."

At least Pfeifer has never lost the team's brooms.

That's another of Pfeifer's jobs.

"I had two conditions when they asked me to join the team," said Rocque. "One was that I used horse-hair brooms. They all started laughing at me over that. The other was that I don't carry the broom bag. I had a thing about that. With most teams the lead carries the broom bag. When you're the one guy who sweeps six straight rocks, at the end of the game you don't want to carry anything. I don't carry the brooms, and there aren't many out there who can say that."

The job fell to Pfeifer because, contend the teammates, Randy is old and the one time they left Nedohin in charge of the brooms, he forgot them and had to drive back home to get them and take a later flight.

"It is true," Nedohin confesses. "Once we were headed to a spiel in the Toronto area. When I reached the check-in counter at the airport, it hit me. I'd left them in the truck. I had no time to get back home to get them, so I missed the only direct flight that had the team arrive early in the afternoon. I went to get the brooms and sweet-talked one of the Air Canada representatives to help me. The person was a curling fan, fortunately, and I was able to get the next flight east without any penalty. The problem was that it was a milk run that stopped everywhere. It got me to Toronto in the middle of the night."

Pfeifer was back in charge of the brooms. He is also the stats guy.

"All the other guys have no clue what's going on with stats. I'm a stats junkie. I think it can be a real advantage, not just in how we play a team but in self-scouting our own team. When we weren't successful at the Worlds in Lausanne and then again for the longest time there in Victoria, the stats showed that we'd started to give up big ends when we didn't have the hammer. We didn't realize that. We looked at the way we were playing the ends in which we didn't have the hammer and found some things."

Rocque has played a part in going after sponsors and projects.

"In the first few years it was tough for anyone to go after sponsorships because nobody knew who we were. They knew who Randy was and after a while who Dave was, too. But the last few years people know who we all are and it's been nice because we can all play a bigger role, and it's a load off Randy and Dave.

"To tell you the truth, to a large extent, I feel spoiled by these guys. They look after me. My wife goes crazy about it. She knows I don't know when we leave, where we play and a lot of stuff. All I do is phone Scott and ask him what time I have to be at the airport."

"Marcel is our official driver whenever we are overseas and need to drive on the wrong side of the road. I think, naturally, being a bad driver to begin with helps immeasurably in a switch like that," says Nedohin.

You get the idea. Nedohin, Pfeifer and Rocque all play interesting parts. Randy…

Gee, what is it Randy does again?

"It's a big job being Randy," said Nedohin.

CHAPTER 17

The Brier of All Briers

Home Sweet Home: Randy Ferbey, Dave Nedohin, Scott Pfeifer and Marcel Rocque pose prior to opening ceremonies at 2005 Tim Hortons Brier in Edmonton.

It would be the Brier they'd treasure above all others, the most ballistic Brier ever held. A Brier in their hometown and their coronation as Brier Kings.

As they headed to Innisfail for the provincial championships, the question was who most wanted them to be successful—the Ferbey Four or Terry Morris, Darwin Daviduk and the 2005 Tim Horton's Edmonton Brier organizing committee.

"Hometown Brier, it's what this is all about. If this year's Brier was anywhere else, it wouldn't have the same importance to us. Our enthusiasm wouldn't be as great. That's certainly the case for me," said Ferbey.

And if they should succeed…

"The Brier people tell us they'll sell more tickets if we're the team that wins this. But it's been so successful, I don't know how many more they could sell."

As the provincial championship was about to begin, the Brier organizers announced that they'd sold more tickets than any Brier in history—and that's before anybody knew who was going to curl for Alberta or who else would be coming to represent the other provinces in Canada.

"Obviously you'd want to play in the biggest Brier ever held," said Ferbey.

"It's going to be the Brier of all Briers," said Nedohin.

It was a provincial championship that had picked up a sponsor and new title, the Kia Cup, and had a new format going from eight teams to 12 with the champion of the previous year gaining a bye to the event for promotional purposes. But, again, no promotion was necessary. The prize of being in the most ballistic Brier of all time in your home province was big enough. For the second straight year, the media coverage was massive.

Unlike the year before in Hinton, where Randy Ferbey vs Kevin Martin was the story line, this year Martin wasn't there.

He'd lost out in the Northerns to fail to qualify for the provincials.

In Innisfail, it was back to a familiar old story line as Ferbey scored six on the first end to clobber James Knievel of Manning 12–3 and followed with an 8–4 win over Terry Meek of Calgary in the second draw.

Ferbey was streaking again.

After two 23-game winning streaks were stopped at the same time at the Saskatoon Brier the year before, it took reporters to remind them that they still had another good one going.

"After what happened to us at the Brier last year, I guess I forgot about it," said Nedohin after they won the first two to make it 29 in a row at the provincial curling championships.

"Streaks are fun to talk about," said Nedohin. "We've had a lot of streaks. But you have to win the last game."

Pfeifer, who keeps track of things statistical, said a five-year run of getting to the Brier was the only streak they had in mind when they drove down to Innisfail, the town 180 kilometres south of Edmonton and 120 kilometres north of Calgary.

"There's no pressure with any winning streak. There's unbelievable pressure to win our last game," added Nedohin.

Not that a winning streak wouldn't go a long way to that end, they all conceded.

In the new Kia Cup, with a 12-team format featuring six-team round-robin groups, one loss in the group could put you in a ton of trouble. One loss could put you second and you'd then have to win four straight in the playoffs to get to the Edmonton Brier. Keep on streaking and they'd only need two.

"Any loss in this format can cause a lot of problems," said Rocque.

"You don't want to lose one," said Pfeifer.

"Win your first five and you get to the 1–1 game and get an extra life," he said of the loser dropping to the semi-final.

Ferbey says if there's a flaw with this team, other than his own advancing age, it's that they know they're the only team here that can beat them. And sometimes, like in the Brier final in Saskatoon the year before when it looked like they had their fourth-in-a-row win, they run into trouble.

"I've said it for the last five years," said Ferbey. "We're our own worst critics.

"We'll lose that edge. It'll happen eventually. It could happen today, it could happen tomorrow. But it will happen."

Good thing. The 1–1 game was tougher to win than any 1–2 game they'd played at the Brier. It felt like the Great Escape. And Nedohin put the "Great" in the phrase.

Nobody would remember the score was 6–5 for Ferbey over Edmonton's Jamie King, and the details would be forgotten almost overnight. That's the way it works at the provincials. Things that happen don't stick to your ribs like at the Brier.

Nedohin curled 97% to anchor the win in the match-up against Brent MacDonald, King's last-rock thrower.

For the fifth straight year, they'd make it to the provincial final.

The story line going into every other year was different for the rink. First was the one-time opportunity to get to the biggest Brier ever, a Brier in their hometown, a Brier that would celebrate their accomplishments and, if they won it, would be their coronation as the greatest. But behind all that was what happened to them the year before in Saskatoon.

Until that momentous event, it was something that was chiselled in granite somewhere: "Randy Ferbey Doesn't Lose Finals."

Then, when you least expected it, it happened. Up 8–4 heading into the eighth end at the 2004 Brier, they gagged on the big game.

Over a span of four provincial championships, three Briers and two world championships, they'd won every final they'd played. And then, with more than a million people sitting in front of their television sets watching what they thought then to be the countdown to their coronation, the greatest run in curling history had come undone.

All year Ferbey, Nedohin, Pfeifer and Rocque had to live with that Brier final loss, a loss that cost them a four-in-a-row run to equal the record of four over five years by the legendary Ernie Richardson rink.

It was that run that provided the backdrop as they had gone into the provincial curling final for the past few years. But not this time. That run was done and it was a different deal.

"Everything we've done in the past doesn't matter," said Pfeifer.

"What happens in the next game is what we'll remember for the rest of the year," said Nedohin, who had been haunted by the memory of his massive misses on the eighth and 10th ends of a Brier final they should have won.

"This year is different than any other year because the Brier is in Edmonton. Now we have one win to get there. We're really motivated by that. But this year we're not the defending Canadian and world champions. We're just another rink in the playdowns."

So was "Randy Ferbey Doesn't Lose Finals" still chiselled in granite somewhere or not?

"I'd hate to play us," said Ferbey.

When it was over, there were 19 sleeps to go before they stepped on the ice for the Edmonton 2005 Tim Horton's Brier.

"I can't wait," said Pfeifer. "I'm going to be counting down the days."

"That was our biggest win at provincials ever," raved Pfeifer.

And not because of the 8–6 extra end nail-biter over King, who bounced back from the semi-finals to get another shot, only to watch the defending champs become the first rink in Alberta history to win the province five times in a row. Nor because it provided Ferbey himself with his eighth purple heart to match Cliff Manahan from the '30s and '40s.

"The first four don't mean anything compared to this one. This one means everything. Getting to play in a home Brier is the ultimate," said Ferbey.

Nedohin, thanks to two double takeouts by Pfeifer, one in the 10th and another in the 11th, had a simple shot in the extra end to win it. But it wasn't until after he sealed the deal that he closed his eyes and tried to picture how it was going to be, playing in front of Oiler-sized crowds in an event that had already sold more than a mind-boggling quarter-million tickets.

"Getting to any Brier is pretty special. But I'm really looking forward to stepping on that ice. It's going to be hard to comprehend playing in front of crowds like that every day."

The team, which won a 34th consecutive game at the provincial championships, headed home with a chance to match Ernie Richardson's four Brier titles in five years, even if they'd failed to become the only rink to win four in a row the year before.

"People don't always want to see the champions win again at the Brier but I'm sure it will be different this year," said Ferbey.

"It's going to be incredible. In Calgary, I had the hairs stand on the back of my neck for the final with all the people in the Saddledome. It's hard to picture that it could be like that every draw at this Brier."

The crowd here wanted it for Ferbey from the start of the week to the finish. And nobody wanted it more than Edmonton 2005 Brier committee head Terry Morris.

"This is just fantastic," he raved. "I want to give them all a big hug."

There were no National Hockey League players to hug in 2004–05. The Edmonton Oilers didn't play a game in Rexall Place. The timing was perfect for Randy Ferbey, Dave Nedohin, Scott Pfeifer and Marcel Rocque to take their place.

In many ways they'd become as big in Edmonton as the Oilers and the Eskimos. Or were about to.

To many sports fans around the country this may not compute. They were curlers! And they were being mentioned in the same sentence as Wayne Gretzky, Mark Messier, Jari Kurri and Kevin Lowe. They'd somehow become Warren Moon, Tom Wilkinson, Dan Kepley and Dave Fennell. Or Jackie Parker, Johnny Bright, Normie Kwong and Rollie Miles. Those guys played on the town's all-time teams, the Oilers who won five Stanley Cups in seven seasons, the Eskimos who won five Grey Cups in a row from 1978–82 and the Eskimos who won three in a row in 1954–55–56.

Ah, yes, 1954. That was a wonderful year in Edmonton's sports history. That was the year the Eskimos won their first ever Grey Cup and Edmonton's Matt Baldwin won a Brier at home. It was 51 years ago. And nobody had been able to do it since.

A big question going into this one was whether the Ferbey Four would suffer the same fate as Mel Watchorn in '73, Pat Ryan in '87 and Ken Hunka in '99.

Ferbey, remember, was on that Ryan rink which, unlike Watchorn and Hunka, was an overwhelming favourite to win a hometown Brier.

He seemed to understand the lay of the land.

"The penalties for performing poorly are worse in front of the home crowd. But the rewards are insurmountably higher."

The home crowd turned on the surly Ryan early.

"Fans are saying personal things, rude things," said Ryan early in that Brier.

They were calling him "Cryin' Ryan."

He headed out the door and went to a post-Brier function where he became Elvis Ryan and sang "Don't Be Cruel."

For the record, Ferbey doesn't do Elvis impersonations. Also for the record, Ferbey still lists the '87 Brier as his most memorable moment in curling, despite what happened.

"It was my first," he explained, as if no further explanation was necessary.

Is it doubly difficult to win at home?

"I don't know about doubly," said Ferbey, "but it's difficult. There are a lot of distractions. You have to learn to say 'no' to a lot of things. At the same time, we've had a lot of success by not changing who we are and what we do. We've always been able to be accommodating to the media and to the fans. We're not going to change that. Hopefully we've seen enough and know enough to solve that problem."

Ferbey said he never really came to grips with what happened in the '87 Brier as the rink went 6–5 and missed the playoffs.

"I think we just stunk the place out. It might have been because of the distractions. Hopefully, we can change all that. We know we're going to be favoured. We know, because we're curling at home, there's going to be a lot of focus on us—probably in this circumstance more than ever before. But I think there are two ways to approach it. One is to be afraid of it and worry about it. The other is to use it for all it's worth."

It's not that Alberta rinks have had trouble winning since Matt Baldwin went 9–1 and made the Brier a big deal back in 1954. Going back to '54, Alberta had won more Briers (17) than any other province (Manitoba is next with 12). And it's not that it's an Alberta-in-Alberta thing. Edmonton rinks had done just fine, thank you, in front of Calgary fans. Hec Gervais ('61), Kevin Martin ('97) and Randy Ferbey ('02) all won Calgary Briers.

It's tough winning a hometown Brier. Not many had done it. Since Baldwin in '54, Garnett Campbell of Avonlea won a Saskatchewan Brier in Regina and Al Phillips and Russ Howard both won Ottawa Briers for Ontario. But they weren't actual hometown guys.

It's a short list of actual hometown Brier winners. Winnipeg's Don Duguid won in Winnipeg in 1970. Transplanted Manitoban Jim Ursel won in Montreal,

curling out of Montreal in 1977. That's it. Duguid and a guy with an asterisk.

Watchorn and Hunka had all the moons and stars lined-up but couldn't finish the job. Watchorn, in the Edmonton 1973 Brier, of course, wasn't in his hometown. He came out of the Peace district. He was 1–5 out of the gate, totally unable to get a handle on the horrible ice, and battled back to end up 5–5. Maybe if Watchorn hadn't made it and somebody else like, oh, Hec Gervais had been there, it would have been different. You could make a case that Watchorn and Hunka (who ended up 6–5) were curlers who just somehow managed to get through the provincials and really didn't have much of a chance when they made it to the Brier.

But not Ryan's rink in '87. They were heavily favoured.

But you can't be much more heavily favoured than Ferbey's rink was going to be for this one. An off-shore betting outfit, www.thegreek.com, which lists curling odds, had Alberta at –200. That means you had to bet $200 to win $100. The actual odds were 1–2. By comparison Ontario was 4–1, Newfoundland 13–2, Saskatchewan 9–1 and Manitoba, Nova Scotia and Quebec 12–1.

On the canoe.ca "slam" sports poll, 45% believed Ferbey would win. Wayne Middaugh of Ontario was at 15% and Brad Gushue of Newfoundland at 13%.

But a more interesting bet, as always, was Ferbey vs the field.

If you took the field in the previous five provincials, the last four Briers and the last three world championships in which Ferbey was involved, you would have lost 10 of the 12 wagers.

In 1954, the first Edmonton Brier drew a record total of 32,000 fans in the old Edmonton Gardens and scribes were writing that the Brier had gone big-time.

For this Brier, people were convinced that they could come close to drawing 10 times that many fans. And there was no question it was going to be a record. They'd broken all the old records before the first rock was thrown.

The home opener was against New Brunswick's Wade Blanchard who had toppled Russ Howard to make it to Edmonton only to find out he had to face the Ferbey Four in Game 1. Oh, yes. It would be the TV game, too.

"The TV game, playing the best team on the planet… we tried to prepare ourselves, but I guess between the competition, the crowd, the mikes and everything else, it was a little more than I prepared for," said Blanchard when it was over in eight ends with the final score 11–2.

"I've never played Randy Ferbey before and maybe there was a little more to it," said Blanchard, who was down 7–1 by the fifth end.

Steal in two. Steal in three. Steal in six. Four-point end in the fifth. This was nice, clean easy work for an Alberta team that worried a bit about butterflies the first time out in front of the Edmonton crowds.

If Ferbey and the boys had a few butterflies, the things flying in the stomachs of the New Brunswick bunch were more the size of eagles.

"They were a little nervous. They struggled a bit. They didn't make as many shots as we did and we took advantage of it," said Ferbey.

The crowd of 14,001 was the largest ever to watch an opening draw at the Brier by almost 3000. This wasn't the Edmonton Oilers vs the Montreal Canadiens down there. This was Alberta vs New Brunswick. This wasn't hockey. This was curling.

"Looking around the place, I don't think I've ever seen a building this full for curling," said Brier boss Warren Hansen. "Despite the number that was announced for the final of the '97 Brier in Calgary, I don't think it was this full. This is easily the biggest opening-day crowd ever to watch curling live in the history of the game."

The Ferbey Four could feel the love.

"They cheered every shot. It was a great feeling," said Scott Pfeifer. "We weren't surprised. We knew it was going to happen here. It seemed like we waited forever to get to this game and find out what it felt like. It was worth the wait. That was an amazing experience."

Marcel Rocque marvelled. "All I can say is, 'Thank You!' from all of us. It really was amazing. Hopefully we can get to the final and play that game for this crowd."

Maybe more impressive was the crowd of 13,872 who showed up for the second draw in the evening, the one without the Albertans even in the building.

The next day there were 13,216 in Rexall Place, the largest crowd ever to watch a morning draw at the Brier. And it was worth the wake-up calls.

It was Ferbey vs Brad Gushue of Newfoundland and for the longest time it was Ferbey in the glue. It was the situation every rink hopes for when they go against the Albertans at the Brier. Have hammer. Hit them with a three-ender in the first end. Try to make every shot after that.

In the end, what Gushue watched defined the Ferbey rink.

"They're the best in the world," said Newfoundland coach Toby McDonald, a man who knows a little bit about underdog upsets, having been on the team that registered the greatest upset in Brier history, the Newfie four skipped by Jack MacDuff that won the 1976 Brier in Regina.

"The way they play the game, I don't care if you get three up or five up, they're going to come back and take you to last rock."

On the eighth end Nedohin made a shot for four—it might have been five but that would have required a measurement and Pfeifer felt that might be a bit unseemly under the circumstances.

It ended up as perhaps the most entertaining 10–6 win in Brier history.

It was a wonderful game. End after end, shot after shot, the complexion of the game seemed to change. Both teams were using the four-rock rule for all it was worth, and Ferbey and mates used the perfect ice conditions in the arena famed around the NHL for its ice to finally make the Gushue crew crack and provide the four-ender to win it.

"The way this ice curls there are going to be a lot of high scores at this Brier," said Ferbey.

Nedohin left the ice shaking his head at Ferbey.

"After what happened to us on the first end, Randy just said, 'Easy, young fella, there's lots of time.' "

At one point the crowd was amazed to see them play Rock, Paper, Scissors to decide which shot to try.

"It was kind of funny to win a game like that 10–6," said Nedohin. "But the way we play, we always joke about it: First one to 10 wins."

The Ferbey Four hit 90% while Gushue and gang were down at 73%, not so much because they played poorly as because they were looking at difficult shot after difficult shot.

"They just play so well all the time," said Gushue, who left the building 0–3 against Ferbey at the Brier.

The next one wasn't quite as entertaining. You could have asked Ferbey. He watched it. Well, the end of it.

When the rink built up a 9–3 lead on Northern Ontario's Mike Jukubo after four ends, Ferbey made a line-up change. He benched himself and gave fifth man Dan Holowaychuk a chance to play in the hometown Brier.

Ferbey said his knee was hurting and decided it didn't make much sense to stay out there. But his knee was feeling fine. The Alberta rink went out and won 9–8 in extra ends against Pat Simmons of Saskatchewan to manufacture some more history.

The Ferbey Four became the first rink in Brier history to win 50 games, not to mention the first team to win 50 games in consecutive Briers.

They'd reached the stage where they weren't just breaking records, they were inventing records.

Individual skips have won more with different line-ups, but when Rocque, Pfeifer, Nedohin and Ferbey scored their 50th win, they became the first line-up to stick together and do that. Just as they became the first team with the same four curlers, playing the same four positions, to make it to five Briers. The rink was on its way to the Brier final to hopefully match the Richardsons' four Brier titles. Remember, only three of the Richardsons—Ernie, Sam and Arnold—played on all four winning teams.

Russ Howard skipped 107 Brier-winning games but fell short of the 50 with his rink of brother Glenn, Wayne Middaugh and Peter Corner. Skips Rick Folk and Al Hackner won 62, Kevin Martin 55 and Pat Ryan 51, but none of them had managed 50 wins with the same four curlers, much less in five consecutive Briers.

No. 50 didn't come easy.

In their record run, the Ferbey rink had only lost one game (to Howard) in which they had last-rock advantage. They had it against Saskatchewan but found themselves down 2–0 after the first end.

Taking a chance on the risk–reward odds in the fourth end, a chance for four or five points turned to a steal of one for Pat Simmons' team.

Simmons made a brilliant shot on the 10th to take the game to an extra frame, but in the end Nedohin had the whole house to shoot at to score the winner. He put it on the button without Huff & Puff putting a broom to it.

"We were muckers and grinders to win that game," said Nedohin.

The glow from establishing the milestones didn't last long. Up next was Nova Scotia and Ferbey left the ice thinking they should just have dipped their noses in blue paint and waved the traditional crying towel Nova Scotia fans hand out to the losing rink every time their boys win one. The Albertans were getting a fair collection of those.

Ferbey and rink walked off the ice having lost only three of their last 33 games at the Brier. Nova Scotia. Nova Scotia. And Nova Scotia.

"These guys are starting to piss me off," quipped Ferbey as he left the ice.

"I don't think it's habitual," said Marcel Rocque.

First there was Mark Dacey's win in the round-robin last year in Saskatoon that broke a Brier-record 23 consecutive victories. Then they gave the final away to Dacey again. And this day they were free and clear, the only undefeated rink left, and up stepped Nova Scotia to bite them again.

The Albertans crashed and burned against Shawn Adams' team, an outfit that beat Dacey three times in the Nova Scotia provincials to get to the Brier. Final score: 8–4.

"Somebody has to beat them," said Adams. "Hopefully we can continue that trend. But that's a great team. We were firing on all cylinders. They struggled a little."

Struggled?

"We looked like rookies out there," said Ferbey. "We looked like rookies with our sweeping, we looked like rookies with our shot calling and we looked like rookies with our shot making. That was not a great thinking game. We looked confused sweeping and throwing."

Ferbey was outshot 91% to 85% by Nova Scotia third Paul Flemming and Nedohin was out-curled 88% to 73% by Adams.

Ferbey refused to blame his knee for having anything to do with the loss. "But if I knew this was going to happen, I would have taken the night off," he said.

He was fine the next morning as Alberta scored a 6–4 win over Rod McDonald of P.E.I.

In the next one, the focus wasn't on Ferbey but the fella he was playing.

If you get the idea that Ferbey was the story, the whole story and nothing but the story at the 2005 Edmonton Brier, that didn't turn out to be the case. Ferbey would be playing the guy who the curling world was going crazy over, much like Guy Hemmings coming out of Quebec a few years earlier.

Randy "The Lunch Box" Dutiaume of Manitoba was one of those stories this sport manages to produce unlike any other. Unlike most other butcher, baker, candlestick maker stories, The Lunch Box was a nobody-turned-somebody before he even arrived in Edmonton.

Some rocks, you just gotta get on early, and the media was all over Dutiaume before he even swept into town.

It was a Brier match made in heaven. Blue-collar sports town meet The Lunch Box.

The guy gave himself his own nickname. "I just go up and down my wing. Call me Lunch Box. I just grab my lunch and go to work," was his mantra.

This was a guy from the same province that gave us Jeff Stoughton, the Human Sleeping Pill, at the 1999 Edmonton Brier.

Dutiaume's occupation really is curling. He makes his living painting ice and selling ice scrapers and curling rocks. "I provide everything for the icemakers. That's why I am so passionate and committed to curling," he said.

This was a guy who had never come close to qualifying for a Brier before, a guy who got rid of half his rink because "we absolutely stunk" in the Winnipeg city zones.

At the last minute he found two free curlers—Dave Elias and Shane Kilgallen, a third and a second who had been to the 2002 Brier in Calgary. Together they then went 16–1 to make it to the provincial finals where they went 7–1 to win it.

"I'm sure nobody has heard of us," he said.

Manitoba hasn't had recent success at the Brier and that hasn't gone down well with the province that had, at least until recently, always viewed itself as the curling capital of Canada.

This was Randy Ferbey's kind of guy. In many ways, between runs with Pat Ryan and Dave Nedohin, Ferbey was a "Lunch Box" himself. But that didn't stop him from eating Dutiaume's lunch.

The guy who came to the Brier saying he was "happier than a pig in poop" left the ice saying, "I feel like the poop today." Six weeks earlier, Randy Dutiaume was pretty much just another club curler in Manitoba. That day he felt like one again.

After facing Ferbey, you could say he was left in what you might call a Red River daze. Except, in a strange way, it almost sounded like he treasured the experience.

"We're 27–4 since we put this team together and that's the first time we had our ass kicked. But who better to have your ass kicked by than Randy Ferbey? Who better to have your ass kicked by than a rink like that?" he said after a 9–5 loss in which he shook hands with Ferbey sitting three and a rock still to be thrown in the seventh end for what would have been a second four-ender in the same game. The Randy vs Randy game was supposed to be a dandy. It wasn't.

"We've never been beat like that," said Dutiaume who looked like a buffalo caught in headlights.

He won his first three games at his first Brier and was 4–1 going into the game against the three-time Brier champions. With Newfoundland's Brad Gushue losing in the morning, it was Alberta–Manitoba for first place. But not for long.

First, Ferbey nailed him with a four-ender. Then the Albertans backed up and ran over the Buffalo Boys again. Steal of three.

Seven points on back-to-back ends!

Alberta 7, Manitoba 1. After three.

"You have that happen to you, you better take away a lesson," said Dutiaume. "If we learned anything from that game it is how Ferbey approaches a game. He orchestrates a game so they have a chance to score four."

It was the fourth four-ender for the Ferbey Four, not to mention a five-ender they also had to their credit in this Brier.

'They're so good, those guys, they make you pay all the time. They deserve every accolade. And everything they say about Randy Ferbey and his rink is true. They're gentlemen. I really enjoyed talking to Randy during the game," said the Manitoba skip.

Ferbey was still grinning and bearing it with his injured knee and Alberta sitting on top of the standings at 6–1. But as the Brier progressed in the two-game-a-day round-robin, Rocque was the Alberta curler visibly playing in pain.

It happened, he said, in the game against Saskatchewan.

"Something just let go," said Rocque. "I can't even bend my arm. It's not affecting my throwing ability, but it's affecting my sweeping a little bit. Somehow, we find it when we need it," he said of sweeping through the pain in his left elbow.

Rocque said it's just another way to prove you're a winner.

"I'll remember for the rest of my life the story about when the Oilers lost the Stanley Cup final and walked by the New York Islanders dressing room expecting to see a bunch of guys celebrating. What they saw instead were a group of guys in there all beat up. They just went to war. It's no different here."

Well, you know, other than the men-with-brooms thing.

The biggest pain would be supplied the next day by Wayne Middaugh when, after a loss to Alberta, he'd whine that Ferbey and friends had all turned pro (as you read in a previous chapter).

"It's like I said at the beginning, Randy's team is the only professional team here and they are head-and-shoulders above everybody else," Middaugh told the media mob. "It's turning out exactly as I thought it would with everybody behind them knocking each other off."

The thing people forgot on the spot was that the score was 6–5. Alberta needed a last-rock Nedohin shot to win it.

With a win over the Territories, the rink moved to 8–1 and clinched a spot in the 1–2 game at the Brier for a record fifth-straight year.

Ferbey kept winning, the crowd kept coming and throughout the week people were wondering if they'd hit the 300,000 mark in attendance.

And they would have, if Nedohin hadn't messed it up.

It was all Nedohin's fault. If he had made one shot, Edmonton would have hit the 300,000 easy.

"If he makes that shot we end up at about 315,000 in attendance" said organizing committee chairman Morris.

When Nedohin missed his shot with the last rock on the 10th end in the last game of the round-robin against Québec, he cost the Edmonton 2005 Brier organizing committee about 29,000 in attendance.

If Nedohin had made his shot, there would have been two draws of tie-breakers and they'd have put up a number beyond belief.

Not that 285,000 would be so shabby.

"They shouldn't be disappointed," said Brier boss Warren Hansen. "This is, without question, the most successful Brier in history. The extra tie-breaker games would have put up a giant number, but the number they're going to end up with will be a new benchmark.

"It's not just a big number. It's the organization. This is by far the smoothest-running Brier we've ever had as well.

Still, when you're Morris, Daviduk, Kennedy Dugan, Ken MacRae, Ron McGowan, Stephen Pelech, Kris Sakowsky, Barry Worth, Janna Tominuk and the rest of the committee, and you set a goal so high…

"It was disappointing to the committee staff," conceded Morris, but he noted that the Ferbey Four sold a lot more tickets for them this week than they cost them by losing that last game. Rather than have eight teams advance to playoffs, four teams got through to the 1–2 and 3–4 Page playoff games.

Nedohin didn't lose any sleep that night. Being a hometown Brier, their sleeping situation became a story, however.

They didn't have to play again until the 6:30 PM 1–2 game against Manitoba the next night. But they decided to stick with their routine in the playoffs.

Nedohin roomed with Pfeifer at the Brier hotel although both had perfectly good homes and beds out in Sherwood Park.

"We don't usually say good night," said Pfeifer. "He's usually in before I'm in."

Randy Ferbey roomed with Marcel Rocque. They've been known to close the Brier Patches together.

The normal routine?

"Go to the Patch. Sleep all day. Watch the 3–4 game on TV…" says Ferbey.

It's what they'd done every year.

The challenge with this year was not to get away from the plan although this Brier was at home. Pretend the Brier is in Ottawa, Calgary, Halifax or Saskatoon. That was the plan. As Brier weeks go, although this one was at home, it had gone pretty much the same.

They went 9–2, scored 90 points, gave up 58 and scored one five-ender and six four-enders while not giving up any big numbers like that. OK, there had been a lot more media to do, but the Ferbey Four had always been terrific in dealing with the sane requests and intelligent about ditching the dizzy deals. And they did take one day away from the regular routine. But that wouldn't be happening on playoff weekend.

The day they gave themselves to get away from each other was the day they didn't play the night draw and didn't play again the following morning. They decided it was OK to get away from each other, go to their homes, or whatever.

Lead Marcel Rocque went home to enjoy a day he'd looked forward to for five years.

"My daughter Gabriella's birthday has always been right in the middle of the Brier. She turned five years old. I missed all her other birthdays. I've been looking forward to this birthday party since she was born. We had a great birthday party for her."

Pfeifer took his wife, parents and grandparents out to dinner. "I didn't go home. My kids have been running around here all the time," said Pfeifer.

"I had a real nice dinner, a hot tub and a glass of Scotch," said Nedohin of his night away from his teammates. "It was nice and relaxing. We all went our separate ways except Randy who was probably at the Patch."

Indeed. Ferbey was the one who stuck to the plan even that day. Pfeifer, after he had his big family outing at the restaurant, ended up at the Brier Patch, too.

At the end of the night they all ended up back at the hotel, Nedohin and Pfeifer sharing rooms and Ferbey and Rocque bunking together as always.

It was a different deal for Randy Dutiaume and his upstart squad as they waited for the 1–2 game against Ferbey.

"We'll be thinking a lot about him but I doubt if he'll be thinking much about us," said The Lunch Box. "He'll probably be thinking about where he can get his next beer and pizza. I don't think he cares. He's been in this position so many times he doesn't care who he plays."

From Dutiaume's side of it, this was ho-ho-holy cow, wow!

"For us this is unbelievable," he said of being two wins away from being the greatest Cinderella story since Jack MacDuff and his Newfoundland shock from The Rock.

"I think that's true," said Toby McDonald, the Newfoundland coach who was a member of the MacDuff team. "I won't say they're a bigger Cinderella story. I think they're better than we were. And let's not get too carried away here. No team from Manitoba should ever be considered a Cinderella story."

Then again, it had been a while for the Buffalo Boys.

"I wish I'd said, 'I'm going to go find a new rink, go 16–1 and get to the provincials, go 7–1 to win the provincials to get to the Brier and then go 8–3 in the Brier to get to the 1–2 game against Randy Ferbey,' " said Dutiaume.

"That's the wonderful thing about our sport," said Ferbey. "You can put together a team in January and get to the 1–2 game at the Brier."

Unlike in their round-robin game, the Manitobans gave them a go.

In fact, there was an emergency meeting of the four-man Alberta team on the seventh end. And despite the objection of Ferbey, they decided not to "Saskatoon" themselves.

It's not always a democracy. Sometimes, as was the case in Innisfail at the provincial playoffs, Ferbey will just say "No!" and away they go. But this was a night for history, and having botched it up in the Brier final with the game in their grasp in Saskatoon the year before, the majority ruled and they decided maybe just this once they wouldn't go for the throat.

The result was a fifth-straight trip to the Brier final with a 7–4 win.

"We'd never thrown a rock yet that we all didn't agree on but we had a good little discussion and we decided to take the safe shot for once in our life," said Nedohin.

Was there a bit of Saskatoon in the back of the mind of Nedohin, Pfeifer and Rocque?

"Oh, I don't know," said Nedohin. "I admit I threw a shot I shouldn't have tried on the eighth end in Saskatoon. No question. You always have to learn from your mistakes."

At the time skip Ferbey disagreed, feeling that Dutiaume, who had just flashed on his first shot in front of 14,921 fans, was in deep do-do and this was the time when they always trip the trap.

After the game was over, he decided the rest of his rink had talked him into the smart move.

"We had a decent opportunity to steal two," he said. "I wanted to go for it.

"We've had some discussions over the years, but that was one of our better ones," he laughed when it was over.

As a result, for the first time in history the same team had won the 1–2 game five consecutive times to go directly to the Brier final.

"We're back in that game again! What a great feeling," said Nedohin of getting the day off to sit back and watch Manitoba vs Nova Scotia in the semi-final.

"It's just unbelievable. I wanted another shot at it."

The win, in addition to being worth $40,000 for getting to the final, gave the Ferbey Four the record for most victories by an Alberta rink at the Brier, beating Kevin Martin's former record of 55 with a variety of teammates.

It was the same old story. Give Ferbey the hammer, and you're likely to get hammered. He'd only lost once in 35 games at the Brier in which he's had last-rock advantage.

Dutiaume didn't get back to give Ferbey another go. But the plot only thickened.

Shawn Adams and his rink of Paul Flemming, Craig Burgess and Kelly Mittelstadt were winners before they threw a rock in the final as their 8–7 win over Manitoba in the semi-final gave them a spot in the Olympic Trials.

Ferbey didn't have to worry about that. Technically he'd qualified five different times.

Adams said winning the Olympic Trials berth thanks to Ferbey's previous successes didn't mean they were going to give him the Brier. "I've watched the Brier every year on TV since I can remember. When you start curling every year, you start thinking of winning the Brier."

Try being Mittelstadt.

"I'm kinda numb," said Pfeifer's old junior teammate. "It's amazing for me. This whole Brier here has been amazing for me."

The Nova Scotia rink making it to the final made it even more compelling in that Alberta lost the 2004 final to Mark Dacey of Nova Scotia after losing to Dacey in the round-robin thereby giving up last-rock advantage. And it was Ferbey defeating Dacey in the final the year before.

"I guess it's Game 3 of a best-of-three with Nova Scotia in the Brier final," laughed a relaxed Nedohin the day before the final.

"It's remarkable that the same two provinces have ended up in three straight Brier finals," he said of splitting with Dacey in 2003 and 2004.

"Their rink matches up very well against our rink. They have a really good rink and Nova Scotia has had our number. Burgess is an amazing second. He ranks right up there with Scott Pfeifer. Flemming and Randy both make all their shots at third. And Shawn has shown me a lot this week," added Nedohin of the last rock thrower match-up.

Ferbey, of course, lost to Adams in the round-robin to make it three defeats to the Bluenosers. The difference this time was that, unlike those three games against Nova Scotia, Ferbey would have last rock this time. The Alberta rink had run their record to 34–1 with last-rock advantage in the past five Briers.

"That's huge for us," said Nedohin. "That is a big advantage for our rink. It gives us a chance to go up 2–0 early. And we're the kind of rink that can take a chance and give up a steal and not think of it as a real bad thing."

Ferbey said everybody, by now, had to know how they'd approach it. "We're going to go out to get that lead. If we get a lead, we're extremely tough to beat. That's the game plan. We're really confident. We're playing well. There are a lot of nerves involved in this game but we've been there before and we handle it better."

The one factor that attracted the curious, however, was how Nedohin would handle it.

He'd have to deal with the demons. This is where he'd have to conquer more than Nova Scotia and history. This is where he'd have to deal with the ghosts of Saskatoon.

Nedohin had to deal with the demons all year to get the chance for a retake with fate. But now it was here. Now it was one game to become the all-time team. Now he was on.

Sometime out there, everybody whispered, the focus would come down to Nedohin and a larger-than-life shot.

If it did, that's when Nedohin would have to deal with gagging on those shots in the eighth and 10th ends at the 2004 Brier.

"Obviously we thought about it. We thought about it a lot for an entire year," said Nedohin. "I don't think what happened in the final last year is going to play any part in the final this year other than to learn from it. I think you saw that in the decision we made on the seventh end of the 1–2 game after all that discussion we had. If it has any effect at all it will be reflected in something like that more than anything."

But it wasn't just Nedohin. They were all going against history again. And they were doing it at home.

"We're not going to think about it as anything but another game," said Nedohin. "We know it is. But…"

Nedohin says that's how it was in the 1–2 game to win a record fifth straight appearance in the final.

"All that other stuff doesn't click in until after the fact. To be honest, when it was over, I was more excited to win the 1–2 game Friday night than any 1–2 game we've ever won. It just blew me away, the fact that we made it back."

Ferbey said he was not worried about his last-rock thrower. He says the guy who has been MVP of all three Briers they've won has long since put Saskatoon behind him.

"Dave got us to another Brier final. He was in those same situations a lot of times and made those shots to get us here. That's all water under the bridge."

And if something were to go wrong, he said, it wouldn't be four over the High Level Bridge.

"This is just curling," he said.

Most anybody who watched the 2005 Tim Horton's Brier final might have suggested they played it like it was a game at the Nelson Mid-summer Bonspiel.

The video of the game should come stamped, "Don't Try This At Home."

It's only wrong if it doesn't turn out right was the story line and the bottom line when Ferbey made it the "Joy Of Six" for himself, and his rink won their fourth Brier in five trips and became the only team of the same four curlers ever to be able to say that.

"It worked, didn't it?"

That was Ferbey's reaction in front of 15,147 fans and more than a million viewers around the nation after making one of the gutsiest calls in the history of the game to become the greatest team in the history of the game.

Who intentionally takes out their own rock with the game tied in the ninth end to not score two so they can score one with the last rock on the 10th end?

Randy Ferbey is who.

He didn't, even for a split second, consider the controversy if it worked out any other way than Nedohin drawing to the button for a 5–4 win over Adams and Nova Scotia.

Ferbey was putting the rock in the hand—history in the hand—of Nedohin. He was making the supreme statement about how he felt about his last-rock thrower.

"Our goal is always the same. Give Dave a draw to the four-foot with the last rock to win the game. That's the kind of confidence we have in him. If I had any question, I'd have taken the deuce on nine."

Whatever, it was wonderful. It set up years of second-guessing and then gave Canada four greats to celebrate.

It was perfect. Nedohin was put in the position to make the shot and manufacture one of the most memorable moments in curling history. And he did it!

"Randy wanted me to have last rock in the 10th," said Nedohin. "That decision in the ninth end showed me Randy had confidence I was going to make it. All year it's been the same. If it comes down to one shot give me the draw on the last rock on the 10th end."

It wasn't exactly ho-hum.

"All I could think about was 'Don't be heavy! I did take a few deep breaths. My heart rate was going pretty good, but I slowed it down."

The great goat of the previous year's Brier was put in a position by his teammates to be the huge hero in the ultimate moment and then paid them off. Then Nedohin was paid off with his fourth Hec Gervais Award as Brier MVP.

"This, by far, is the most unbelievable," said Nedohin of the Brier wins.

"We've been excited thinking about winning this Brier in our hometown and taking that walk down the sheet after we won and finding out what that felt like. It felt unbelievable. I don't know if this feeling can ever be matched," added their ace.

"Never in my wildest dreams did I think I'd ever win one Brier, let alone six and four, with a team like this," said Ferbey. "I wouldn't trade any one of these guys for any other curler in the world."

Brier history is littered with people who couldn't handle the pressure and some figured this day involved just about the most pressure you could ever put on a rink considering the history and being at home.

"What is pressure?" said Ferbey. "I don't know what pressure means. Is it being afraid? We're not afraid."

Matt Baldwin won it here in 1954 in front of 32,000 during the Brier. Ferbey and rink did it in front of 281,985 fans.

"This was so special," said Ferbey. "So many people were behind us. To hear that crowd roar when Dave made that shot and we'd won the game…I don't think it was any louder when the Oilers won their Stanley Cups in this building."

To those in attendance, those moments will be treasured along with other memories in the arena that maintains Edmonton's legacy as the City of Champions.

To those watching on TV, the indelible memory will be of Ferbey making the call to have Nedohin take out their own rock to not score two on the ninth, however.

"I've never seen that before," said former Brier champ Ed Lukowich.

"Now junior curlers all over the world are going to be out there taking out their own rocks for two on the ninth with the game tied."

CHAPTER 18

The Great Escape

Bringing Home Another Winner: Marcel Rocque, Randy Ferbey, Dave Nedohin and Scott Pfeifer pose in front of sign on way back from airport.

The big story back home was the big breakup of the Ferbey Four.

It was on CFRN TV in Edmonton.

Dave Nedohin was caught on video back home. Randy Ferbey was on the phone from Victoria, the site of the 2005 Ford World Curling Championships, saying they'd had a major row and Nedohin had decided he had had enough playing second banana. The team was in a shambles. They didn't know what they were going to do.

It was April 1. April Fools.

Who knows when they'll eventually break up. But clearly they were having too much fun for it to happen for a while.

They arrived in Victoria telling themselves they'd been history chasers for years now, so why stop here?

"When we lost in our first World Curling Championship in Lausanne in 2001, if we had said 'Let's get back three more times and see what happens,' it would have sounded ridiculous," said Nedohin. "It would be like saying right now, 'Let's win this and get back four more times.' "

Ferbey, who was going to quit five years earlier, said, "It would be nice to have some more of these things on our resumés."

Nedohin said the last one was for him in his old hometown of Winnipeg. This one was for Ferbs.

"I'd like to see us win this for Randy. It would put him in exclusive company at the world championships, too. It would be his fourth. If you don't count the old Scotch Cup days when it was just Canada vs Scotland, nobody would be able to say they'd done that either."

Ferbey said whoa.

"The Scotch Cup counts. That's where this all started. If the Richardsons hadn't taken the trip over to Scotland for those best-of-five series all those years and been such wonderful ambassadors, who knows if there would be a world championships and if curling would have ended up in the Olympics."

The Richardsons won four according to Ferbey's scorecard. Next on the chart, the only Canadian to have won three world titles was Ron Northcott. Both rinks didn't do it with the same four curlers on board, however.

The year before in Sweden, in his eighth trip to the championships, Peja Lindholm of Sweden won for the third time with the same four curlers. That's the record Ferbey said they were chasing.

"It's so much tougher to get here as a Canadian," said Nedohin. "We won't get the chance to come here seven, eight, nine and 10 times like some of these guys."

On the other hand, come to think of it, Ferbey was in Victoria for his sixth Worlds. Hmmmm.

"Success followed both times I've lost a World Championships," said Ferbey of the two losses with the two different teams from two different eras, both in Lausanne, Switzerland.

"In both cases it made my teams stronger and able to come back better and follow with more success. It's an experience factor. Things happen at the world championships. You have to be ready for these guys. I think it has affected a lot of Canadians in the past."

As he arrived in Victoria for the Worlds, Ferbey found himself engaged in debate.

The 2005 Brier had just been held in Edmonton. The next men's World Championship, in 2007, was also going to be in the City of Champions. Has the degree of difficulty become higher at the Worlds than Canada's grand national rockfest?

Better than the Brier? Tougher than the Tankard?

Ferbey said he thought it had become a truth Canada didn't want to hear.

"It shouldn't be. But it is," he said. "These teams are using our resources—resources we're not even using ourselves—to beat us," said Ferbey.

"The Europeans are doing more progressive things in the sport than Canadians now that curling is an Olympic sport. They're using all the modern sports training methods, video, sports psychology—all those things elite athletes in other Olympic sports use.

"They're taking coaches from Canada and using them to beat us. That's not new. But now they're taking it to another level. When they lose, they go back and look at the video with the coaches to learn how it happened."

The rinks arriving in Victoria, essentially, were the same ones that would be in Torino the following February for the Olympics. And they were in Canada adopting the Page playoff system that had been used in the Brier for the past decade.

In recent years Canada had been doing a lot of the adapting to the European game, which resulted in more rocks in play and a much more watchable game. But this year there would be a change to adopt something that had been working on this side of the Atlantic.

The decision by the World Curling Federation to go with the Page playoff system for the first time in Victoria was A-OK with 2002 Olympic Games gold medal winner Trulsen, for one.

"It's a big advantage for the best teams, isn't it? It gives the top two teams two chances to get to the final. Fair enough," said The Troll.

Trulsen, the Norwegian who has won the Olympics but has never won the Worlds in eight previous attempts, said he hoped to end up as one of the top two teams that would play in the 1–2 game, the winner to advance to the final and the loser to drop to the semi-final.

"The big favourite, of course, is going to be Randy Ferbey. But it's a pretty deep field this year. I'd say there are five or six guys who are capable of getting to that 1–2 game, too."

Ferbey lost to Trulsen in the bronze medal game at the 2001 World Curling Championships in Lausanne, Switzerland. Ferbey, after having three rocks pulled on highly controversial hog line violation calls against Switzerland's Andreas Schwaller in the semi-final of the 2001 Worlds, would get rematches against both of them.

There was another thing the WCF adopted from Canada, the electronic device in the handles of the rocks that eliminated free trips to the World Championships for a host of hog line officials.

Also in the field were David Murdoch of Scotland, Eric Carlsen of Sweden, Markku Uusipaavalniemi of Finland, Pete Fenson of the U.S.A., Andy Kapp of Germany, Johnny Frederiksen of Denmark, Sean Becker of New Zealand, Hugh Millikin of Australia and Stefano Ferronato from Italy. With Ferbey, Trulsen and Schwaller, that totalled 12. The reason for going to the Page system was the decision to separate men's and women's World Championships. It allowed the events to go from 10 teams to 12.

"The teams in the Worlds are getting better. Like New Zealand. The gap's closing. Five years ago they would have been a walk in the park for us. Not now," said Ferbey, who said he'd seen this movie before.

"What we're seeing happening here with the rest of the world happened at the Brier 10 or 15 years ago. You used to be able to go against one of the teams from the Maritimes at the Brier and know if you curled respectable you were going to win," said Ferbey. "Not any more."

Ferbey said their own stats made the point. In five Briers the Edmonton rink went 57–8. In their first three Worlds they were 24–9. And every morning of the event, Ferbey's statements would be remembered when you looked at the standings.

Of course, at least until Edmonton 2007, there was no debate about the Brier compared to the Worlds in terms of size and atmosphere.

You've heard of people riding off in a cloud of dust? For this one, they rode *in* on a cloud of dust. It was an ice-maker's nightmare as curlers took to the pebble while construction workers painted, sawed and swept, creating a cloud of dust throughout the new Save-On-Foods Memorial Centre.

"Look up at the lights," suggested ice-maker Hans Wuthrich. "That's unbelievable," he said of the haze of dust while the curlers had their practice session.

"You put the broom down and the rock goes somewhere different every shot. Dust a problem? @ $% yes!" said Wuthrich.

"The sweepers are saying the dust is filling their lungs. Scott's eyes were watering with his contacts," said Nedohin of Pfeifer.

"I can smell it and I can taste it," said Rocque. "It makes me light-headed. It's like cleaning out your vacuum then giving it a big whack and then going out and running. Hans should be getting a bonus for making ice in these conditions. We can't even walk from the dressing room to the ice. We carry our curling shoes and put them on out here."

"No worries, mate," said Sean Becker of New Zealand who was due to play Canada's Randy Ferbey in the second draw of the championships. "If we were playing in New Zealand, anything could be happening. Skaters could be skating around. This spring they were doing construction in the arena.

"At one point out there the ice had 4½–5 feet of curl. It's going to be interesting," said the curler who lost 9–3 to Ferbey at the 2001 Worlds.

The great thing about covering the Worlds is talking to an international curler when the subject of ice conditions and curling rinks come up.

Canadians learn quick to zip their lip.

This year they should have put the curlers on stage at the Extra End Pub in a comedy club format.

It all started with Trulsen talking about how tough it is to get curling going when your curling rinks keep being blown down. It was "I can top that" storytelling for hours.

"They built a new curling rink in this one particularly windy area of Norway," began Trulsen standing around waiting for his turn to practice. "A big wind came up one day and blew the building over. They rebuilt it and another big wind came up and blew it down again. They built it again and so far it's still standing."

Becker, the New Zealand skip, who has a flock of 4000 sheep, said that the rink is about 30 kilometres from where he lives in Ranfurly on the south island.

The Kiwis don't see each other for more than a few weeks a year and spend more time curling overseas together than at home. They spent a 10-day stretch in Calgary before they came to Victoria.

There are a couple dozen accredited curling clubs in New Zealand. They all play on outdoor ice.

With the inclusion of curling in the Olympics, the sport is now being played in 46 countries. But there are growing pains.

Hugh Millikin of Australia says you're not going to hear him complaining about the ice in Victoria. In Oz, he says "it's not even good enough for playing hockey."

To get here, Millikin had to emerge from the Australian nationals and conditions that he described as "ridiculous."

He said having a roof on your rink isn't necessarily a good thing.

"We had drips from the roof that left little moguls on the ice," he said. "We used them as guards.

"The variables of having little moguls around makes it very difficult. You can throw a great shot then it hits a bump on the ice in the wrong spot and it's gone.

"We have a scraper out and there's no rule about when you can scrape, so you scrape it, dump it and throw your rock. Our nationals are a challenge."

You'd think it would be better in Finland where Markku Uusipaavalniemi had emerged to make it to his eighth world championships.

The state of facilities in Finland are so bad that M-15 built his own curling rink. The previous "rink" consisted of two sheets of ice covered by a tent.

"I had to build a curling club," he said and explained how he raised money from the federal government and the city of Helsinki to do it—adding some cash of his own.

"I risked everything," he added as he checked in with his story.

Uusipaavalniemi, a former computer store owner, now lists his occupation as curling club manager and even makes the ice at his six-sheet Oulunkyl Curling Club.

The Ferbey Four opened against Andy Kapp of Germany.

Kapp made his debut on the international scene in Victoria at the World Juniors in 1987. This was his eighth world championship appearance. His name resembles Andy Kapp, the famous comic strip character. So when Ferbey lost the opener to Kapp, the story line in headline type was "What In The Worlds…"

It wasn't that they lost to Kapp, who had an 0–9 record on his resume in one of his eight trips to the Worlds and was 1–7 for Germany at the Nagano Olympics.

No, the disturbing thing was that they lost so big. Got clobbered. Were humiliated. Looked like a bunch of farmer's bonspielers. The, er, formerly Fab Four gave up four on one end, three on another and lost 10–5.

Kapp didn't suggest it was anything but a massive upset.

"When it's Germany–Canada, we have about a 10% chance," he said.

If that wasn't enough, the guy who herds 4000 sheep from New Zealand, the country that was just now building its very first curling rink, beat Sweden, the defending world champions.

And the U.S.A. needed a *steal* on the 10th end to beat *Australia!*

The opening draw at the world championships was an eye-opener and a jaw dropper.

How does Canada, especially this Canadian team, lose to Germany for openers in a home-country Worlds?

"After we stole two in the sixth end, we stunk the joint out," Ferbey explained without expression.

Actually they started stinking it out on the first end. And if you wanted to point fingers, you would have started with Scott Pfeifer curling 69%.

Dave Nedohin said he can't remember Pfeifer, a four-time Brier first team All-Star—considered the best player at his position in the world—playing so poorly.

"No, I don't think so," said Nedohin, who was equally bad with the same 69% figure compared to Kapp's 89%.

To regain their sense of humour, they decided to pin it on Pfeifer, not for the way he played but for losing the coin toss.

The last time they gave up four and lost a first game was back at the 2002 Calgary Brier to Russ Howard. The team, which hadn't lost a game with the hammer since that game, didn't have last-rock advantage against Kapp.

Unlike the Brier, where they draw to the button to determine last rock for the first draw, at the Worlds they flip a coin.

Pfeifer was sent to call the flip for Canada. "When I went out for the flip, I wasn't mentally ready," Pfeifer quipped.

Next up, a New Zealand team that would become the darlings of the crowd much like Randy Dutiaume of Manitoba at the Brier as the Victoria crowds cheered for the Kiwis, who were there to try qualifying for the Olympics, an accomplishment they managed to succeed at with no thanks to the Canadians on the ice.

The Kiwis didn't come to Victoria thinking they could make it to the finals, but they were hoping to finish high enough that they'd qualify for the Torino Olympics and "double the size of New Zealand's Winter Olympic team."

They would go on to do just that. But it was no thanks to Ferbey and friends who scored a 10–5 win to even their record to 1–1.

Most would have expected Sweden's Carlsen to give Ferbey his first big game of the tournament when they first glanced at the schedule. It was Carlsen who had defeated defending champion and three-time world winner Peja Lindholm in the Tre Kronar final to get to the 2005 Worlds.

> **"Our team doesn't go out there and say 'Good try' or 'Tough luck' when we miss a shot. We say, 'Pick it up, you're stinking the joint out.'"**
> **—Randy Ferbey**

It wasn't a game. Canada scored a 9–1 slam over the Swedes.

Ferbey described Canada's performance as "probably our highest percentage game in five years together as a team."

They were 95% in the game that was abridged to six ends.

"I don't remember anybody missing a shot."

Somebody asked Ferbey if it was a good thing they'd lost the opener to Germany.

"No," said Ferbey, who looked at the interviewer like he was a loon. "I'd rather be 3–0."

They weren't out of the glue. Soon enough they'd be in a real Sticky Wicket, and we're not talking about the name of the bar in downtown Victoria.

The trouble with the Ferbey Four for a sports columnist is that you can't carve 'em. Occasionally they soil the sheets, but when they do, they're tougher and rougher on themselves than any scribe is going to be. They're a remarkable group of guys to cover.

Of all the events the Ferbey Four had ever played, curling fans would never have a better look at what makes them tick than they'd have in this one.

Like their tough love.

There's no team in the world that "tough-loves" itself quite like this one. Watching these guys interact during these Worlds was more interesting than watching them curl.

After they lost the opener to Germany, Ferbey was ripping Pfeifer for not being able to "make two shots in a row" and the rest of his rink for "stinking the joint out." His Canadians responded with two solid wins and looked like the greatest curling team in history again.

"That was a performance!" said Ferbey. "That's the best game we've played in a long time. That was better than any game we played at the Edmonton Brier," Ferbey raved about the win over Sweden in which Dave Nedohin and Ferbey both hit 96% and Pfeifer and Marcel Rocque scored 94%.

"I thought Scott probably bowled 100%," said Nedohin.

"I felt a lot better," said Pfeifer who curled 69% in his first game.

Ferbey, who had been on his game from the get-go, was grinnin' instead of pickin' on his players as they eviscerated the Swedes.

"Our team doesn't go out there and say 'Good try' or 'Tough luck' when we miss a shot. We say, 'Pick it up, you're stinking the joint out.' Each player has taken their turn. We don't look at it as a guy being in a slump or having a tough day. We look at it as not being ready to play. We have the attitude you should be able to do it all the time or be very close," said Ferbey.

Rocque said it's not mean-spirited.

"We don't need a hug," he said. "We need a kick in the butt. You never say 'Nice try' on this team. Randy is not going to be on a guy any more than the guy is going to be on himself. We have high expectations to produce. Look at the Europeans. They're high-fiving when they miss. I understand it. I'm not being critical of them. They're trying to be positive and supportive to each other. But if Randy misses, I'm not going to say 'Nice try' because he'd look at me like I didn't have my head screwed on straight. Can you imagine how I'd look at one of these guys if I'd put a guard in the house and somebody said 'Nice try'? Can you imagine how Scott would look if he was bonking peels and one of us said 'Nice try'? If Dave misses a draw and one of us said 'Nice try,' can you imagine the look you'd get from him? It happens. If there weren't misses it wouldn't be sport. But we're not huggy-feely when it happens to us. You watch us after a loss. We bounce back after a big loss. We take a note of pride in not losing two in a row. I can't remember the last time we lost two in a row."

Again and again in these Worlds the Ferbey Four had to bring their team policy into play.

Team policy?

"Don't lose two in a row," said Marcel Rocque.

There was that. The fact that they twice had to enforce it early in the tournament was a worry.

The Worlds were just getting going, and the Ferbey rink had their second loss. It was a little early to have two losses, especially for a team that sometimes goes through Briers with no losses.

"Obviously we're behind where we hoped to be," said Nedohin of the team, which coughed and sputtered and jerked their way to a 1–1 day, which began by blowing a 6–3 lead and losing 8–7 to Fenson's Yankees.

The Ferbey Four had gone 9–2, 9–2, 11–0, 10–1 and 9–2 in the round-robins of five consecutive Briers and 6–3, 6–3, and 8–1 in their three previous world championships. To get out of the gate at 2–2, and have to invoke the club policy to get to 3–2, was a bit of a bother.

"We haven't been in this situation in a long time," said Pfeifer. "I guess the last time we had two losses this early in the week was in Lausanne."

That was the one in 2001 when they came home without so much as a medal.

"This is not good. Not good at all. A little too soon to panic but…If we'd lost both, I don't know if I'd be here," said Ferbey in the post-game scrum after an ugly 8–6 win against Finland following a morning draw loss to the U.S.A.

For the rink that is usually on top of the standings, finishing first or second to get to the 1–2 game of the playoff was in definite danger.

They absolutely gave a game away to start their day. The Americans scored three on the 10th end. Fenson didn't even have to throw his last rock to win 8–7.

They hadn't given a game away like that since they blew a four-point lead against Mark Dacey in the final three ends of the 2004 Brier.

While they bounced back with the win over M-15 (M. Uusipaavalniemi), their fans didn't go to the rink completely confident after what they had watched in the morning.

Hey, in 2001 in Lausanne, it was Uusipaavalniemi 8, Ferbey 2. That's giving up almost a point for every vowel in the guy's name.

Despite the Ferbey win over the Finn with the 15-letter name, there was room for real concern for the Canadian team trying to win a third Worlds in four attempts with the way they'd started in Victoria.

The loss to the Americans was only the second time in the history of the event in which Canada has lost to the U.S. The two nations have played at Worlds eighteen times, and both losses were by Ferbey & Co.

"We had full control of that game. If they think they outplayed us and deserved to win that game, they have another thing coming," said Ferbey.

"I don't know what it is," moaned Ferbey. "We're in total control of these games and then all of a sudden, we're not. We're just not making the big shot to get us out of an end. I can't remember the last time we made a double peel or a run-back. That's what we normally do, and Scott and I haven't done that yet."

Nedohin sailed his last rock through the house on the 10th end.

"That whiff was a surprise," said Fenson who put up three points on the end for the win.

"We just let that one slip away," said Ferbey.

When the team curled 95% in the six-end win against defending champion Sweden, Pfeifer declared they'd "arrived in Victoria."

Well, maybe Nanaimo.

As a team they curled a pathetic 77% against the Americans, the lowest percentage of any team on the ice in the morning draw. And Ferbey took his turn in the toilet. He shot 66%.

One thing about the loss to the U.S.A., it provided an answer to the question of when the Ferbey Four last lost a game in which they had last rock. Then and there.

At least they didn't also provide the answer to the question of when they last lost two games in a row or two games on the same day.

"I don't think we've ever done that," said Rocque.

The Canadians scored three in the first end and three in the ninth to claim a 9–3 win over Denmark to keep the team policy in play. But Trulsen was up next and they were back to being hit-and-miss again.

A 5–4 loss was their third loss in seven games. It didn't even end with any real drama. Trulsen had hammer heading home and threw a quiet tap to the Canadian shot rock at the back of the button for the win.

"Maybe they're playing our old game of possum," joked Trulsen.

Trulsen, after losing his first game, was on a roll. He'd win eight straight. The Canadians were hanging on for dear life.

In the Wednesday morning draw they were down 5–3 to Italy before they cracked back-to-back three-enders to win 10–7.

"We were up only from the mistakes by Nedohin," said Forronato.

With three losses, you have to go out there believing one more will take you out of the tournament. And this was a rink not used to curling from the edge of a cliff much less on life support.

The word "burnout" started as a whisper but became a shout when Canada went six ends looking like a bunch of newsmen's bonspielers and Nedohin like a jam-pailer in the game against Italy, a team that hadn't managed a win in the tournament until the night before against New Zealand.

While they'd end up having their first two-win day of the tournament, that was thanks to Switzerland's Schwaller coming up short with the last rock to donate them a steal of three.

The more the Canadians had struggled during the week, the more they became the focus for the other curlers as the week went on.

Even Trulsen couldn't help but check in with his thoughts. "I can see them shaking their heads a lot," he said. "Ferbey doesn't look too happy. I wouldn't want to be joking with him out there now.

"Are they burned out? No. But they are tired. Randy told me that. They have a lot of pressure. They have to curl at a high level all the time. None of the other rinks here have to deal with what they have to deal with. These guys don't get many easy games."

While the wheels were wobbling, Trulsen went out of his way to say he didn't think they'd fallen off. "I still think they're going to be OK."

It had become a subject discussed from within.

"I think it's burnout more than anything," said coach Brian Moore. "They're tired. It's been a long year."

Media Scrum: Columnist/author Jones (centre) gets the lowdown from Ferbey

Ferbey himself said he was at a loss to explain it.

"People are saying burnout and a lack of concentration. I don't know. Hopefully it's just being tired. We can work through that. What other sport asks you to play at 3:30 PM, again at 7:30 PM and then have six hours sleep and be back to play at 9 AM?

"We've been as good as anybody here. We've been no better or worse. We're just used to being better."

Nedohin, who missed a couple of simple shots to give up steals on the first and second ends against the Italians to put the Ferbey Four in a hole they couldn't climb out of until the seventh end, went on record as saying he, for one, wasn't burned out.

"I'm good physically and mentally. But this is the most out-of-synch I've been for a while."

The Canadians left the rink that night hoping for a match against the Schwaller Swiss rink, which beat them in the medal round in Lausanne in 2001 when a Swiss official, backed up by a Swiss judge, called Ferbey for three hog line violations.

"We got cheated out of that game," said Ferbey, seconds before he headed on the ice to claim what turned out to be 7–3 revenge.

"We're not used to scrambling to get back into things," said Nedohin, a much-improved 94% against the Swiss. "It was nice to extract a little revenge. It was a bitter loss in Lausanne."

Two games from the end of the round-robin tournament they were 6–3 and in definite danger of failing to win a medal at home.

Twice on the last day of regular-round play they pulled off a great escape but ended up walking off the ice like zombies. There was certainly no sense of euphoria as they miraculously ended up alive and part of an unprecedented six-way tie for first place with 8–3 record.

If David Murdoch of Scotland hadn't come up dreadfully short on his first shot and then sent one up the kilt of his vice-skip and through the house with a draw to give up a steal of three with his last rock on the 10th end, the Canadian goose would have been cooked.

Ferbey gave up two in the first end and had to battle all the way to the 10th to end one up without the hammer. They knew when Murdoch took his place in the hack that they were going to be either dead or alive. He missed both of his shots, leaving Canada with three to win 8–4.

"I would have never bet against him on that draw," said Nedohin. "He was on the button all week. But we'll take it."

Murdoch said missing the shots bothered him more than the actual result.

Ferbey moved on to the last game against Australia. If it hadn't been for a Canadian expatriate from Orangeville, Ontario, who flashed 6137 fans with his last rock in the 10th end, the four-time Brier champs would have been toast.

If Ian Palangio hadn't missed a relatively easy double takeout, the Canadian bacon would have been fried. The Australian last rock thrower had half a rock to shoot at and sailed it off toward Australia to allow Nedohin the entire house to throw at for three and an 8–7 win.

Nedohin couldn't watch when Palangio was in the hack.

"There was a moment there I thought we'd lost the game," said Nedohin. "I didn't watch. I stared at my feet. I waited for the crowd reaction. All week we've been behind the eight-ball. It felt really good to get that break and go down to the other end of the ice and make that draw. I just took a deep breath when he missed and didn't even think about it when I went down to make my shot."

Pfeifer watched it horizontally.

"I was laying down on the ice. I'm speechless," he said.

"That was a very makeable shot in the end," Aussie skip Millikin said of Palangio's miss. "He could see three-quarters of the rock. All he had to do was make half a rock and they're both gone and the game is over."

Ferbey stood there shaking his head when it was over.

"We got a break. A huge break. It's been a wacky week. What do I say. It's sport. Stuff happens."

Sorting out a six-way tie for first place is not something the World Curling Federation had ever planned on being necessary. While it left most involved shaking their heads, Germany and Scotland landed in the

1–2 game. Canada was slotted against Finland while Norway would play the U.S.A.

Uusipaavalniemi had won seven straight since losing to Ferbey in the round-robin.

Ferbey, who won the last four games of the round-robin just to qualify for the playoffs, knocked off M-15 9–5 in the first tie-breaker with little of the drama of the preceding games.

"They didn't make the crucial mistakes they were making during the week," said Uusipaavalniemi.

Well, not against him. Not in that one.

Trulsen, who had won eight straight before causing the six-way tie for first by losing both games on the last day of the round-robin, made it to the 3–4 game with a 10–6 win over Pete Fenson in the morning tie-breaker.

That set it up. Canada–Norway. Ferbey–Trulsen.

It would be a game, like several before it, that would be remembered as much for a shot missed as a shot made. The shot made was by Nedohin. It was so spectacular that Trulsen took a deep bow. Then he bowed out. And the world was yet again left wondering how many great escapes were possible for the Canadians.

The Norwegian skip was so impressed with Nedohin's almost impossible circus shot to score two in the ninth end, he took two exaggerated deep bows to pay the Canadian off. Then on last rock in the last end, The Troll appeared to buckle coming out of the hack then shook his head before his rock was half way down the ice.

As a result, the Ferbey Four, who were on life support for days, won another game standing at the back of the hack watching somebody miss their last shot.

This wasn't a nobody like Ian Palangio of Australia. This was the Salt Lake 2002 Olympic gold medal winner.

"I missed it," said Trulsen. "That was a fairly easy shot and I missed it," he added of the double takeout that sent Ferbey to the semi-final with a steal of one for a 7–6 win.

"I saw him wobble," said lead Marcel Rocque of Trulsen's wonky knee. "I feel for him. He played such a great game."

Asked if he in any way felt like they were a team that had just won six straight games, Ferbey said, "No way."

Ferbey said they've been trying to convince each other that they're in "C" event of a bonspiel. "We've always done well in 'C' event."

While so much surrounded the game, Nedohin's two shots would be remembered from this day.

Trulsen raved at Nedohin's seventh-end draw to a sliver of the four-foot and even more so at the shot in the ninth to take the game to the 10th end with Canada still alive. "It was fantastic," said Trulsen of the ninth-end shot by Nedohin. "That was the shot of the whole game. If he missed that one, it would have been over."

"I'm just thankful I could make the big shots to save a couple of ends," said Nedohin. "I hadn't been doing that this week."

In an act of sportsmanship, Nedohin signalled the crowd to be quiet for Trulsen's final shot—the year before in Saskatoon, he missed the shot to lose the Brier final.

"Pal is a great guy. He's the kind of guy curling is all about. A lot of curlers could learn a lot from Pal."

Trulsen said he was beginning to believe there was something at work against Canada all week but now he was beginning to think there was something at play the other way.

"I think somebody has decided they're going to win it and win it by winning every game by as little as possible."

Nedohin said there were so many times when it felt like it just wasn't meant to be.

"Now we're getting the feel that it's destined," he said.

Dodging bullets, pulling rabbits out of hats, finding horseshoes in their pants, they'd been a crazy combination of the Flying Wallendas and the Four Houdinis. But somehow, someway, they managed to make their way to the final with an 8–6 win over Germany's Kapp in the semi-final.

Rocque said the plot had taken so many twists and turns he felt more like a co-author than a curler.

"It's a hell of a read," he said. "It's a whale of a story already. It'll really be a hell of a story if we win this."

Game after game it was the same story starring somebody new.

Kapp took his turn in the barrel, managing to miss two Canadian rocks welded together side-by-side. Missed 'em by half a foot!

Three points on the 10th end resulted in a win by two.

"It's amazing," said Ferbey of all the freebies. "It's definitely been interesting for the fans."

Scoring two in the first end, the Ferbey Four were in control until they hit the fourth where Ferbey missed both his shots and Nedohin sailed one through the house to put them in the position of chasing the game again. Nedohin botched two attempts to blank ends and left Canada down 6–5 heading home.

Kapp was looking at two rocks side by side at the top of the button and a biter at four o'clock. With eight seconds on the clock when he released the rock, he sailed a high, hard one a full six inches wide.

Why he didn't attempt to draw to the edge of the button, and at least make Nedohin throw his rock, left a lot of curlers in total disbelief.

"The end was over anyway," said Kapp.

"The sitting of the rocks made it impossible. To draw, I'd have to put it on that piece of paper," he said referring to the size of a reporters notebook in front of him.

Ferbey and mates seldom second-guess shots by opposition curlers, but they shook their heads about this one.

"He could have nosed one of them and made me draw the four-foot to win," said Nedohin.

"I don't know why he tried that shot," said Ferbey. "That wasn't there even if he hit something. He made Dave take his gloves off early."

With 0:00 left on the clock and the shot rocketing through the house way wide, it was a different definition of hurry hard.

"Another chapter," said co-author Scott Pfeifer.

> "It'll really be a hell of a story if we win this."
> —Marcel Rocque

Nedohin, who had taken Canadians on a roller coaster as he'd gone from brilliant to brutal to brilliant at different times, said it would be delicious if they won it.

"It'll be pretty sweet if we win now. A lot of people counted us out."

They'd never had to do it the hard way before. But they'd made it to the final against Scotland with a chance to win a third World Curling Championship doing it the hard way every day.

"We're 11–3 right now," said Nedohin of their record in the terrific tournament.

"I don't know if it feels like we're 11–3. But we're 11–3. It's amazing that we've won seven straight games knowing it would be over for us if we lost any one of them. They've been some pretty interesting games. It'll probably be another last-rock finish."

The Ferbey Four had spent most of the year making history and if they were to win the final they'd do it again. If you don't count Ernie Richardson in the days of the Scotch Cup (a best of five series against Scotland), only Calgary's Ron Northcott and Sweden's Peja Lindholm had won three world titles.

In the 10 years of the Page playoff system being used at the Brier, never had a team come from the 3–4 game to win. It was the first year the Page system was being used at the Worlds, and one would.

It would be their 13th final of the curling season. They were 8–4 in those finals, which included provincials and the Brier. They were four for five in Brier finals and two for three World Championship finals.

"When we get to finals we tend to relax more than earlier in the events," said Nedohin. "Personally, I think when we get to the final we tell ourselves, 'We're the best rink here. Somebody has to win. It might as well be us.' "

A Scotland–Canada final was just fine with the folks of Victoria, who sometimes see their locale as a wee bit of the old sod.

The place to be in Scotland, said skip David Murdoch, was in Lochmaben.

"At the Railway Inn. Ah, and it'll be prime drinking time, too. That gives them most of the day to get primed up," said Murdoch.

"It's my local. There will be 80 to 100 people jammed in there. I might get a free beer when I get back. And if we win it, it'll be colossal. It'll be absolutely huge."

The last time the Lockerbie Curling Club was big in the news nationally was when the Pan-Am 747 flight crashed in December of 1988 in what became known as the Lockerbie Catastrophe, and the curling club was used as the morgue because it was cold.

Murdoch, a farmer in the area, and his rink of treasury manager Craig Wilson, veterinarian Neil Murdoch and farmer Euan Byers were over the moon to be playing Canada's Ferbey in the final of the World Championship in Canada.

"We wanted Canada to win," said Murdoch of the semi-final against Germany's Kapp, the team the Scots beat on the Friday in the 1–2 game to go directly to the final.

"We wanted to play the final against Canada with 6000 Canadians cheering against us. It's going to be electric."

They'd already witnessed it once as Murdoch missed his last two shots and Canada stayed alive to make it to the playoffs in a six-way tie for first place.

"We definitely should have beaten him," said Murdoch of the 8–4 Canadian win.

The game set up to feature two different styles of curling. The Ferbey Four is famous for making the most of the four-rock rule and putting as many rocks in play as possible. The Scotland rink likes to keep it clean and keep the number of rocks in the house to a minimum.

"They play that game all year-round," said Murdoch. "We can't. We don't have this ice to play on back in Scotland. We have to play our game."

Not that he didn't like the ice.

"Not many people see ice like this," he said of the amazing job, especially considering the construction site conditions they were dealing with at the time, which Hans Wuthrich's icemaking team managed to pull off. "The amount of swing here is tremendous. I wish we had it every day of the year."

Canada's Nedohin said they'd definitely be going for the jugular in the final.

"We'll be aggressive with them. They don't want as many rocks in play as we do."

"Hopefully they don't sleep too well. We know we'll sleep well."

In the end everybody had to wonder how it was that the week that had been so difficult ended up looking so easy to win.

"The Aussies pretty much had us down under and now we're on top of the world," said Pfeifer of where they were and where they ended up.

On top of the world with an out-of-this-world pair of five-enders to win the final, the Ferbey Four had again gone where nobody had ever gone before.

With an 11–4 win in the final, they completed the 2005 Ford World Curling Championships—an event that was being called the greatest curling competition ever held—with the ultimate display of their greatness.

"We've definitely left our mark on the game now, I know that," said Ferbey after winning his personal fourth World Championship to go with his individual six Brier titles while skipping the rink to four Brier titles and three world titles in a five-year run.

"It's so satisfying. Halfway through the week we didn't know if we'd be up here. We were definitely human this week," said Nedohin, who returned to being the world's greatest shot-maker to manufacture the ultimate moment for curling's all-time team.

"The way we had to fight and scrap to get into the playoffs, the way we were able to win eight straight, probably makes it sweeter. And two five-enders. Isn't that something?" said Nedohin.

"I don't think we've ever had two five-enders before and we got them in the final of the World Championship," said Rocque.

There had never been a five-ender in the final of a World Championship before, much less two.

"The way we went this week, with all the ups and downs, I'll never forget this. Absolutely, this is the best for me so far. We were lucky to be alive. For that reason it made this one better than any other.

"We stuck it out as a team and fought it out for Canada."

Pfeifer said it would take all summer to sink in.

"We were 4–3. To come back like this by winning eight straight is something we've never experienced as a team before," he said.

"Not bad for a bunch of burned-out curlers," Ferbey told the crowd during the closing ceremonies.

"We didn't want to spend the summer thinking about losing," said Rocque of the way it was the summer before gagging on the final of the Saskatoon Brier.

"We went from cliffhanger to cliffhanger and kept telling ourselves we were due for a big one. It didn't come, didn't come, didn't come but it finally happened in the final. We made all our shots," said the lead who hit for 93%, second only to Nedohin's eye-popping 95% on a rink that curled 90% as a group in the final.

There's no room on the trophy for the story of the missed shots by Murdoch, Palangio, Trulsen and Kapp that put the Ferbey Four in the final. In the record book it will show a dominating rink dominating the final.

History will record that Canada became the first nation to win four playoff games. History will also now show this rink, playing their 148th game of the season, went 12–3 at the Worlds despite only having last-rock advantage in six games. They went 7–0 at provincials and 11–2 at the Brier. That's 30–5.

History would record that the Ferbey Four had to win eight straight games, six of them facing elimination, to equal the record of Sweden's Peja Lindholm and

Canada's Ron Northcott as three-time world winners.

The final was a best-of-one against Scotland. Ferbey stole one in the first, gave up two in the second and then manufactured the most amazing end in the history of the final when Nedohin made the shot heard 'round the curling world.

It was skip Ferbey setting it up and last-rock thrower Nedohin executing a tricky tap-back to score five. No team had ever scored five in a final before.

Four ends later the record was equalled as Nedohin executed another delicate shot for five more!

"They just made all the shots and we didn't," said Murdoch. "It was a bit of a disaster, wouldn't you say?"

"It was a great final…for three ends," World Curling Federation president Roy Sinclair told the crowd.

That said, it would be remembered for greatness. They weren't great throughout much of the 2005 World Curling Championships, but in the end their greatness was achieved.

CHAPTER 19

Oh, The Fun They've Had

Colleen a lot of laughs: Colleen Jones (right) and teammates Kim Kelly, Nancy Delahunt and Mary-Anne Waye (lighter-coloured jackets, right to left) with Ferbey rink at Worlds.

So there they were, the curling kings with the Queen of England.

"We had her laughing pretty hard," said Dave Nedohin about Her Majesty the Queen after they won their fourth Brier and third World Championship.

Queen Elizabeth happened to be in Alberta's capital to celebrate Alberta's 100th birthday. So it wasn't like she made the trip special to meet them, or anything.

But still. What a thrill.

"We had about four or five minutes with her. We were certainly the only ones to get her laughing. Everybody else was pretty stuffy," said Nedohin.

"I asked her if she ever curled. She said 'No, no. That's much too difficult with all that sweeping.'

"And then Queen Elizabeth stood there pretending she was sweeping with a corn broom.

"We have a really great photo of her pointing at Marcel Rocque and laughing. We're not sure if she was laughing with him or laughing at him."

Curling royalty meets real royalty.

"What a great experience," said Rocque. "In fact, it was the only time in all the years of our successes that my wife thanked me for all of the opportunities it has given us. That might have been the best part of it."

Scott Pfeifer was the one who found out first.

"I was the one who got the e-mail. I was the first one to know. I had to read it twice. It wasn't just a chance to meet the Queen, it was a private reception to meet the Queen. That was a fun one to tell the guys about. Telling our wives was even better. How good a guy are you when you tell your wife you're going to take her to meet Queen Elizabeth!"

Randy Ferbey said the guys took it more in stride. At first.

"Our wives were totally thrilled. But I think I was more thrilled about it two or three days after we'd met her. That's when I realized it was a once-in-a-life-time thing. I thought we shouldn't talk too much about it because maybe it would sound like we were starting to think we were getting a little carried away with who we thought we were or something. I didn't make a big deal about it.

"I couldn't believe how many people were to-tally thrilled for us. And the people who were there couldn't be-lieve how we were talk-ing to her. Kinda like she was our grandma or something. And she obviously had a good time talking to us, so we just stayed ourselves."

Before the team went to the 2005 Worlds, I set up a picture for the *Edmonton Sun* of the curling Fab Four, recreating the Beatles "Abbey Road" album cover. The team presented the Queen with a framed, auto-graphed copy of the picture with the inscription 'The Real Fab Four.'

"She started off with Scott and Chantelle and came through the line shaking hands," said Rocque. "Then she started chatting with us. It was nice. Then Dave asked her if she'd ever curled before. That's when it re-ally got to be an experience. People couldn't believe she stood there pretending to sweep with a corn broom.

> "I asked her if she ever curled. She said 'No, no. That's much too difficult with all that sweeping.' And then Queen Elizabeth stood there pretending she was sweeping with a corn broom."
> **—Dave Nedohin**

"Dave started talking about the grand match that is held in Scotland ever year and how it's played out-doors. I said that I'd never curled outside. The Queen said that surely we have outdoor curling in Canada. That's when I leaned in and whispered to her, 'It's much too cold in this country to curl out-doors.' That's when she started pointing at me and laughing as illus-trated in our photo.

"The rest of the greet-ings that night seemed to be very formal. We occupied her time more than any of the dignitaries by far. I overheard her asking Ralph Klein what our team name was again. Obviously we had some kind of impact for her to inquire further."

The rink had met King Ralph, as the premier is known in Alberta, on several previous occasions. But after winning their third world title in Victoria they were invited to visit him in his office in the provincial capital.

"He presented us with personalized plaques and we presented him with a team photo. He showed us where he'd put it, next to all his other photos of fa-mous dignitaries and celebrities," said Rocque.

"We took a picture of him and he insisted Randy sit down at his desk with the rest of us around him. Ran-dy told him how he could get used to that seat. They joked about being in the hot seat and Ralph men-tioned that the curling hot seat is probably more en-joyable. We all agreed.

"Then he escorted us into the Legislative Assembly and introduced us as being great ambassadors, not only for Alberta but for all of Canada. They gave us a standing ovation, banging the tables and getting way more carried away than we expected. But nothing tops Queen Elizabeth pretending she was sweeping with a corn broom."

If it wasn't the Queen of England, it was the Queen of Track & Field.

In Edmonton for the 2001 World Championships in Athletics, the team was chosen to present the medals to the winners of the women's 4 x 100 metre relay. Huff & Puff presented the medals to the bronze medal winners, Nedohin to the silver medal winner and Ferbey to the gold medal winner.

> "How good a guy are you when you tell your wife you're going to take her to meet Queen Elizabeth!"
>
> —Scott Pfeifer

"We had Ferb convinced that you had to kiss each girl, no matter what. That it was protocol," said Nedohin.

"When Scott and Marcel presented the bronze medals, they both gave them a kiss on the cheek. I followed and also gave the silver-medal winners an even bigger peck on the cheek. But there was also a representative of the world governing body who presented the flowers to the gold-medal winners and, following our lead of giving them a little peck, he may as well have used his tongue kissing them. So when Randy went to present the gold medals, they were a little hesitant to receive the kiss from The Ferb. Randy almost had to pull Marion Jones off the podium but he didn't want to mess up protocol."

Ferbey said he couldn't let his teammates upstage him.

"I kinda grabbed her, pulled her to me and gave her a great big smootch."

That was just the kissing.

Then there was the sex.

At the final of the 2004 Continental Cup, CBC colour commentator Joan McCusker made arrangements to come into their dressing room for a pre-game interview. A member of Sandra Schmirler's 1998 Nagano Olympic gold medal-winning team, which also won three world championships, McCusker was supposed to ask Ferbey a question referring to all the team's success over the years. However, her tongue got all tangled up.

Nedohin tells the story.

"Joan began interviewing Randy and said 'After all the great sex you've had over the years...' Never saw Joan turn that colour of red before."

Ferbey said it could have been so much better.

"It's too bad it wasn't live. It's in their blooper library and maybe some day they'll show it. But when she said that, I didn't miss a beat. I'd love to see her blooper shown with my reply."

The rink suggested it was something along the lines of 'Nah, you weren't that good.'

Ah, who needs great sex when you've got great success?

"The fun is what makes the entire experience more worthwhile than anything else," says Pfeifer. "More than the titles and the notoriety, the real payoff is in the moments most fans don't see.

"When this is all over and I sit back in a rocking chair someday, I'm sure most of my memories are going to be about all the good times we had off the ice.

"I definitely wouldn't be playing if it wasn't for the good friends and the socializing afterwards. Having accomplished what we've accomplished so far with these guys is genuinely what this has been all about."

Not that winning isn't any fun.

"Never in my life have I seen anyone so excited about winning anything as Marcel was when we won our first Brier in Ottawa," said Pfeifer.

"After our victory that night, Marcel was phoning everyone at home yelling out 'I'm a @ *%ing Brier champion!,' while being pushed around in a laundry cart someone found in the hallway."

Pfeifer says when they won the first Continental Cup, a Europe vs Canada format featuring the top men's and women's teams in the world, he couldn't believe what he saw.

"Randy Ferbey and Kevin Martin hugging! We witnessed a sight we will probably never witness again!"

Curling, with the Olympics, has become a truly international game. And as the world's top team, the Ferbey Four have been invited on several occasions to travel the world. After winning their fourth Brier and third World Curling Championship in 2005, they were invited to take two trips, one to Spain and another only a couple of weeks later to Switzerland.

"What possessed us to sign up for the third annual Madrid International Bonspiel, I'll never know," said

Meeting the Other Fab Four: Queen Elizabeth II shakes hands with Ringo...er...Marcel.

Denis Drever/Canadian Heritage

Pfeifer. "Maybe it was the four bottles of cheap Spanish wine we took home for winning the tournament after outscoring our opponents 49–19. Maybe it was the wacky modified Schenkel system they were using to rank teams after each game—the only system we know where you can win all your games and still lose the bonspiel.

"In all reality, it was a terrific trip, a valuable team-building experience and an opportunity to promote our sport in a nation where curling is still in its infancy.

"Our most amazing experience was attending a Real Madrid game with the likes of David 'Bend it Like' Beckham, Zinedine 'Head Butt' Zidane, Ronaldo...

"We also experienced another side of Spanish culture by attending a bullfight one day. We were glad to experience it one time," said Pfeifer. "But cross our team off the list for a return trip unless the matadors aren't allowed to hide behind stone walls while they're stabbing the bull to death.

"Normally a trip to Switzerland is routine, but for that one, Dave couldn't make it, so we pulled Kerry "Bubba" Burtnyk out of retirement. Before arriving in Swizerland, we decided to take a three-day detour trip to Rome.

"I booked our hotel on Via Torino, hoping the street would be a good omen for the Olympics.

"Rome was an amazing experience. We even had a chance to see the Pope close up. Not quite as close up as the Queen, but…

"We went 7–0 in the Switzerland tournament to give Kerry his first undefeated season ever," laughed Pfeifer.

In January of 2005 they'd also taken a trip to Scotland where they were hosted by 1967 world champion Chuck Hay and family.

Nedohin tells the story.

"One of the great things we did was tour a couple of distilleries. At the Famous Grouse, the tour ended up with a sampling of their scotch. The lady hosting the tour toasted us in the traditional manner. Then she asked if there were any other toasts for other parts of the world that anyone on our tour would like to offer. Randy had just gulped down his scotch, looked up in classic Ferb manner, and said 'Got any more of this *@!* shit?' The room fell silent. Then everybody burst out in laughter."

As part of that same invitation to compete in a bonspiel in Scotland, the team took advantage of Hay's membership at the Old Course in St. Andrews to play a little golf.

"Some of our best memories as a team involve Randy playing golf," says Nedohin. "I've caught them on camera.

"Randy's shot going off the hotel on the 17th hole at St. Andrews and back to the 16th green was about the funniest thing I have ever seen on a golf course. This was followed closely by his attempts to get out of a sand trap at Carnoustie. Six tries. And the ball got deeper in the trap with every swing."

Before a game at the 2005 Edmonton Brier in front of a capacity crowd, Nedohin slipped the video of Ferbey on the legendary golf courses to CBC's Don Wittman. The veteran play-by-play man then informed the officials that CBC would run it on air after the fourth end so the officials wouldn't start the clocks and the feed from the telecast could be shown on the video boards.

Nedohin, Pfeifer, Rocque and the lead, second and third from Brad Gushue's Newfoundland rink were also informed. So there they sat, on the bumper boards at the back of the house when the video was shown across the nation and went up on the video boards in Rexall Place.

There was Ferbey in the bunker at Carnoustie.

One. Two. Three. Four. Five. Six.

The players from both teams fell backwards off the bumper boards in delight as they watched Ferbey flail away. It made for great pictures.

In the same game that the golf video was shown— and this was a game against Brad Gushue of Newfoundland in which the Ferbey rink was losing 3–0 after the first end and didn't take the lead until much later—they actually played a game of rock-paper-scissors to decide which shot to try.

And it wasn't the first time.

"The first time was at a Canada Cup when Dave and Randy did it to decide a shot," remembers Rocque. "We were split 50–50 on a shot and I told them that I used rock-paper-scissors all the time in my phys-ed classes. So they did it! The crowd picked up on it. It was pretty funny. The only time we do it, though, is when the consensus is that both are good choices and we just couldn't agree on which was the best choice."

Not agreeing on things is a team trait. In fact they go to great lengths not to agree. Put enough miles together in a van driving around the frozen tundra of Canada and things can get goofy.

"We debate about everything, even if we don't want to," says Rocque. "Generally, when there is something on the team that two people don't agree on, the other two pick sides, no matter how you feel about the issue, so it's two against two," said Nedohin.

"One perfect example was the day when we drove past a Christmas tree lot somewhere in Saskatchewan or Manitoba and saw a sign that read 'Live Christmas Trees.' So the discussion starts about whether Christmas trees are alive and when they actually die. Are they dead when you cut them down or when the needles fall off? This has been an argument going on with the team for over two years and we often poll people at a curling club when it comes up."

Rocque said that one had the longest life. "Scott ended up talking to professors at the University of Alberta about it.

"Just stupid stuff, but it would last for weeks," said Rocque.

"I remember one time in Brandon I saw the signs for herbicides and pesticides. Next thing you know we're coming up with words that end in 'cide.' Ferbs ended it with 'fries and gravy on the 'cide.' "

The team has a three-votes majority policy to decide an issue when it gets to the serious stuff such as Ferbey dealing with the media.

"There have been so many media situations that have been funny, but the best stuff is when we had to put Randy on 'verbal probation,' " remembers Rocque.

"This has been an ongoing thing when Randy has been goaded into saying negative stuff in the press. The next day he'd have a rant about being misquoted or saying the media didn't take it the way he meant it or however he was trying to weasel out of it. Somebody will always say, 'Ferb, we're going to put you back on verbal probation if you're not careful.' "

Practical jokes have always been part of the fun.

Rocque tells of the time in Lausanne when Jim Waite showed up as the national coach and the boys decided to have a little bit of fun with him.

"The first time we practiced we made Jim hold the broom. The rest of us agreed to miss the broom by a foot. We all kept straight faces. It was great to see his reaction and give us his positive feedback. He only lasted five or six throws before he suggested that Randy knew how to ice us and that Randy better hold the broom for us.

"Then he suggested he'd make sure we weren't going over the hog line. We just looked at each other and knew what we were going to do then. We all started going over the hog line by about a foot and looked back to ask him if it was OK. He was so stressed. We finally couldn't take anymore and burst out laughing, so he knew he was had.

> **"Randy Ferbey and Kevin Martin hugging! We witnessed a sight we will probably never witness again!"**
> **—Scott Pfeifer**

"Hey, I got Ralph's autograph!" Alberta Premier Ralph Klein signs special proclamations in his office.

they didn't know what to do. They were all afraid to come too close. One of them muttered that she 'knew something like this would happen.' They were just heading down the stairs for help when we burst out of the room. They almost killed us."

At that same Worlds there was also the Canadian Curling Association (CCA) dinner plans prank on Colleen Jones and her team.

"Team Jones = Gullible," laughs Pfeifer.

Nedohin tells the story.

"In Colleen's mind they were a little hesitant about a big dinner with the CCA during the event in case it would throw off their games the next day. As such they arranged to have their dinner with the CCA at a pizza parlour, where they'd be for about an hour and then return to prepare for their games the next day.

"When we heard about the pizza deal, we concocted a story that we rented a boat for our dinner, were sailing around Lake Geneva, picking up a chef in France and spending the evening on the water. The girls were so jealous they were almost in hysterics.

"We continued on with this for a couple of days until we finally let them in on the joke. As it turned out our team had an amazing dinner that took the better part of four hours at a wonderful restaurant on a peninsula of Lausanne and it still remains one of my favourite meals of all time."

Jones and her rink have been the Scott Tournament of Hearts Champions six times and regular representatives for Canada at the world championships where Jones, Kim Kelly, Mary-Anne Waye and Nancy Delahunt have won two world titles. As a result, they've spent way too much time around the Ferbey Four.

The two teams had been taken to Wildhaus, Switzerland, for a pre-Worlds camp prior to the 2001 championships in Lausanne.

"Of course, in the end the joke was on us as the Swiss officials kept calling Randy for going over the hog line in our playoff game against Switzerland."

At those same Worlds they pulled another one on Colleen Jones and her rink representing Canada in the women's championship.

"We didn't win those Worlds but at least we can look back and remember we had a great time, particularly because we had so much fun with Colleen Jones."

"At the Worlds the teams were on the same floor in the host hotel. After one of the women's draws, we knew they'd be coming up the elevator," remembers Rocque.

"We stuffed a pair of curling pants with towels and put shoes at the end of them and an empty bottle of wine on the floor. It was Brian Moore's room and we'd put 'the body' there as if he'd fallen and was lying halfway out of his room. When we heard the hotel elevator doors open, we would make 'Brian' moan and groan. Lots of people were had with that and we had tons of laughs. But it was all set up for Colleen, so when her team came up the elevator, 'Brian' started moaning from inside the room where we were hiding. Colleen screamed for her team to go back down and get some help. Her teammates were panicked, saying

Pfeifer remembers playing a game cross-sheet with them there.

"What's the best way to prepare for the world championship? Play another world-calibre team, of course. We did just that against Team Jones but did so from the home end of sheet 1 to the away end of sheet 4. There were no boards on the ice there, of course."

Diagonal curling. Could catch on.

"On our way from Wildhaus to Lausanne, which was a three-hour drive, Dave was getting bugged by members of Team Jones for reading *Maxim* for the pictures, not the content," recalls Pfeifer.

"So we thought it was appropriate to stop at a convenience store to pick up something worse. When we all piled back into the van, Dave brought out his new magazine called *60 Plus* featuring naked women over the age of 60. You think Colleen Jones yells loud on the ice?"

Pfeifer has another story about Wildhaus.

"They'd taken us there to get used to the time change and get ready for the event. After a few too many drinks, Brian Moore noticed Dave had a rip in his jeans and proceeded to tear his jeans all the way up the pant leg. What to do with all the material? Create our own drink, of course. Cut it up. Put it in our glasses. Called it the 'Denim Vodka.'

"After a few too many Denim Vodkas, Dan Holowaychuk thought it would be funny on the way back to the room to lock Dave's door while he was in the hallway in essentially only his underwear. With the front desk closed, it looked like Dave was going to be sleeping in one of our rooms. Being the nice guy that I am, I was the only one who answered his pleas for help from the hallway. Since my room was next to his, I had the brilliant idea of crossing from my balcony to his and opening his door. Yes, we were about four floors off ground level. A little balcony-hopping in the middle of the night may or may not be considered team-building. But it happened."

With drinking more or less mandatory in curling—the Brier Patch being a national institution and all—the team has ended up having the odd libation together over the years.

The official bar of the Ferbey Four was Mo's on the southern end of Edmonton. Many a celebration of success has been held there.

"The oversized cheques from some of our biggest paydays, like the Skins games, were hung at Mo's," said Pfeifer. "They routinely threw Team Ferbey celebrations after our victories. The round table closest to the door was painted with curling rings. It was usually our gathering spot when our team had things to discuss."

It was at Mo's, no doubt, where the streaking incident at the provincial championships in Hinton was hatched.

Doug Munro, the bartender at Mo's, was somehow convinced to streak a Ferbey game at the Hinton provincials. It was the final game of the round-robin against John Morris and turned out to be meaningless because of the results in other games. Ferbey was up by a bunch when suddenly a streaker raced naked between the sheets.

"What streaker?" asked Ferbey when the game was over. "Streaker? I didn't see any streaker. I was totally focussed on the game."

It was pointed out to the skip that there were pictures. And Ferbey was captured on one with a priceless expression on his face.

"It was the toque," he said, referring to the merchandise the team was selling that year to help raise money to cover their costs.

"He's keeping that baby. I'm not buying that one back," he said. The man from Mo's was holding the toque over his private parts as he made the trip from one end of the rink to the other.

Pfeifer remembers the golf game at Bear Mountain, the Jack Nicklaus course near Victoria, prior to the 2005 Worlds.

"Dan Holowaychuk, Marcel, Randy and myself went golfing in the pouring rain. When it started to really pour, that was enough for Randy and Marcel. Dan and I kept playing. Randy put down our shots on the scorecard and the number of drinks he and Marcel had for their score on the remaining holes."

After winning those Worlds the team was invited on a fishing trip with Dave Cutler, the former Eskimos kicker.

"He and his friends arranged for a 50-foot yacht for a fishing expedition to celebrate our third world title. But there wasn't much fishing done. The rods hit the water for about a half hour. We were too busy sharing stories, eating crabs and smoking cigars," said Pfeifer.

At an earlier world championship in Lausanne, the Ferbey Four ended up in a karaoke bar with the American team.

"Dave broke our cardinal rule of karaoke, 'Always Follow Someone Worse Than You.' People were belting out wicked renditions of Pavarotti, complete with back-up singers. Then Dave and Team U.S.A. got up to sing 'Great Balls Of Fire.' No sooner than the song was done, which felt like an eternity, did the lights turn on and the bartender kicked us out," said Pfeifer.

On another occasion they extended last call a couple of hours by negotiating to buy the bar.

"They were making last call and we were still thirsty," laughs Ferbey. "So we started talking to the manager of the place about buying the bar. He knew we were the curlers from Canada and just assumed curlers must make a lot of money and could afford to just up and buy a bar in Switzerland. We negotiated until 4 AM or so. And, of course, he kept pouring us drinks."

Pfeifer remembers the time they were in Norway, having replaced Nedohin, who couldn't make the trip, with the two-time Brier champion Al Hackner.

"I'll never forget trying to put Hackner to bed in Oslo," says Pfeifer. "My goal for the week was to try to outlast Hackner for just one night. Needless to say, after several attempts, I was unsuccessful. I don't know how he does it."

On that same trip, Pfeifer joined Don Bartlett "fjording."

"Paul Gowsell had completed the task earlier in the week. Bartlett and I wanted to add our name to the list of those who had stripped down naked and waded in the Atlantic Ocean. After a few drinks to build up our bravery, we became the second and third Canadians to complete the task within a week."

The Ferbey Four has plenty of trains, planes and automobile stories. On one trip to Kamloops, their flight from Vancouver to Kamloops was grounded by weather, so Rocque and Nedohin took the bus while Pfeifer and Ferbey took a train. Rocque and Nedohin won 'The Amazing Race' easily; Pfeifer and Ferbey didn't arrive until 2 AM.

They're the only curling team in the world with their own pilot.

"To get to some of the locations we've curled, such as Swan River and Nipawin, we've hired one of Marcel's family friends, Jack Kindermann," said Pfeifer. "Jack is in his mid-70s. He loves coming along to the spiel and enjoying himself with Marcel's dad, Roland. When we introduce him as our team pilot, people get some pretty weird looks on their faces. First, a curling team with a pilot. Second, a 70-some-year-old guy who is a pilot. A great guy, though, and a great supporter of the team."

At the Brier, each team is provided with a well-marked van and a driver.

"We showed up in Saskatoon and our driver was the same one Pat and I had when we were in the '89 Brier in Saskatoon. John. He was a former police officer," remembers Ferbey.

"He was great. He was an older gentleman, and we were worried our antics may be too much for him to handle," said Pfeifer.

"No way!

"On the first day we had him convince Brian Moore and Dan Holowaychuk that his hearing was poor and the music would have to be played very quietly. In addition, he said, he could not be out after 10 PM.

"This caused a panic attack right away.

"For the cherry on top we also had him convince Brian and Dan that he intended to take our team to church Sunday morning before our 9 AM game. He said he'd arranged for a special service and sermon at 6 AM.

"Dan and Brian went to Team Services to have the driver changed and made every call possible for two days. But we had everybody in those groups involved in the joke as well.

"That driver was great. We've always had a lot of fun with our drivers. In Calgary, our driver Rick was terrific. He was also tuned into our superstitions. We always listen to a special CD that Scott makes up for every Brier. We never know what's on it until the first time it's played. There have been some shocked looks on some drivers faces when they hear the CD. Another thing we do is take the same route every time. Every time! We informed Rick of that. Wouldn't you

know it, on the first day Rick accidentally drove through a red light on the way to the Saddledome. Without asking, he continued on each trip to run through one red light."

You can always recognize the Alberta van at the Brier.

"We have to have the right colour," said Nedohin. "We have to have gold."

Great pains are taken by fifth man Holowaychuk to make sure that happens.

Inspired by their Sherwood Park neighbor Trent Evans, the Rexall Place icemaker on loan to the Salt Lake Olympics who became famous for burying a loonie in the ice that became part of the lore of Canada winning Olympic hockey gold for the first time in 50 years, they buried an Alberta pin in the ice in 2002, and they won their second Brier. They also had it under the ice for their first world title in Bismarck.

"Holowaychuk found a way. He always finds a way," said Nedohin.

Just one of the reasons the rink always has Holowaychuk and Moore in the first few snapshots of their championship pictures.

The Ferbey Four are champions at getting their pictures in the paper without even trying.

They've been asked to perform ceremonial face-offs at Edmonton Oilers games again and again to celebrate championships. Click. Edmonton Eskimo ceremonial kickoffs. Click. First pitches at Edmonton Trappers games. Click. And parades. Click. Click. Click. Click. Click.

"I can't say no to a parade," says Pfeifer.

They've been in so many parades they feel like the Shriners.

While Rocque says the best one was at his hometown in St. Paul, the rest of the team roll their eyes on that one.

Four times they've been in the Klondike Days Parade, three up front as parade marshalls to celebrate Brier wins. The other time they were featured on the Edmonton 2005 Brier float after they lost in Saskatoon.

"They didn't even ask us when we won our fourth Brier and third world championship," said Pfeifer. "Maybe they got tired of us. In our place, they went and put somebody by the name of Ralph Klein as parade marshall. Something to do with the centennial celebration or something. Can you believe that?"

Considering the Edmonton–Calgary rivalry, they were stunned to find themselves in the Calgary Stampede Parade.

"That was big," remembers Ferbey. "That's when we realized curling is different than hockey and football. Hockey and football is Edmonton vs Calgary and the Battle of Alberta. In curling, we *are* Alberta," said Ferbey.

"It's a curling-mad province and when you're curling at the Brier, Albertans cheer for Alberta. Period. We won a Brier in Calgary and the fans were really behind us."

When the province was looking for a sports team to help head up the centennial celebrations, they picked the Ferbey Four. They spread them around the province to be hosts of a multimedia celebration.

"To me that was especially flattering. We really do see ourselves as Alberta's team," said Ferbey, who helped host in Medicine Hat.

"I think most people see our team uniform as being the blue and yellow of Alberta. Just being in the Calgary Stampede parade, to us, said it all," said Pfeifer.

"We were treated pretty well the night before the parade. They took us to a local country bar where someone recognized me and asked to see my world championship ring," said Nedohin.

"I took it off to let the person have a look and turned away for a moment to have a chat with someone else. As soon as I looked back, the person with my ring was gone. I thought for sure that was it. About an hour later, another girl came up to me and asked if I was David Nedohin. I said yes. And she handed me my ring, mentioning it had been passed around the whole bar for all the curling fans in the place to take a look at. It really reinforces the honesty and down-to-earth nature of the curling fans in this country."

They've been inducted into the Edmonton Sports Hall of Fame and, along with bobsledder Pierre Lueders, were responsible for a new award being created for continued achievements after already having been recognized by the City of Edmonton.

All four members of the rink, Rocque who went to school in Sherwood Park, and Pfeifer, Nedohin and Ferbey who live there, have received the Pride Of Strathcona Awards presented by the county.

The lead had a "Marcel Rocque Day" in St. Paul and Pfeifer has been recognized in his hometown of St. Albert on repeated occasions as well. Together, Huff and Puff were given a special award by the University of Alberta Alumni in September of 2005.

Ferbey is already in the Canadian Curling Hall of Fame and the rink is like Mark Messier, guaranteed to go in as soon as they become eligible. Ferbey is also in the Alberta Sports Hall of Fame where, again, there is a space reserved for the entire group.

The team says they know they've become sports celebrities in their own right from the number of celebrity golf tournaments and appearances they've had to make.

"But it still seems strange being around Henry 'Gizmo' Williams, Ryan Smyth, Jamie Sale & David Pelletier and all those people in Edmonton," says Nedohin.

The group also hung around with "Men With Brooms" stars Leslie Nielsen, Paul Gross and Molly Parker at a promotional event.

Whether you'd count Brynn Griffiths and Jake Daniels of Team 1260 radio in Edmonton as celebrities is open to debate, but the team has treasured their "Team 1260 Death Matches" with the morning radio hosts.

"Every year before the Brier we play a fun match against Brynn and Jake," explains Pfeifer. "Every year there is a different handicap. In 2003 Randy had to throw a frozen turkey instead of a curling rock. Team 1260 actually won that game. The turkey lost by a measure.

"One year we had to throw with an eye patch and a big banner in front of us so we couldn't see the other end.

"The game became larger than life in 2005 with the Brier in Edmonton. They built an outdoor rink in front of City Hall and had us throwing jam pails. We cracked a seven-ender on them in the second end."

Ferbey and Nedohin were invited to do a cameo on the CTV hit sitcom *Corner Gas*, which is set in rural Saskatchewan, in a curling episode.

Now, most people would remember it as "the time I was on *Corner Gas.*"

Not Randy Ferbey.

"That was when I saw the ghost. I swear! I've stayed in hundreds of hotel rooms over the years and I've never seen a ghost. But I saw a ghost there.

"Dave and I had separate rooms in the Hotel Saskatchewan and I heard a bunch of noise in the hall. I thought that was unusual for that hotel. But I tried to go back to sleep. Eventually I got up and looked out the door. Nobody. Nothing. Totally quiet.

"Then all of a sudden a radio comes on in the room. I roll over to turn it off, except there's no radio in the room. I'm thinking, 'Oh, Randy, you're losing it.'

"Then, I swear to God, I felt something jump on the bed…"

Nedohin says Ferbey looked white as a ghost the next morning.

"Randy asked if I had heard any noises," remembers Nedohin. "Randy looked very odd, so I asked him what was up. He told me about the ghost. He said it was about the size of a dog when it jumped on the bed. It moved across him and his bed, jumped off, and all was well again. He said he just about shit his pants. He said he would have come to see me in my room if he hadn't been so scared. He spent the night wide awake.

"The next morning Randy, feeling pretty embarrassed, went to the concierge and asked if they had ever heard strange stories from his room in the hotel. The guy asked him which floor he was on, and Randy said six. The guy said these ghost stories were fairly common but not on that floor recently."

Ferbey said he felt like a fool asking the hotel people about ghosts.

"They said I certainly wasn't the first, but he said that was a first for that floor."

As for being on *Corner Gas?*

"We were surprised that all the cast members knew us. It took two days to film. I think they paid us $700 each," said Ferbey.

"When we watched it, it seemed like we were in it for about four seconds. It was like 'That was it?' "

When you become a curler you don't picture yourself being invited to Las Vegas by somebody like Real Michaud of the World Financial Group for a speaking engagement at a convention of 15,000 people.

"We spoke twice. The first time was 15 minutes to all the brass. Then we spoke for about an hour to 3,000–4,000 members of a Canadian contingent. Our message was what it takes to build a championship team," said Rocque.

For the rest of the time in Vegas, they had a blast.

"It was a fantastic trip. That's where Randy lost the moustache," said Nedohin of Ferbey coming home with a clean-shaven face into the 2005–06 curling season. "We'd been bugging Randy to lose that moustache for years. We finally convinced him."

Ferbey said he lost it on a kind of a dare.

"I've had that thing all of my life. I said I'd shave it off if Dave coloured his hair, so I lived up to my half of the bargain."

The rink struck it rich in Las Vegas. They hit the jackpot.

"Speaking for 15 minutes each in front of thousands of people is a bit unnerving," said Ferbey.

"We hadn't really done any motivational speaking before, but we prepared, broke it down into areas like team building, commitment and applied it to their business. We spoke for a little over an hour. We didn't really know how we'd done but it seemed to go OK, we thought.

"After it was all over, the executives talked to us and told us they'd brought guest speakers in from all around the world and we'd been the best they'd had in seven years. Then they made us believe the compliment by becoming a major, major sponsor with us.

"We went down there because we had the Edmonton branch of the World Financial Group as a minor sponsor. It was the local branch manager who came up with the idea of having us as speakers in Las Vegas. Coming back with major sponsorship was something we certainly didn't expect."

CHAPTER 20

Forward to the Future

Svelte and shaved: A new-look Randy Ferbey.

Randy Ferbey lost his moustache. Dave Nedohin coloured his hair. And Curling's Fab Four spent the off-season attempting to acquire the look of Olympians.

The missing moustache was the first thing you noticed, but there was more missing from Ferbey than his moustache as the team began the Torino 2006 Olympic year.

"He's probably lost 20 pounds," said Nedohin of the then 46-year-old Ferbey as the team headed out to different locales around the province to participate in Alberta's centennial celebrations.

"We worked hard on an off-season training program with former Toronto Blue Jays' trainer Jeff Krushell. Our team has been at it five days a week all summer.

Our training also included a nutritionist. Ferbs is in the greatest shape of his life," reported Nedohin.

"There's going to be a lot of double takes when people see Ferbs this year," predicted Pfeifer.

"He's looking good, the old guy," said Rocque.

Maybe Ferbey just wanted to look good for the women. Their season would begin with a national telecast of "The Battle of the Sexes" skins game against the Canadian women's curling champion Jennifer Jones' Manitoba rink.

It wasn't the first time curling had staged their version of the event first made famous in tennis by Bobby Riggs and Billy Jean King. When Marilyn Bodogh faced Ed Werenich there was a lot of show business involved. Bodogh entered the arena doing cartwheels in a kilt. This time they'd play it straight.

There was $60,000 in prize money for the game. Televised live on Rogers Sportsnet, it was serious stuff. For the Ferbey Four, the thought of winning big bucks to launch their Olympic-year season was tempered by the thought of losing to the ladies.

"Obviously we'll take a lot of ribbing from the guys if we lose this thing," said Nedohin when he arrived in Brandon.

"When it comes to the 'Battle of the Sexes,' the men have everything to lose and the women have everything to win," Pfeifer explained. "Everyone remembered the old Bodogh–Werenich battles, and we weren't about to join the notorious list of losers, especially when Canadian junior men's champ Kyle George lost to Canadian women's champion Andrea Kelly in the preliminary.

"We'd normally feel pretty confident in a regular game but with the skins-game format, all it takes are a few carryovers and missed shots at inopportune times and you'd easily find yourself on the losing end," he continued.

Pfeifer bottom-lined what would happen.

"There was a Brandon crowd cheering for Jennifer Jones' Manitoba team. Jennifer's team played well. But Dave made everything."

When it was over, the men had a cheque for $52,050 and the women had one for $7,950. While the men won the money, the women won the respect.

"We certainly had our hands full. There wasn't a big difference in the two genders. The difference was Dave shot the lights out. Jennifer's team proved elite teams are elite teams," said Pfeifer.

After taking a trip to Switzerland for a tournament, the rink was back in Canada with a countdown to the Olympic Trials in Halifax in December.

"We felt we were more ready than ever for a successful season," said Nedohin. "After the 'Battle of the Sexes,' our season continued on very well with wins in Bonnyville and Yorkton. Our off-ice training continued in the gym right until the final week before the Olympic Trials. We felt we were very well prepared."

Four years earlier, fresh from their first Brier win, the Ferbey rink didn't see itself as more than one of the challengers to Wayne Middaugh, the team that had qualified for the Trials four times. But this time around it was Randy Ferbey who had qualified on multiple occasions.

Ferbey and rival Kevin Martin were favoured to end up in the final. And they were scheduled to meet in the opening draw.

"Right now we're ranked No. 1 and No. 2 and that's the way it has been for quite a while," said Martin. "So what in the world are we doing playing each other in the first game? It's insane. The game should be saved for later in the week. To have these two teams playing each other in the very first game doesn't make any sense."

For Ferbey, many commentators felt that their team had earned the right to represent Canada at the Olympics over the previous four years.

"Randy had so many spots that he should at least get the hammer for extra games," offered Colleen Jones, the two-time world women's champion who should have been on Canada's women's Olympic team, based on her body of work over the past four seasons.

But there was room to wish Martin success as well. He was a two-time Brier champion, the first skip to hit the million-dollar mark in earnings and had spent four years waiting to do what he didn't get done representing Canada at the 2002 Olympic Winter Games in Salt Lake City.

"I'd love to get that inch back," said Martin of coming up one inch short on his last rock shot on the final end that made Pal Trulsen of Norway the Olympic gold medal winner.

"Getting back to get that inch back isn't it by itself. It's about getting back to enjoy the Olympic experience again. It was the ultimate experience of our lives," said Martin who was also at the 1992 Albertville Olympics back when curling was just a demonstration sport.

The knock on Martin was that he'd never won for Canada, having failed to bring back gold from two trips to the World Curling Championships as well.

The event was titled "Roar of the Rings" and from the Nagano Olympics to Salt Lake to Torino it seemed as though the event had multiplied exponentially by 2006.

"You're going to see a lot of frustrated people. You're going to see a lot more broom-tossing than normal," Ferbey explained on the eve of the event.

"This is not like a Brier or a World Curling Championship when, if you lose, you walk away to reload and try to win it the next year. Maybe it was before but not anymore. This is every four years. This is the ultimate bonspiel."

Everybody on the property was making the case that this edition of the Olympic Trials was a tougher tournament to win than the Olympics might be themselves.

Among the favourites were Jeff Stoughton, Glenn Howard, Mark Dacey, Shawn Adams and John Morris. And by adding veteran Russ Howard to skip and throw second rocks, Brad Gushue's Newfoundland rink was certainly not considered long shots.

But it was still Martin vs Ferbey at the git-go. Martin went into the Trials with a 26–10 record for the season and $37,000 in prize money while Ferbey headed in with a 40–8 record and $106,791 including money from the "Battle of the Sexes" skins game.

"I think we've done everything we can do to get ready for this. It's been three years coming. We were the first of the 10 rinks to qualify and we qualified again and again and again," said Ferbey. "We're looking at this as being bigger than anything we've ever played in before."

As for going against Martin in the lid-lifter, Ferbey uttered what would qualify as famous last words: "No matter if it's the first, third, seventh or 10th games, we have to play them. The thing about playing each other first is whoever loses better be able to turn the page and get on with trying to win the next one."

There was what you'd be tempted to call a "Halifax Explosion" or a "Roar on the Shore" on the seventh end of the opener when Martin made the shot that caused 6,764 fans to erupt in amazement and appreciation. You can make a case that one shot turned the tournament for Ferbey.

Actually the crowd roared twice on the end at both Martin shots that would result in four points and an eventual 8–5 win.

But it was the first shot, not the second, that was the one.

"The first shot he made was brilliant," said Ferbey. "That game was about one shot. I thought we played well but for one shot, two shots if you want to count the second one, but there wouldn't have been a second one to make if he hadn't made the first one…that was the difference. That shot won the game."

Somebody suggested all the first-game losers were tied for second.

"You can tell yourself that," said Stoughton, who had lost his opener to Morris. "But you're really tied for sixth."

After Ferbey and crew scored their usual win to make it a 15–1 lifetime record against Morris, always the free space on their bingo card, they sunk to 1–2 with a loss to Gushue. And the question was what was wrong with Scott Pfeifer?

"I'm playing like spit," said the second, who gave his son the middle name of Torino and spelled out an inspirational Olympic message with his kids' plastic letter magnets on his fridge. "I sucked. I missed a shot on the 10th end. Marcel and I overswept one. I've got to pick it up."

Pfeifer was shooting 78%, the second-lowest number in the tournament at his position, up from last place after the first two draws.

"We're concerned about it," said Ferbey. "If he doesn't pick it up, we're out of here in a hurry. It's ridiculous. We're not making enough shots. We've had chance after chance to take advantage and we're not doing it. We have to snap out of it. We're not setting anybody up. We're missing simple shots."

When they lost the next one, to Glenn Howard, they were 1–3 and in deep, deep trouble.

"We're close to being dead," admitted Ferbey.

Russ Howard, out of the gate at 4–0 with the Gushue crew, shook his head at what was happening. "I predicted carnage, I just didn't think it would happen to Randy," he said. "You don't expect to see somebody

> **"They kicked the living crap out of us. It's done. It's over. It didn't work. It's four years of preparation down the drain."**
> **—Randy Ferbey**

like that 1–3. But you wouldn't expect us to be 4–0. You wouldn't have bet on that either."

Brother Glenn believed he was a benefactor of the Ferbey Four being too tight. "They're the best team in the world, but they've struggled. They've missed a few key shots. We got a few uncharacteristic misses out of Dave."

The team that was 48–7 at the Brier and undefeated at the one held in Halifax, was now 6–7 at Olympic Trials and in definite danger of being just another rink mopping up a bonspiel.

That's the way Jeff Stoughton wanted it. "We wanted him to get four losses—to get rid of him," said Stoughton.

But he didn't want it the way it was going down. Stoughton made the statement when he was making a public plea to prevent the crowd from reacting the way they did in their loss to Howard.

"For some reason Canadians seem to hate a winner," said Stoughton. "Those guys are out there trying their best and the fans are cheering misses. I think that's pretty ignorant and rude of the crowd to do that to a true champion. I don't know why. It seems the Canadian mentality is that they don't seem to love their winners and these guys are certainly big winners. It's disappointing to see that happen to such a great team."

The next day both Colleen Jones and Randy Ferbey declared themselves dead after suffering their fourth losses.